William Empson and the Philosophy of Literary Criticism

CHRISTOPHER NORRIS

With a Postscript by
WILLIAM EMPSON

UNIVERSITY OF LONDON
THE ATHLONE PRESS
1978

Published by
THE ATHLONE PRESS
UNIVERSITY OF LONDON
at 4 Gower Street London WC1

Distributed by Tiptree Book Services Ltd
Tiptree, Essex

USA and Canada
Humanities Press Inc
New Jersey

British Library Cataloguing in Publication Data
Norris, Christopher
 William Empson and the philosophy of
 literary criticism.
 1. Empson, William—Criticism and interpretation
 I. Title
 820'9   PR6009.M7Z/
 ISBN 9 485 11175 6

Printed in Great Britain by
WESTERN PRINTING SERVICES LTD
Bristol

For Alison and my parents

Acknowledgements

My thanks are due to Dr Keith Walker, for his generous discussion of this work in its earlier stages; to Professor Karl Miller, for his encouragement in revising it for publication; and to Professor Frank Kermode, whose graduate seminars were a source of enlivening interest and fresh ideas. My debt to William Empson can hardly be summarised, except by saying that this book owes much to his personal kindness, and even more to the wisdom and inspiration of his writing.

A Note on Texts

I refer throughout this book to the most recent, complete and accessible editions of Empson's works. The 1961 edition of *Seven Types* incorporates the Preface to the previous (1947) reissue, along with Empson's 'Note for the Third Edition', defending the book against its early critics, and this I have taken into account. *Some Versions of Pastoral* (1935) was republished in 1966, also bearing a preface which helps to define Empson's later thoughts on the subject, and this therefore is the text I refer to.

The Structure of Complex Words now contains Empson's 'Comment for the Second Edition' (pp. 444–5), although the title page mentions only a Fourth Impression. This, anyway, is the text I have used; the edition of 1951. *Milton's God*, first published in 1961, reappeared in 1965 with 'minor changes to improve the argument', and with a lengthy appendix (pp. 288–318) supporting Empson's assumption that Milton was involved in Cromwellian intrigues against King Charles. I shall have something to say about the relevance of this piece of tactical argument, and I therefore refer to the latest edition. *Collected Poems* (1955) contains all that Empson wished to preserve from two previous collections and various single publications. Also among the 'basic texts' is Empson's almost book-length Introduction to *Coleridge's Verse: a selection*, co-edited by Empson and David Pirie.

Reference is therefore made to:

William Empson, *Seven Types of Ambiguity*, 3rd ed. (Penguin, Harmondsworth, 1961)—usually abbreviated to *Seven Types*.

William Empson, *Some Versions of Pastoral*, 2nd ed. (Penguin, Harmondsworth, 1966)—usually abbreviated to *Some Versions*.

William Empson, *The Structure of Complex Words* (London, Chatto and Windus, 1951)—abbreviated to *Complex Words*.

William Empson, *Milton's God*, revised edition (London, Chatto and Windus, 1965).

William Empson, *Collected Poems* (London, Chatto and Windus, 1955).

William Empson and David Pirie, eds., *Coleridge's Verse: a selection* (London, Faber and Faber, 1972).

I have also referred at several points to copies of I. A. Richards' *Practical Criticism* (1923) and *Principles of Literary Criticism* (1924), belonging to Professor Empson and bearing his marginal notes. Most of these were apparently made while preparing for the writing of *Complex Words*, where Empson acknowledges Richards as 'the source of all the ideas in this book, even the minor ones arrived at by disagreeing with him'. I am grateful to Professor Empson for access to these texts, and for all the help and encouragement he has given me, over the past few years, in writing this book.

May 1977

Contents

Introduction

William Empson is perhaps the best known and least understood of modern critics. *Seven Types of Ambiguity* (1930) was a brilliant first book but tended to strike attitudes and pile up examples which Empson has too often been called to defend, in later years, from humourless scholarly attack. *Some Versions of Pastoral* (1935) avoided this provokingly obvious subtlety by absorbing it, translating its ingenuities and complications, into a basic metaphor and, by extension, an entire genre of literary history. *Some Versions* invited misunderstanding, not because its subtleties seemed too insistent, but because, on the contrary, they were so far left implicit and unspoken.

In *The Structure of Complex Words* (1951) Empson gave his readers further reasons for disquiet. Here he returned, through the structure of attitudes learned from Pastoral, to a linguistics of criticism which was more accountable, more historically secure and philosophically generalised, than anything in *Seven Types*. *Complex Words* is beyond doubt Empson's critical *summa*. Yet it, like the other books, has attracted little more than superficial or downright hostile attention. In this case it is perhaps the rather abstract theoretical machinery, prominent in his first two chapters, which has cost Empson his readers' sustained application. These theoretical sections of the book are inevitable by way of philosophic completeness—and *Complex Words* is, as I hope to show, a real contribution to the philosophy of criticism. But they do come to seem inessential, at times, to the chapters of practical criticism. They provide both the assumed background and the ultimate formalisation of the insights gained in Empson's 'practical' chapters, the major part and central section of the book. *Complex Words* is, among other things, a rationalist theory of language and interpretation. In this respect it demands philosophical treatment and comparison, such as I intend to provide in the following chapters.

In the end, however, the theory is justified only by its fruits in finer, more assured understanding. I shall therefore try to show how the theoretical implications of Empson's work enter creatively into the methods and responsive cast of his criticism.

With *Milton's God* (1961), the point of such commentary becomes necessarily more detached and diagnostic. Like much of Empson's recent writing, the Milton book incorporates an outspoken hatred of Christianity which largely governs and sometimes appears to distort his reading of the poetry. Muriel Bradbrook thought that Empson might pass for 'the wisest fool in Christendom if he did not take every opportunity to cock a snook at theology'.[1] Empson's humanistic rationalism is present in his earliest writings, and forms a coherent and developing background to each of his books. But in *Milton's God* and the later essays it becomes such a palpable design that one must, in fair assessment, try to sort out the biassed from the merely unorthodox in his criticism. Whatever the balance, it is I think possible to show that Empson's 'eccentricity', as remarked upon by many of his critics, is less disabling—more a positive, consistent set of alternatives—than is commonly recognised.

This purpose has determined the relative priorities in my treatment of Empson's books. *Seven Types* is discussed mainly as a testing-ground and source of ideas for his later themes of Pastoral and Complex Words. By finding out the limits of verbal analysis as practised in *Seven Types* (and by the book's many imitators), Empson used Ambiguity as a pointer to more expansive regions of criticism. This has not been recognised by critics who consider him, true to the handy prototype, as the originator of those rhetorical ideas which took hold among the American New Critics. It may therefore be helpful to begin by examining what has been made of Empson's example, often against the grain of his own intentions.

Empson and Present-Day Criticism: a Chapter of Misunderstandings

Empson's critical 'influence' has been a passage of literary history from which the man himself has characteristically dissented. *Seven Types* did not actually inaugurate the New Criticism: Cleanth Brooks, for one, recalls how he came upon Empson's early writing more as a useful support than a starting inspiration for his own work.[1] But he and the others of his movement were quick to recognise affinities and to point out its signal virtues and limitations, to their way of thinking, when the book arrived in its first American edition (1931). He became a part of their common orthodoxy but, they found, a tricky and often subversive part. Brooks subsequently took the tone of gentle tolerance: let Empson read the founding fathers, Wimsatt and Beardsley.

So, when Empson returned from China in 1951, he found himself referred to (as he wrote at the time) 'with a kind of pitying fondness, as the wild old man who still doesn't know the rules which have been invented for the game'.[2] Empson's differences with the New Critics are far-reaching and will occupy me later. At this stage they illustrate more generally the way in which Empson has distanced himself from the ruling orthodoxies in modern criticism. In 1955 he reviewed a clutch of American critical books, all of which served to confirm his suspicions. Wimsatt's anti-intentionalism is seen straightaway as the philosophic prop of a more or less uniform 'movement'.[3] This mistrust of official creeds is strong in Empson; it associates with his loathing of orthodox Christian dogma. He was a member of the Cambridge 'Heretics' as an undergraduate, and the character of dissident rationalism has marked all his later writing.

His criticism seems, in retrospect, to have roused such opposition, and to have raised such a case in its own defence, as would situate it more than marginally in a stream of theological argument. Empson would not at all agree with this. He regards *Milton's God* and much of his recent work—essays arguing that, for various authors, religion was no blessing but a torment to their moral conscience—as necessary spade-work to clear the critical air of a creeping, misconceived pietism. Certainly this resigned address to the job in hand explains the main puzzle of Empson's later work. Why should the brilliant, ground-breaking critic of Ambiguity and Pastoral now be so occupied with scholarly quarrels, attempting (for instance) to re-establish, against heavy textual odds, the earlier, more libertine versions of Donne's love poems? Why expend such labour, against the weight of received opinion, to justify his editorial omission of the pious marginal glosses to 'The Ancient Mariner'?

The reasons to be distinguished here are, firstly, the force of a ruling preoccupation; secondly the workings of a rationalised 'heretic' outlook, constant with Empson throughout his writings; and thirdly a distinct though allied bias toward unpresuming dialogue and 'open' literary forms. Here I wish only to suggest that when Empson opposes his liberal brief to more orthodox formalist doctrines, it is generally a Christian critic and implicitly Christian-traditional aesthetic that he objects to. Cleanth Brooks is, one gathers, a Methodist or low-church Anglican; his tone of reprimand with Empson is that of a religion which has contained and more or less thrived upon heresy. Not so with Hugh Kenner, whose hostility towards Empson—and through him, towards the whole spirit of modern rationalism—would justify something of Empson's intransigent atheism.

There are good reasons for Empson's reticence in matters of explicit critical theory. Formalist criticism constantly states and re-confirms its theoretical premises, as defined by the working alliance of Wimsatt, the aesthetic philosopher, and the various New Critics who applied his doctrines. As Cleanth Brooks habitually reads it, poetry is always a model example of its own, critically sanctioned, unique status; its formal autonomy, inviolable resistance to paraphrase, and above all its removal from contingent spheres of 'intention' and biography. Poetry confirms the theory, just as the theory, quite literally, 'confirms' the poem by closing it off within its own formal limits.

I shall later examine the presumptive logic of this operation by direct comparison with Empson's more open-minded practice. Meanwhile one notices how the poetry of, for instance, Allen Tate and John Crowe Ransom—themselves New Critics by general persuasion—is highly wrought and ironically fortified, perfectly conforming to the New Critical disciplines. Never would they be seen trailing a companion 'note', like the poetry of Empson, supplying the kind of useful hint and detail which might not quite have been 'got into' the poem itself. The critical intrusion may be to point out, as with Empson's 'Letter IV', that at some stage the 'basic feelings' have seemed to have 'nothing to do with the moral', prompting him to attempt revision (*Collected Poems*, p. 103). Or it may, more intrinsically, extend the relevance of some particular conceit to a general truth about the apprehension of poetry. Thus in his note to 'Letter V', Empson glosses the pun 'knot chance' as an instance where 'the connection of thought [it makes] possible spreads itself into an actual meaning' (p. 104). In both cases the note functions as an extension, almost a genetic stage, of the poem itself.

By appending these prose glosses to his poems, Empsom is in effect running counter to all the New Critical assumptions about poetic form. His notes are not, like those which Eliot supplied to 'The Waste Land', keys to esoteric points of reference, separate and dispensable once the poem's private allusions have been grasped. Empson's notes are integral; they are the poem's *literary* complement, and often supply the context and tone for a relatively thin structure of conceits. The implicit point here is that the language of poetry is continuous with—directly qualified by—the expository language of prose. Empson decisively parts company with the formalist doctrines of discontinuity and poetic autonomy. John Crowe Ransom was true to critical form when he objected, in a generally admiring essay, that Empson's readings of poetry might often apply equally to 'a piece of infinitely qualified prose'.[4]

Here, perhaps, is the main reason why Empson's criticism does not readily pass into abstract statements of principle. The most natural, endemic kind of literary theory is that which produces—and finds itself constantly confirmed by—an ontology

of poetic form. Given the basic tenets of formalist criticism—
multiplicity in unity, autonomy of form, personal disengage-
ment—poetry can only confirm the critic's leading predilections.
He will reckon it worth close attention only if it seems to embody
these principles; otherwise he will find it lacking in structural
coherence. Coleridge, who provided the New Critics with many
of their central definitions, had the light touch and discursive
energy to escape their rigid application. But for a critic like
Cleanth Brooks, the chapter-length essay gives just sufficient
space for a neatly-turned reprise from critical theory to poem and
back again to theory. 'What Wordsworth wanted to say
demanded his use of paradox, . . . could only be said powerfully
through paradox.'[5] Once accept paradox as an absolute aesthetic
value, and this kind of argument takes on a perfect circularity.
Paradox is seen to be constitutive of all good poetry; a formal
principle with its own privileged rules of elucidation.

In *Seven Types*, Empson constantly reverts to paraphrase,
albeit multiple paraphrase, as a means of critical explanation.
He insists that Ambiguity belongs to a normal, not a uniquely
poetic order of thought and language, accessible to prose explanations which must perhaps lessen its concentrated *point* but not
its specific complexity. At one stage he finds an ambiguity of
the seventh type—'perversions of the negative'—in the way an
editor of Shakespeare faces about among various possible
emendations of a difficult passage. Empson, in some famous pages,
works his way back *through* the discarded suggestions, to arrive
finally at the complex, perhaps obscure word or phrase which
most likely satisfied Shakespeare himself (*Seven Types*, pp. 81–8).
I shall show later how close this process comes to the view of
poetic 'intention' which Empson assumes in his recent editorial
work on Donne and Coleridge. For the moment it serves to
indicate that Ambiguity is essentially a part of the normal,
rational-deductive habits of thought. Empson's reading of the
lines from Shakespeare uses material that 'three centuries of
scholars and critics' had collected. The claim is that Ambiguity
fits their conjectures into a new genetic unity, effectively re-
constituting Shakespeare's intentions. It is not, clearly, the kind
of specialised rhetorical theory which sets poetry apart from the
normal process of reason.

The idea of 'continuity', as here defined—chiefly the continuity between poetry and prose discourse—is important in Empson's writing. The doctrine is inconspicuous, as a matter of belief, since only in its negative form does it need to be stated at all dogmatically. T. S. Eliot took this negative line, influenced to some extent by the doctrines of T. E. Hulme. Following up its echoes among the pronouncements of the New Critics, one can see how variously were the bye-laws drawn of the classicist division between aesthetic and rational realms of discourse. Hulme wanted a clean break between our conceptions of the scientific, the human and the divine. Eliot amplified the distinction between psychology and ethics, finding Freud—and perhaps the complexities of his own emotional life—disturbingly at odds with his religious conception of ultimate values. Allen Tate speaks for the New Critics in thinking religion 'the only technique for validating' the belief in a separate realm of 'quality'.

On this disjunct scale of values, the poem has to know its proper place. Hulme wanted it to be descriptive, brief and precise, with no misplaced pretensions to knowledge on the higher, moral or religious plane. In his essay 'Romanticism and Classicism', Hulme connects 'the perverted rhetoric of rationalism' with the Romantic poetry which, in his opinion, had already had its day. Romanticism is 'spilt religion', whereas the new classical poetry knows its limitations and conceives of itself, apparently, as affiliated to the purely 'mechanical' on Hulme's discontinuous scale. 'Certain extremely complex mechanisms, subtle enough to imitate beauty, can work by themselves—I certainly think that this is the case with judgements about beauty.'[6] From here the way points clearly enough to Eliot's theme of 'impersonality' in poetic creation.

These ideas of Hulme are at the root of Empson's differences with the New Critics. Ransom's real objection to Empson's style of reading is that Empson takes poetry too *seriously*; takes it, that is, as a species of argument, with all the responsibilities of truth-telling prose, whether or not 'infinitely qualified'. Ransom's defensive tactics show clearly through the mixture of alarm and admiration which makes up his response to Empson's writing. The metaphysical procedure in poetry was, he suggests, curiously like the theological, with one vital difference: 'the poet was playful, while the theologian was in deadly earnest'. Metaphysical poetry had to 'suggest' theologies, not to imitate or in any way rival them. Ransom shares Hume's anxiety that poetry should not trespass upon serious grounds of moral or religious argument. His case against Empson encapsulates the means by which formalist criticism avoids such blasphemous implications. Poetry in Ransom's account translates the 'profoundest passions' into 'crisp, objective constructs'. Its seriousness of purpose is thus transformed into a non-committal, self-absorbed play of ideas.

Eliot's revived 'classicism' and its potent influence has seemed to Empson the source of all that he most dislikes in modern criticism. He sees it as a 'cult of unnaturalism', of precious immoralism in poetry and irresponsible foolishness in academic criticism. Hulme's principle of keeping 'the divine and the human absolutely separate' amounts, he thinks, to an excuse for 'boasting about seducing shopgirls and then boasting about revelation'.[7] At the same time one can feel the pull which Eliot exerted, for all his antipathetic doctrines, upon the intellectual values and the view of literary history taken in *Seven Types*. At one level the book is principally a 'decline and fall' of the metaphysical conceit, outlining its fortunes from the witty precision of Donne and Marvell to the diffuse, pre-Romantic metaphors of Henry Vaughan. To this extent, the book did reflect T. S. Eliot's idea of tradition and the formalist tenets by which later critics refined and consolidated it.

Possibly this conflict stems from the mixed character of Eliot's 'tradition'. In it, the English metaphysicals were oddly yoked to the French Symbolist poets, a pragmatic combination suited to Eliot's own poetic purpose. On the face of it, these two lines of descent are scarcely compatible, since the kind of witty argument that delighted the metaphysicals cannot have access to the opaque, purely intuitable Symbol. Empson, as poet and critic, is a great believer in poetry which argues its way, and a great doubter of the claims of literary Symbolism. The whole Symbolist tradition has, he suggests, 'grown up completely divorced from the tradition of fair public debate'.[8]

This appeal to 'public debate' typifies, in various ways, the moral and intellectual character of Empson's criticism. It is squarely opposed to the related orthodoxies of discontinuity, Symbolism and formalist doctrine. These represent a cultural nexus which Empson identifies—rightly, I think—with the prevalence of a highly orthodox Christian critical concensus. The Symbolist side of Eliot's allegiance, in his poetry as well as his criticism, limits and suppresses the role of active reason in exactly the way that Ransom prescribes. *The Waste Land* and the *Four Quartets* carry this programme into practice. Discursive connections are deliberately suppressed; the poem's structure, through its juxtapositions of irony and paradox, is felt to cut off its meaning from any possible sequence of reasoned argument.

Empson's books all seek, in different ways, to make terms between poetry and the normal conditions of language and commonsense discourse. This is the linguistic equivalent of the history of 'public debate' invoked against the doctrines of Symbolism. In *Complex Words*, Empson tends to single out the same kinds of words and phrase which claimed the attention of Wittgenstein and the 'ordinary language' philosophers. Wittgenstein investigated 'the grammar of those words which describe what are called "mental activities" . . . which comes to the same as saying . . . the grammar of "phrases concerning sense-data" . . .'[9] *Complex Words* has several chapters on 'sense', its occurrences in Shakespeare and Wordsworth, its normal and deviant uses. The chapter 'Sense and Sensibility' builds up a whole machinery of complex semantics for the basic word and its cognates, defining what must be the normal—balanced and active—sense of possibilities inherent in the word.

The main examples in *Complex Words* fall into two broad categories, according to the mode of semantic argument they suggest. 'Sense' refers to an implicit epistemology, a relation of thought to perception and of both to the intelligible forms of language. The word's semantics mime the condition of its rational self-interpretation as what Empson calls a 'compacted doctrine'. On the other hand, words like 'honest', 'fool' and 'dog'—all of which Empson shows to have a mutual, self-implicating tone about them—take on a social and ethical dimension. The first point to notice about 'fool', in Empson's 'hearty' sense of the word, is that 'it is mutual, and it claims an escape into some broader way of judgement or larger air' (*Complex Words*,

p. 109). This 'larger air' represents, in a general way, the background of elementary human sympathies. But also, more specifically from Empson's critical viewpoint, it is the medium of rational social exchange or (as he uses the word) of 'intellectuality'.

This forms a bridge between the moral and the epistemological premises of Empson's writing. *Complex Words* has three appendices on 'Theories of Value', marginally relevant to the main chapters unless this connection is recognised. Empson is up against the same widespread doctrines in ethics as in critical theory: mainly the emotivist theory which makes 'good' simply a container-word for any kind of suasive moralising purpose. Empson places his trust in a hopefully 'intellectual'—a rational or cognitive—theory of moral reasoning. Its logic is simple enough. 'Good effects are the same when I am there as when I am not, like the rest of the external world . . . Hence, it is good for me to produce good effects in you' (*Complex Words*, p. 127). This follows, Empson believes, from the 'intellectuality of the creature'.

These elementary notions would not be of much account if they were not so closely tied in with the linguistic and literary arguments of Empson's book. The starting-point of this rationalist ethic, as of Empson's criticism in general, is what he calls here 'an extremely rich and confused experience which is gradually analysed . . .' (*Complex Words*, p. 428). This could equally serve as a description of Empson's approach to poetry in *Seven Types*, where the richness and confusion are a part of the critical style, or again of *Complex Words*, where analysis plays a more orderly role. 'Intellectuality' means precisely this measuring-up of reason to the wealth of immediate experience. In criticism as in everyday judgement, this is the rule of generous interpretation.

These arguments contain, more than incidentally, a shrewd blow at the behaviouristic theory of mind, always within Empson's sights when he attacks 'emotive' doctrines of meaning. Such had been the philosophic exit chosen by I. A. Richards in *Science and Poetry* (1925) and its better-known sequel, *Principles of Literary Criticism*. Richards based his theory of poetry on the behaviourist model of emotive response and satisfied impulse.

He accepted the poets' claims to serious attention—a matter, he thought, of the utmost modern importance—only when completely divorced from the realms of logical discourse or truthful statement. Poetry, he believed, had an emotive, not a logical content. Its value lay in the power it possessed to organise our emotions by creating complex and finely balanced states of feeling, the effects of which might restore something of the imaginative wealth stolen from nature by the progress of modern science.

Empson's reaction to this doctrine crystallised the rather diffuse theoretical interests of the essays collected in *Complex Words*. He rejects what seems a last-ditch retreat, on Richards's part, into emotivist theories of meaning. Richards reduces the workings of language to an account of the 'sign-situation', or the context of behavioural response which associates word with object on a purely reflex model of language development. In *The Meaning of Meaning* (1924), he and Ogden dealt dismissively with the 'mentalist' philosophies of Meinong and Husserl, denying that subjectivity could ever be included in a science of language, except by introducing impossibly vague criteria. The New Critics, oddly enough, thought Richards a chief perpetrator of the 'affective fallacy', since he frankly took for his standard of poetic value the number and variety of 'impulses' a poem could satisfy. Yet Cleanth Brooks later stretched a hand to the prodigal—'not a renegade but a pioneer who started out from a different set of assumptions'.[10] In fact Richards's simplified psychology of response was transferred and modified easily enough in the New Critics' various objectifications of poetic form. The psychology of 'impulse' involved only a null subjectivity, a mechanistic philosophy of mind which offered little resistance to this process of assimilation. The same poetic virtues of complexity, balance and internal resolution governed both Richards's affective criteria and the various formal priorities of the New Critics.

An essay of 1948, sketching the background of *Complex Words*, shows how these questions came to be associated in Empson's mind. Of the word 'sense' he suggests programmatically that 'on the basis of such a word you could hint at a whole theory about how men *should* or *do* interpret their experiences'.[11] It is here that Empson's critical interests join on to the modern philosophy of 'ordinary language' descending, in various forms, from the later writings of Wittgenstein. It is as easy to miss the point of *Complex Words*—to regard it simply as an exercise in historical semantics—as to take Wittgenstein's *Philosophical Investigations* as merely a descriptive guide to the finer points of philosophic usage. Such indeed is the widespread objection to Wittgenstein's approach: that it answers nothing, simply pointing us back to comfortable habits of language which evade all the deep-lying issues of philosophy. One can see that Wittgenstein to some extent invited this objection. He expresses an interest in language which infers the 'grammar' (as he calls it) of sense-data and mental experience. But he, like Richards, avoids 'mentalistic' criteria by insisting that these usages interest the philosopher only as part of the 'system of language', and not as indicating anything in 'the mind of the speaker'.[12] Thus Wittgenstein can talk of 'sense-data' without the philosophic need or inclination to examine more closely the epistemological claims on which such usage rests. The 'system of language' of which he speaks corresponds to Richards's 'sign-situation', and carries the same deliberate limitations of scope. Empson, on the other hand, conducts a critique of 'sense' which also undermines the assumptions of behaviourism and lays the ground for a rationalist philosophy of mind, self-evident in the cognitive semantics of language.

Stanley Cavell moves in a similar direction when he sets about the appropriation of Wittgenstein's ideas for a worked-out philosophy of criticism. In his excellent summary: 'The problem of the critic, as of the artist, is not to discount subjectivity, but to include it . . . to master it in exemplary ways'.[13] Cavell argues, in the spirit if against the strict letter of Wittgenstein, that the elucidation of 'deep' distinctions in usage can properly be called a linguistic phenomenology. It involves not merely language as a system of significations, but language as an operative medium of thought, the 'rules' of which entail some important philosophic truths. As Empson more simply puts it, some degree of 'intellectuality'—of intelligent self-understanding—must operate in language, as in all human experience.

J. L. Austin, the linguistic philosopher, states the case of *Complex Words* when he sets out to demonstrate that 'a peculiar and intimate relation' exists between 'the emotion and the natural manner of venting it'. Empson also believes that the 'emotive' is not some separate, irreducibly affective mode of understanding; that it involves structures of implicit assertion, open to rational explanation; and that this implies a basic sanity about the general habits of usage. Austin likewise, in his essay 'The Meaning of a Word', calls for investigation into the difference between the predicates 'being a part of the meaning of' and 'having the same meaning'.[14] Empson stresses a similar distinction as part of the basic logical machinery of his Complex Words. It is this tightened grasp of the logic of multiple meanings which marks the book's advance on the somewhat makeshift logical 'types' of Ambiguity.

It is therefore in the nature of Complex Words that theory should at best be unobtrusive. As with 'ordinary language' philosophy, the problems should eventually give way to the immanent logic of commonsense reason as embodied in practical usage. This, I think, explains why the 'practical' chapters of Complex Words seem to be largely independent of the elaborate conceptual machinery of the first part. The theory is more a background of assurance, a generalised set of assumptions, than a rigid logical frame on which to hang the later chapters. Complex Words discovers much more than can be got, neatly and squarely, into the listed forms of equation. The typology of 'A=B' serves mainly as dissolved into the philosophic background of Empson's resistance to irrational theories of meaning.

POET AND CRITIC: A CHANGE OF HEART?

It may be useful at this point to consider the working relation between Empson's poetry and his developing critical interests. Many commentators, including F. R. Leavis,[15] noticed a falling-off in Empson's poetry after 1935 (when the first volume Poems —mostly the early Cambridge productions—was published). The later poems are less concentrated, more matter-of-fact and prosaic, often with the seemingly deliberate effect of having nothing to say and saying it. I disagree, as will soon become clear, with Leavis's opinion that Empson for some reason lost his poetic nerve in these pre-war years. But it does seem that his mental energies were concentrated elsewhere at this time, and it happens also that this was the period of gestation for *Complex Words*. The first hint of his new theoretical interests came in 1936 with the essay 'Feelings in Words', followed closely by 'Sense and Sensibility'. Empson has written of the sheer exhilaration, the creative satisfaction, he found in his critical work at the time.

Of course, one could speculate endlessly on the possible connections here. What does seem relevant is the philosophic temper of *Complex Words*—the way in which it leads criticism down into regions of verbal experience characterised by the common-sense assumptions of 'ordinary language'. Cavell remarks of Wittgenstein's philosophy that:

> the more one learns, so to speak, the hang of oneself, and mounts one's problem, the less one is able to say what one has learned; not because you have forgotten . . . but because nothing you say would seem like an answer or solution; there is no longer any question which your words would match . . .[16]

The thought, mood and style of this—offhand, slightly surprised to be still talking at all—echo remarkably the tone of Empson's poem 'Let it go' (first published in 1955):

> It is this deep blankness is the real thing strange.
>> The more things happen to you, the more you can't
>>> Tell or remember even what they were.
>
>> The contradictions cover such a range.
>>> The talk would talk and go so far aslant.
>>>> You don't want madhouse and the whole thing there.

The poem has a strange, oblique intensity of feeling, hardly related to the flat, listless quality of its language, the various one-line pot-shots at meaning. One is pulled up at last by the staring specificity of 'madhouse' and the vague but total statement of 'the whole thing there'. The poem seems to strain in two directions, both leading out of poetry. 'The talk would talk'—which takes the casual looseness of language to the point of sheer redundancy. And in the last line one feels just the opposite: a self-locked private intensity of meaning which

Empson the critic, with his mistrust of private symbolism, would surely consider an obscure and unachieved piece of writing.

The language of the poem mimics the 'deep blankness' of its theme. There is something apt in a review Empson wrote, in 1955, of The Way of Deliverance, a rather morbid study of the last days of condemned Japanese war-criminals. One of them—'so very much like the corresponding Englishman'—said before dying: 'No, I haven't written anything. There doesn't seem to be anything to write about. Thank you very much.'[17] This lets it go with the same achieved patience as Empson's poem, which perhaps he had in mind when writing the review. The poem says, I think, not that reason cannot reach some ultimate assurance, but that sometimes it matches commonsense so completely that poetry seems beside the point.

In short, the 'crisis' in Empson's poetry was as much a matter of poetic means, or of what Empson could, at the time, get satisfactorily into language, as of anything recalcitrant in his mood or experience. This is, of course, a crude distinction; the two kinds of problem are inseparable, and doubtless the poem's blank gestures in its final line face up to some private defeat or misgiving. But the point for criticism—for the sort of criticism Empson writes in Complex Words—is that their understated emotion passes outside the normal ambit of adequate expression. It hints at a state of wise self-acceptance which even its flat mono-syllables rhetorically disturb; then, in the last line, admits to private perplexities equally beyond communicative reach.

Possibly these were the problems and perceptions which channelled Empson's interest away from poetry into the kind of criticism attempted in Complex Words. An increasing mistrust of the 'emotive', the private and unaccountable in language, would tend to produce the sort of close attention to poetic logic which hardly facilitates the writing of poetry. The view of creative psychology in Complex Words—or the critic's attitude toward it—scarcely corresponds to anything resembling a dynamics of literary creation. 'There is something like an impertinence in calling a good poet's work "emotive"; he makes it look emotive because that is the right relation of the emotive to the cognitive part.'[18] This seems alarmingly remote as a piece of descriptive psychology. But in the context of *Complex Words* it becomes a matter of intellectual tact, or of commonsense practical judgement. It attributes to the poet a mood 'like those pretences of humility which it is more sensible not to take at their face value'. This is the Pastoral attitude, carried over into the basic mechanisms of critical response. It involves the Pastoral irony of 'putting the complex into the simple', along with the knowledge that any such treatment must seem absurd from another point of view. It has the additional effect, however, of cutting the critic off from the natural roots of poetic expression, forcing him out on an intellectual limb; like that avatar of Pastoral, the gentleman-scholar, who becomes increasingly central to the *genre*, but intellectually more and more 'critical' and remote.

So while, on the one hand, the development of Empson's criticism may have inhibited his poetry, there was also the rationalising activity of *Complex Words* to provide a focus for his new-found interests. Cavell talks of Socrates' aim to 'coax the mind down from self-assertion—subjective and private definition—and lead it back, through the community, home'.[19] This could just as well stand for the philosophic project of *Complex Words*. It offers some reason for the direction of Empson's intellectual effort since the nineteen-thirties.

I feel that this rather negative connection is the main bridge between Empson's poetry and his criticism. His critical interest has now been in the ascendant for at least thirty years. In any assessment of his work to date, the criticism must take first place as the main and continuing vehicle of his literary thought. There is, of course, a more obvious connection between the earlier poems and criticism. The 'Cambridge' poetry bears out, more or less deliberately, the ideas advanced in *Seven Types*; its meanings dense and logically rewarding, intended for the reader who enjoys the challenge of a philosophic chase. But only within the conventions established by this early writing—habits of response slightly artificial in kind—can such connections be usefully pursued. Ambiguity is mainly a subject for rhetorical explication, dealing with its local devices and subtleties of style; not with its relation to language at large, which becomes the dominant theme of *Complex Words*. Ambiguity, as I have already suggested, leads on naturally to the refinements and distinctions of formalist theory, removed as a matter of principle from the generalised nature of verbal intelligence.

In 1961, when he came to write a preface to the third edition of *Seven Types*, Empson was content to define Ambiguity very broadly as 'a feeling of generalisation—an appeal to a background of human experience . . . all the more present when it cannot be named' (*Seven Types*, p. xv). In this description, echoed in additional footnotes throughout the text, Empson seems to modify Ambiguity through the knowledge gained in the meantime of Pastoral and Complex Words. These categories have their roots, not in the clear-cut cases of Ambiguity, but in the dubious readings where Empson's rhetorical treatment does not wholly exhaust the richness of his text. I shall later be taking one such case—a passage from Wordsworth's 'Tintern Abbey'—to show that Empson's dissatisfaction, his awareness of somehow falling short, was a spur to the much deeper explorations of *Complex Words*.

Georg Lukacs, in his book *Writer and Critic*, calls for an aesthetic which can recognise in Ambiguity 'the inexhaustibility of man (the subject) and of the objective world encompassing him'.[20] This carries the main argument of his Marxist-humanist case against critical formalism. For Cleanth Brooks, 'irony' and 'paradox' are operative only within a closed poetic structure, contained in manageable compass by the tensive play of contradictions. This method precludes exactly that 'inexhaustibility' which Lukacs demands as the basic assumption of a humanistic criticism. Cavell states the philosophic point at issue when he insists that 'intension', the *analytic* property of complex meaning, cannot be a substitute for 'intention'. Analysis cannot replace meaning, which eludes the explanatory power of 'definitional equivalents'. Cavell speaks of the 'pragmatic implications', 'categorial declaratives' and possibly the 'difference between grammar and rhetoric' which suggest the bearing of linguistic philosophy beyond the reach of formal analysis. Cavell's 'grammar' and 'rhetoric' are the equivalents, respectively, of the kind of poetic *intentionality* which Empson discovers in his Complex Words, and the formalist inventory of structural norms laid down by the New Critics.

Therefore, on the strength of Empson's later work, one can
take issue with those critics who have chosen to develop what
they see as the formal or ontological dimensions of Ambiguity.
According to their various persuasions, these theorists have
pushed the logic of multiple meaning in different directions.
For instance, Winifred Nowottny, in *The Language Poets Use*,
rejects 'ambuiguity' as too vague a term and supplies in its place
the concept of 'extralocution'. This implies more firmly than
Empson's term 'a stopping short of complete specification' and a
rhetoric which transcends 'the limitations of ordinary language'.[21]
Such, certainly, would be the logical consequence or fullest
achievement of Ambiguity, considered as a formal, rhetorical
category. Philip Wheelwright fits Ambiguity into a full-blown
Symbolist aesthetic by much the same argument; that multiple
meanings must completely forego the rational 'either-or' and
embrace the poetic 'both-and'.[22] Like Brooks, he treats poetic
language as completely specifying, by means of intensive collocation, the rhetorical terms of its own acceptance.

Empson would not for a moment accept, with Nowottny,
that poetry is a matter of 'not entering into the full commitment
of unequivocal assertion'. He insists, on the contrary, that poetry
is answerable to the quotidian logic of rational prose statement.
So far as it eludes or defeats that logic, its deviation means something more than merely to label it 'poetic'. In Wordsworth, for
example, Empson meets the limits and beyond of rational argument. He carries the critique of 'sense', as used in *The Prelude*,
to the same point as reached by the 'ordinary language' philosopher when he shows how a problem arises through philosophic
language becoming specialised beyond commonsense usage.
Wordsworth's verbal equations make false claims, being logically
unable to erect the 'third concept' which their idealism
promises. All the same, as Empson admits, 'the result makes
very good poetry, and probably suggests important truths'
(*Complex Words*, p. 305).

The individuality of Empson's approach may be gauged by
comparing it with the philosophic treatment of Wordsworth's
ideas, similar in its point of departure, undertaken by Geoffrey
Hartman.[23] Hartman's theme is the 'unmediated vision', the
poet's striving for an intuitive and unwilled fusion between

nature and the creative imagination. Hartman therefore expounds from Wordsworth, as a matter of imaginative creed, what Empson finds embedded in the poet's semantic 'equations'. According to Empson, Wordsworth's mystical tonings result from his play on the senses of 'sense'—'jumping over' the middle term in the word's normal range (common sense) to effect a startling and paradoxical conjunction of the outer pair ('sense-data' and 'the divine imagination given by love'). In this way, 'good sense' is pushed into the background of the word's equations (*Complex Words*, p. 296). Hartman also sees that Wordsworth's philosophic point was to establish 'identities' rather than logical arguments of 'relation'. His poetry shows 'the mind's capacity for non-relational and simultaneous apprehension'. Hartman is attempting a persuasive description of a system of metaphysics. He therefore gives Wordsworth his argumentative head, and takes the poet's language on its own terms as realising, in point of achieved meaning, all that it states or intimates of his idealistic vision. Empson, on the other hand, is more interested in the language-strategies than the content of ideas in Wordsworth's poetry. The rhetoric is, he admits, indispensable to the high prophetic tone of Wordsworth's language. But judged in terms of a rational semantic, it proves somewhat wilful and evasive in its way with Complex Words.

Reviewing Dylan Thomas's *Collected Poems* in 1954, Empson sums up this attitude in simpler terms: 'I assume on principle there is something there which I feel and can't see, but *could* see.'[24] *Seven Types* already suggests this mood by constantly stating both points of view. It is addressed to those with courage enough to rationalise their own, perhaps delicate modes of response. At the same time this rationalism is continually chastened by an awareness of the impossibility of ever achieving its ambition. In Pastoral this mood is captured in a socialised metaphor and a somewhat pragmatic view of intellectual history. *Some Versions* chronicles, in effect, the rise and social vicissitudes of the rationalising, 'critical' consciousness. Complex awareness, a kind of remnant aristocracy, working out its conscientious scruples in the decade of Spain and the 'pylon' poets—such is the critical lens through which literary history is viewed as Pastoral.

These generic transformations are my main topic in Chapter 2. I have sketched them here to suggest their connection with the mood of chastened rationalism in Empson's writing. In this light, the equivocal 'rules' of *Complex Words* still seem logically puzzling, but in some way rightly and inevitably so. Empson put the case most succinctly in 1931, in reply to John Sparrow's criticisms of I. A. Richards.[25] We must accept 'verbal fictions', Empson wrote, and yet at all costs subject them to the test of 'true beliefs'. In criticism it is 'essential to analyse beauty; essential to accept it unanalysed; essential to believe that the universe is deterministic; essential to act as if it was not'. Determinism is the outlook most obviously congruous with verbal analysis. Both suppose a confidence in rational explanation; a directive rightness of understanding matched by the essentially normative character of its object. Some such metaphysic—a notion of harmonious adjustment—seems to subtend the formalist doctrines of discontinuity. Without it, and discounting all possible access to the poet's intention, there would simply be no hold for critical understanding. For Empson, the crucial departure comes with the qualifying doubt. No such elaborate logic can really be sufficient; no formal analysis really hope to uncover the roots of poetic beauty.

Empson's answer to Sparrow epitomises the classic problems of philosophy, as enounced for example in the 'Antinomies' of Kant's *Critique of Pure Reason*. For Kant, those unthinkable complementarities—free will and determinism, the finite and the infinite, the 'cosmological' paradox—marked off the realm of empirical fact from that of reflective reason. Empson's early writings often seem, in a less formal, more exuberant way, to juggle with contradictions which lift the process of reason onto a higher, more creative plane. His Cambridge poems (for example, 'The World's End'), explore the paradox of 'finite but unbounded' space in the same exhilarating style. There is some suggestion, even in the rather flippant reply to Sparrow, that these intellectual conflicts *can* be resolved in some useful and important way. Empson's defence of Richards is not without its pointed reservations. The psychologistic approach, treating poetry as a means of 'self-completion', tends to obscure what Empson calls 'the element of objectivity in criticism'. Thus

Empson's argument casually outlines the stages of enlightenment described by Kant in the *Critique*: from Sparrow's naïve and restrictive certainties, through Richards's basically sceptical subjectivism, to a properly 'critical' attitude which restores rational confidence to the act of judgement.

This, then, is something of the intellectual mood behind the 'rules' of verbal implication suggested in *Complex Words*. It gives rise to the slightly devious, familiarly Pastoral tone of critical address, whereby the 'emotive' part of poetry is seen as a 'pretence of humility', not to be taken too much at face value. This can be seen also in Empson's dealings with Milton, from *Some Versions* to *Milton's God* (1961). He treats *Paradise Lost* as laying claim to the rational prose virtues of justice, consistency and moral generosity. Refusing to make the usual allowances, either for its somnolent verbal music or resistless theology, Empson makes the poem continuous with the ordinary language and values of human experience. In *Some Versions* his entry had been by way of Bentley, the rationalising eighteenth-century editor of Milton. Bentley was often wrong-headed, and Empson can relish his more absurd lapses of judgement. But at root, Empson argues, this is the right way to read poetry. Bentley is an early model for the 'absurd' rationalist philosopher, one of the constituent types of Pastoral, much in evidence in the later chapters. There is something of this character in Empson's own writing; frankly acknowledged in the piled-up examples and wire-drawn reasoning of *Seven Types*, and present in a more subdued way—as a part of the founding metaphor—in *Some Versions*. Hugh Kenner, always hostile to Empson, applied to him an image drawn from Pastoral: that of the Victorian natural scientist and philosopher, 'patiently labouring at his absurd conceptions'.[26] For all its belittling intention, there is a grain of acute sympathy in Kenner's remark.

This openness to experience, the readiness to get it all down and, perhaps, risk one's intellectual dignity, is very strong in Empson's early criticism. He told Richards[27] that *Seven Types* had simply made a 'heap' of all his interests at the time, and that the main reason for publishing was to see what readers would make of it. He relied on common sense to sort out the more or less logical claims of the book's general plan. In his later writing, this chastened rationalism is the basis on which Empson moves away from a formalised rhetoric of poetry, and explores instead the generalised logic of poetic language.

Of a reading of Shakespeare in *Seven Types*, Empson explains: 'I am sorry to appear so fantastic, but I can form no other working notion of what this unique mind must have been like when in action' (p. 84). Empson arrives at his 'working notion' by comparing textual variants, and then reconstructing the associative jumps of Shakespeare's mind, from the obvious to the more recondite—and potentially richer—word in context. Clearly the general outlook of *Seven Types* is the attitude Empson associates with the nineteenth-century editors of Shakespeare, those who 'secretly believed in a great many meanings at once' (p. 81). However, it is the eighteenth-century scholar, the rational man with 'none of this indifferentism', whose object was 'to unmix the metaphors as quickly as possible' —it is this maligned figure who really beckons to Empson. 'We no longer have enough faith to attempt such a method', he confesses. But this kind of rational confidence, keenly aware of its own limitations, is what the book finally tries to inculcate.

Empson's rationalism is therefore a complex of ideas and attitudes, scarcely to be understood apart from the Pastoral metaphor. Questions of methodology are always to some extent pragmatic, known by their fruits in finer shades of response. Empson can even regard the theoretical props of anti-intentionalism—which, on the whole, he considers a metaphysical nonsense —as having a sort of 'flat good sense' about them.[28] It is indeed difficult, in literature as in life, to judge fairly and accurately of other people's intentions. But again, 'flat good sense' has the familiar Pastoral ring. In *Seven Types*, discussing a poem of Herbert, Empson speaks of the 'flat and as it were pastoral' effect of the imagined situation; 'a sort of humility and reality, something of the conviction of steady prose' (p. 120). This counts as an instance of the Third Type, but one which Empson cannot categorise to his own satisfaction. Read in a slightly different way, its Ambiguity lies 'deep within the obscurity of the First Type'. It amounts in fact to a kind of complex 'generalisation' which only 'an absurd stretching of the idea of ambiguity' could accommodate to his scheme. It is, I shall argue, precisely his impression of these 'flat' poetic devices and effects of context that points the way toward Empson's ideas of Pastoral and Complex Words. The fact is that Ambiguity meets its limit, not in those extreme complexities of meaning to which paraphrase cannot do justice, but in the realisation that often the simplest forms of expression evoke the most resonant contexts of experience. Thus to speak of the 'flat good sense' of the anti-intentionalist case is to understand it, not as an absolute or 'metaphysical' argument, but as a token of the elusive complexity of all human relations.

Complex Words is therefore nothing so reductive or self-defeating as a logical analysis of the orders of poetic statement. Empson's implicit claim for the permutations of predicative logic—the topic of his first two chapters—is that they provide a more confident working notion of the limits of intelligibility. They lend weight to Empson's case against the view (as taken by Orwell in 1984) that language can be adapted without resistance to any perverted rhetoric or creed. Empson, on the contrary, believes and sets out to prove that 'the human mind, as expressed in language, is not irredeemably lunatic and cannot be made so' (p. 83). The book takes its cue, and finds much of its literary material, in that eighteenth-century temper which 'let them prune down so far towards rationalising their emotional life without killing the roots' (p. 169). This is not to deny anything of their importance, variety or partial independence to the life of the emotions. It does not refer directly to any plausible model of genetic or descriptive psychology. The pragmatics of Complex Words are indeed far removed from any 'inside' account of creative process. Empson's is distinctly a philosophic or heuristic point of view, entailed by a level of argument quite distinct from that envisaged, for the most part, in Seven Types.

All later attempts to consolidate Ambiguity—to regularise Empson's logic and pigeon-hole his categories—miss this complicating factor and are therefore untrue to the spirit of Empson's criticism. Such are the formal extensions undertaken by Wheelwright and Nowottny. Similar, although taking a different nominal direction, is the worked-out psychology of multiple meaning described by Ernst Kris.[29] Kris invents a number of

logical distinctions, speaking of the separate orders of 'con-
junctive', 'additive' and 'integrative' ambiguity. These represent
an ascending scale, the last most typically and completely
characterising the 'poetic' use of ambiguity. Kris, like Richards,
refers aesthetics to psychology, placing his relative values on the
various kinds and degrees of complex mental response. But,
again like Richards, his theories transfer without problem to a
purely formal, objectivistic view of literary meaning. His psychological gradings are simply a formal logic of complication, shifted
onto an affective plane.

Empson's attitude to questions of literary psychology is altogether more circumspect and qualified than those of Kris and
Richards. There is an indicative turn of thought in his essay on
Tom Jones, where Empson takes it that Fielding 'refused to
believe that the "inside" of a person's mind (as given by
Richardson in a letter, perhaps) is much use for telling you the
real source of his motives'.[30] Empson forms a working notion of
Fielding's mentality, its moral generosity and invincible balance
of judgement, in the course of interpreting the author's attitude
to his hero. In effect, this essay brings out all the critical assumptions of *Complex Words* without any use of the book's verbal
machinery. Fielding's 'homely, commonsense temperament' is
the field of elementary sympathies within which the novelist,
his characters and the like-minded reader have a certain community of interest. Empsom describes the technique of 'double
irony' whereby Fielding contains and expresses the ambiguities
of his own moral involvement. The capacity to see all sides of a
question, and at the same time to refer one's judgement to honest
self-appraisal—this is the evidence of moral generosity which
Empson finds in Fielding, and which also provides the ethical
basis for many of his examples in *Complex Words*. He deduces
Fielding's intention and, indeed, his moral character as a man
'fit to sit on a magistrate's bench, prepared, in literature as in
life, to know and judge any situation'. Statements of this sort
have struck many critics as mere 'eccentricities' in the later
Empson. It should I think be recognised that they follow on
directly from the theme of Pastoral, where Double Irony is a
staple of the *genre*, and from the social-semantic investigations
of *Complex Words*.

Empson has always defended A. C. Bradley against the attacks on his notion of dramatic 'character', led by F. R. Leavis; so he would probably not welcome any too subtle or qualified account of his own approach to the subject. Nevertheless, it can be seen that Pastoral and the approach through Complex Words throw a crucial paradox into the whole idea. The characters of *The Beggars' Opera* 'are plausible if they don't mean all that the play puts into their words and delightful if they do, and the shift between the two theories is so easy that we take them as both' (*Some Versions*, p. 137). The emphasis here, as in most of Empson's Pastoral interpretations, is on the socialised process of reception and the appeal of complex meanings to a broad and generous variety of viewpoints. Dramatic 'character', in this context, is a conception qualified and expanded through the inbuilt ironies of a literary *genre*.

The essay on *Tom Jones*, although published in 1957, looks back to Pastoral in its attempt to give an answerable, common-sense account of the moral element in literature. So with *Complex Words*: the 'generality' of Empson's equations—their intellectual validity—is underwritten by the same structures of response as affirm the basic 'generosity' of human impulse. Thus the Erasmic sense of 'fool', in its manner of self-implicating irony, allows 'a black little piece of fun' to find 'two ways out into a larger air, the idea that tragic experience may lie behind wit, and the idea that simplicity is learned through adversity' (p. 122).

Again, this shows how Empson continually reverts to the authority of common sense and ordinary language, this time couched in the social currency of words which imply their own colloquial register. *Complex Words* is largely devoted to interpreting what Empson calls the 'flat', the apparently simple but in fact indefinitely complex uses of language. The critic has to realise their inexplicit background, those hints they contain of a subdued and somehow *normal* state of feeling, rather than fit them into some specialised theory of poetic meaning and structure. Empson therefore avoids the ontological constructions placed upon poetry by the New Critics. He treats the poem as a concentrated species of ordinary language; drama and the novel as complex solutions to typical problems of social conflict and adjustment. Pastoral is an encompassing mode of imagination which cuts across the boundaries normally drawn between literary forms. What seemed to many critics (especially the Chicago Aristotelians[31]) a culpable laxness in matters of formal classification, indicates in fact a much greater interest on Empson's part in the means of communication common to all forms of literature. Pastoral has its own typology, an historical series in ascending order of complication. But this is far from the rigid division of *genres* demanded by the Aristotelian critics and observed by the New Criticism with its rhetorical definitions of poetic structure. The Pastoral procession of forms grows out of, and leads back to, the social mediations of language and ideology from age to age.

Complex Words are essentially 'democratic' in so far as they invite the kind of interpretation—based on a commonly available stock of response—which Empson sets out to explore. The 'hearty' feeling of words like 'sense', 'fool' and honest', referring their users to a background of shared understanding, comes to suggest an implicit ideology. Civilisation, as Empson interprets it, 'is slung between the ideas of Christianity and those of a half-secret rival . . . one that stresses pride rather than humility, self-realisation rather than self-denial, caste rather than the communion of saints or the individual soul' (*Complex Words*, p. 159). Empson effectively demonstrates that these, as well as the 'official' values, can give the critic what Walter Stein—a Christian and a follower of Leavis—thinks that Empson lacks: a consistency of 'analytic tact' joined with a 'purposive centrality of judgement'.[32] Stein envisages a criticism rooted in metaphysical, religious and moral sanctions. The 'purposive judgement' of *Complex Words* is that of a rationalist philosophy more apt to undermine than to strengthen the values of received belief.

Empson puts the rationalist case most simply in the opening chapter of *Milton's God*. 'We could not use language as we do, and above all we could not learn it . . . unless we were always floating in a general willingness to make sense of it; all the more, then, to try to make a printed page mean something good is only fair' (p. 28). This makes the critic's attitude of rational meliorism a matter of plain sense and decent obligation. It is for these reasons that Empson has habitually rejected any 'rules' of criticism which threatened to become an iron-cast orthodoxy. He has mostly reacted by renewing, in various ways, the appeal to commonsense standards of judgement. In Helen Gardner's edition of Donne he objected to textual readings arrived at 'by the grim authority of a scientific law'.[33] This comes surprisingly from the author of *Seven Types*, where allusions to modern science were not merely ornamental—where they assumed, in fact, something of the significance and depth of implication which they had for Empson's poetry at the time. However, the phase of scientific thought which bore most urgently on the early writing—the Cambridge science of Empson's university years—worked out philosophically as a case for the *indeterminacy* of many of the phenomena newly available to observation. In the last chapter of *Seven Types* the practice of specific verbal analysis gives way to speculations about modes of poetic meaning more diffuse, or less demonstrably anchored in particular details of 'the text'. Literature, Empson reflects, 'demands a sense, not so much of what is really there, as of what is necessary to carry a particular situation off' (p. 245). The concept of Pastoral was to explore the various social modalities of such 'particular situations'. And *Complex Words*, as I shall try to show, carried on these social intimations into the study of poetic language and logic.

Empson's defection from verbal analysis, strictly defined, goes with his increasing interest in questions of authorial 'intention'. Stanley Fish has remarked acutely that the interpretations in *Milton's God* 'developed in the spaces *between* the explorations of verbal texture rather than as a result of them'.[34] At its most suspect, this comparative disregard of verbal detail can amount to a mere excuse for handy misquotation. In reply to some sharp criticisms on this score, Empson urged that 'the idea of checking your quotations is fairly recent, and not always relevant'.[35] Hazlitt, he remarked, often quoted inaccurately but still very much to the point. The appeal is rather suspect, but it does help to suggest how Empson had moved away from detailed verbal analysis toward a more generalised style of criticism. Poetic effects, as he comments at the end of *Seven Types*, are 'not easily disturbed by altering a few words' (p. 241).

In his preface to *Coleridge's Verse: a Selection*, Empson repeats from *Seven Types* his point about the impasse in theoretical physics; the fact that science often requires the postulation of mysterious 'forces' which may be fictions but have to be accepted, at least provisionally, if the problems are to be worked out. The imaginary 'forces' are

> eliminated from the equations by being absorbed into the Equals sign, on the basic assumption that cause equals effect; and maybe they are a delusion derived from feelings in our muscles; but nobody could learn dynamics without thinking about forces ... (p. 15)

It is this aspect of the new science—quantum physics and the Indeterminacy Principle—which leaves its mark on *Seven Types*. In *Complex Words* also, a measure of tactical presumption is 'absorbed into the Equals sign', the book's official schemes of logical assertion being only the speculative instrument of subtler penetration. Empson's example of 'physical forces' bears directly on the question of authorial intention. Such things, he concludes, 'can always only be guessed at', but the guess 'should always be made'.

This is the point of Empson's reference, in *Seven Types*, to the modern shift in scientific knowledge, which now prefers to allow for 'a probability [attaching to] the natural object' rather than 'the fallibility of the human mind' (p. 81). Of course this can lean over into dubious tactics; as when Empson defends his misquotations by saying that such ideal precision as his opponents want is no longer a part even of the exact sciences which (presumably) they have in mind. This lends itself all too plausibly to the admission elsewhere that, in criticising a *long* poem, one might be 'tempted to fudge a detail to fit an overall interpretation'.[36] But this is, I would argue, only the more dubious extreme of what remains a wholly consistent ethic of interpretation.

This aspect of Empson's criticism has not been much noticed, despite its explicitness in *Seven Types*. In many ways the epistemology of Empson's final chapter anticipates the more recent reflections of Michael Polanyi on the status of scientific knowledge. Polanyi rejects the idea of exactitude or positive certainty as the goal of science. 'You cannot formalise the act of commitment . . . to attempt this is to exercise the kind of lucidity which destroys its subject-matter'.[37] Empson also is nagged by the likely objection that too much close analysis may spoil a reader's unimpeded enjoyment of poetry. In *Seven Types* he argues such doubts away, but not without some lengthy and searching discussion of the relative claims of 'taste' and 'understanding'.

Finally, of course, Empson sides with those whose intellectual curiosity outweighs their more delicate scruples. But he seems to be still dissatisfied with this answer. The 'surrealist type of critic' might reject such knowledge altogether and argue that Pope, for instance, 'would have written just the same if he had had no critical dogmas' (p. 254). Empson disagrees, but sees that this argument might hint at an important truth about the puzzle of priorities: 'the dogma produces the sensibility, but it must itself have been produced by it'. Empson's most convincing answer is the chapter on Pope in *Complex Words*, where the 'dogmas' of Pope's critical opinion, defined through his use of 'sense' and 'wit', are shown to be a part of the operative style of his poetry. The hint of double-take about using the explicit assertions of the *Essay on Criticism* to demonstrate their own semantic logic is, of course, very much to the point of Empson's argument. He does, however, make it plain that Pope's equations, though peculiarly neat and self-contained, typify the resources of covert statement in all such 'complex' (witty yet rational) uses of language.

Complex Words has learned to use practical criticism as an object-lesson in its own philosophic premises. In *Seven Types*, with its rather detached discussion of these problems, Empson finally justifies the book by the vague hope that it provides 'a belief that all sorts of poetry may be explicable' (p. 256). On these terms, criticism remains a curious and paradoxical enterprise. In his later books Empson finds a working solution on the pragmatic levels of Pastoral and Complex Words. The chapters on theatre in *Some Versions* rely on the idea that 'an appeal to the circle of a man's equals' corresponds to 'the fundamental escape into the fresh air of the mind' (p. 59). The social mobility of Pastoral, expressed in a series of dramatic metaphors, replaces the rather vague appeal from Ambiguity to the wider human background of knowledge and experience. And in *Complex Words*, the semantics of Wordsworth's 'sense' or of Pope's 'wit' hold the same invitation to an exercise of readerly tact which is also a form of self-giving generosity. Poetry is not an object of knowledge as such, but an occasion or (literally) a *pretext* for the attentive reader's agile sympathies.

Again, the obvious parallel here is with the interests and claims of 'ordinary language' philosophy. In reply to the extreme sceptical argument that one can 'know' only one's own sensations, J. L. Austin remarks that in sensitive common usage the verb 'to know' cannot take a direct object. ' "I know what he is feeling" is not "there is an X which both he and I know and he is feeling" but "I know the answer to the question What is he feeling?" '[38] This argument has an important bearing on the question of Intention in literature. It also helps to define the kind of 'knowledge' Empson seeks of his texts in *Complex Words*.

There is an introductory note to *The Gathering Storm*, Empson's second volume of verse, which shows him trying to puzzle out the sometimes obscure connection between his poems and their prose glosses. The argument takes an interesting turn which parallels, to some extent, the process of reflection which led from Ambiguity to Pastoral. Besides their argumentative 'point', his conceits (Empson thinks) have something to do with the pragmatic, broadly social aspect of literary communication. 'Puzzle interest' is connected with 'the old snob interest', and distinguished only by the fact that the puzzlers 'are not offended by seeing the answer in the Notes'. For the author's part, Empson reflects that 'the motives behind making the puzzle are themselves very mixed'. In fact, the conceits and elements of recondite knowledge in Empson's poetry are often the props, or at most the convenient intellectual frame, for a much more complex play of attitudes.

Seven Types was early to recognise this background complexity in its dealings with the Metaphysicals. Donne, in 'A Valediction: of Weeping', is found to be writing out of a total situation irreducible to verbal detail, precisely because it would seem 'ungenerous' for the poet, in such intimate verse, to set out his equivocal feelings in plainer terms. Donne's conceits are all the more pregnant for *not* completely expressing the implied situation (*Seven Types*, p. 145). Even more in the case of Hood, the inveterate punster: 'wit is employed because the poet is faced with a subject which it is difficult to conceive poetically' (p. 109). Empson admires Hood for his sheer verbal neatness, but even more for the courage and fine social tact which lie *behind* the witty technique. The scope and subtlety of this implied background—almost independent of the witty technique—cause Empson to question even the basic importance of 'wit' in such a connection. He wonders whether 'the same effect could not be conveyed without an overt pun at all'. These speculations are within easy reach of Pastoral, where the refinements of social tact and class-manoeuvring take over from pure verbal intricacy as the main topic of attention.

It is in this way that *Seven Types* occasionally brings out the element of 'indeterminacy' which, according to the analogy with modern physics, attaches to the 'object' of critical perception. Criticism, like science, admits the impossibility of giving a certain account of what is objectively 'out there' on the page. I have suggested—perhaps too dramatically—that a 'crisis' comes on in Empson's poetry when the mass of these background feelings, sometimes spread out in the Notes, threatens to force itself *out* of the poem, leaving what amounts to a private nexus of meanings and associations. In 'The Beautiful Train' (*Collected Poems*, p. 64) the obscure image of the ballerina does more to offset, or to compensate, than actually to express the knotted complex of feelings supplied by Empson's Note. The situation was, we learn, the Sino-Japanese war; the Japanese, Empson felt, were in a 'tragically false position', and the Chinese 'with their beautiful good humour were always patient when I told them I was more sorry for the Japanese'. The poem can only resolve this into a tortured attempt at self-analysis—'And I a twister love what I abhor'—and a privately associated image. It is Empson's criticism, most of all *Complex Words*, which now finds a place for the complicated feelings and baffled rationality sensed behind the poem. As Empson treats it, the ironic but humane use of 'fool' catches precisely this moment of transition from the tragic to the humorously sympathetic.

Empson arranged the poems of *The Gathering Storm* to begin with 'Bacchus', the quintessence of his early 'clotted' style, and to end with 'Autumn on Nan-Yueh', a 'somewhat prattling long poem', written whilst a refugee in China. If the collection was read straight through, Empson wanted the change of style to seem connected with the 'gathering storm' of pre-war world politics. 'Bacchus' is pre-eminently an intellectual poem, based on consecutive argument through multiple conceits. 'Nan-Yueh' and 'The Beautiful Train' have no such firm argumentative basis. In the face of such painful tugs of loyalty as Empson's during the Sino-Japanese conflict, poetry is perhaps likelier to 'prattle', to keep talking regardless, than to try to bring experience perfectly into focus.

Among the Notes to *Collected Poems*, there is one piece of self-criticism in particular which seems to indicate the perplexities of Empson's writing at the time. Of the sonnet 'Not wrongly moved by this dismaying scene', Empson comments in retrospect that the final word 'free' now sounds 'an offensively false use of the great emotive term'. At this point, it seems, the critical scruples of *Complex Words* combine with Empson's tugs of loyalty to inhibit, at least in hindsight, the emotional sources of his poetry. The Note on 'Reflections from Rochester' brings out further painful connections:

> The mind uses unconscious processes (mining underground) and an outpouring of loose words, sometimes poisonous (gas); the reasons that make the thought of a country succeed can be as queer as the reasons that sometimes make war good for it, and a mere change of proportion might make either fail to work any longer. (p. 112)

This suggests, I think, on what precarious bases the spirit and logic of the poetry rested at this time. It is too much to argue that Empson's sanity is in the balance in these poems. However, the poetry itself is clearly at risk, as a medium scarcely adaptable to such tortuous mediations of meaning and conscience. This makes it the more understandable that Empson's interests were increasingly channelled into criticism rather than poetry.

Among Empson's reviews for the Cambridge magazine *Granta*, there is a piece on the 'English way of thinking', inspired by Bertrand Russell, which shows him already aware of both the normative character and the emotive temptations of language. A decent English style 'gives great resilience to the thinker, never blurs a point by too wide a focus, is itself a confession of how much always must be left undealt with, and is beautifully free from verbiage. To an enemy it looks like sheer cheating'.[39] In this last sentence, with curious prescience, there speaks the B.B.C. propagandist of Empson's wartime career. *Complex Words* likewise holds a delicate balance between its working faith in the ultimate rationality of language, and the practical understanding of how it can be manipulated to suasive ends. Doubtless his experience of Allied propaganda had a part in the interests of *Complex Words*. It must have intensified the clash of loyalties in the man just returned from teaching in China and Japan, and already torn between these two attachments. The published excerpts from his B.B.C. broadcasts show how difficult it was for Empson, on the one hand to ridicule the self-conceived destiny and racial purity of the Japanese, and on the other to allow them the national dignity needed for their eventual recovery.[40] Again one finds a confluence of reasons, mainly biographical, for the rationalising turn taken by Empson's criticism and—possibly—for the signs of emotional retreat in his poetry.

At this point I had better make some answer to the question whether criticism can, or legitimately should, express what amount to the critic's private involvements and sympathies. Of course Empson, like any critic, takes up poems which interest him and so give him something worthwhile to say. This defence covers the ground for *Seven Types*, where Hood rubs shoulders with Pope and Wordsworth, enabling Empson to make a general point about certain uses of poetic language; or again for *Some Versions*, where Gay's and Carroll's work happen to represent— a usefully ambiguous word—as much complexity of social poise as a sonnet of Shakespeare or Marvell's 'The Garden'. In such criticism, the idea of 'objective' or veridical judgement meets a testing paradox. A line must of course be drawn between the critic's own virtuosity—meanings patently 'read into' the text— and the content he can claim to have uncovered. But then, Empson's practice and the force of his example in these first two books would suggest that the line be drawn so as to include such subtleties as might, on a more conservative view, be counted highly subjective. There is no absolute distinction, no possible demarcation between what is 'in' the text and what is produced by the critic's active involvement.

Some Versions has at least the root notion of 'putting the complex into the simple' by which to organise its ascending scale of complications. Yet this merely postpones the issue. *The Beggars' Opera* and *Alice* are in many ways much simpler works than the poems of Shakespeare and Marvell. Empson, on the contrary, treats them as later and more subtle—because socially more complicated—variations on the Pastoral theme. It is not sufficient to invoke the supposed commonsense standards of disciplined perception and historical plausibility. Empson is claiming in effect that any competent reader, knowing the relevant history, and versed in the politics of the imagination, will understand more by elementary sympathies than the sceptical theorist of literature thinks he can possibly know. Reviewing Arthur Waley's *Secret History of the Mongols* in 1964, Empson remarked that the scholar 'probably does not realise how much interpretation he is putting in when he savours it [the cultural past] as literature'.[41] This observation could lead either to a completely sceptical relativism or—as it does with Empson—to a renewed confidence in the general human capacity for enlightened understanding.

Undoubtedly Empson's rationalistic humanism lends a strong ethical colouring to the detail of his readings. I would argue, however, that the opposite set of ideas—the formalist notion of poetry as an autonomous verbal structure—rests on an equally presumptive philosophy. Combining the various pronouncements of Hulme, Eliot and the New Critics, one gathers that poetry is set off completely from matters of moral and rational argument. It best serves its purpose by disciplined use of 'analogy' or 'collateral form', its closed limits of contextual statement reflecting (as R. P. Blackmur believes) its small portion of the 'substance of God'.[42] Such an outlook is quite as likely as Empson's to add its moralistic shading to the critic's practical judgement. On the whole, the proto-theological bias tends to be hidden by the plausible circular logic which I deduced from Cleanth Brooks's remarks on Wordsworth. However, it remains at bottom a theoretical *parti pris*.

THE RATIONAL MOTIVE: EMPSON AND THE
LITERATURE OF CONFLICT

Most of Empson's recent, uncollected essays have been intended as rehabilitations of some sort, usually with the aim of 'rescuing' a particular author from the damaging misrepresentations of the Christian exegetes. His arguments are sometimes too predictable and betray—especially in the latest essays—the force of a ruling obsession. Still, it should be realised that Empson is rejecting a whole modern school and connected ethic of criticism, as well as countering what he sees as a falsely pietistic drift of literary opinion. One of his strongest cases, on both counts, is his protest against Hugh Kenner's readings of James Joyce.[43] Kenner, for example, finds Joyce's Stephen Dedalus such an insufferable young man, and (above all) his theology so garbled, that he assumes Joyce to have been satirising his cast-off, unregenerate youthful self. The effect of this is to make *The Portrait* just such a closed, ironically fortified literary structure as the New Critics typically demand of poetry.

Empson's objections to Kenner have the somewhat offhand, colloquial manner which goes to enforce his instinctive mistrust of any such orthodox position. He is frankly trying to find 'decent feelings' at work, and at one point (speaking of *Ulysses*) he pauses to make sure 'you understand I am trying to interpret this frightful text'.[44] 'Interpret', here, carries all the forementioned puzzles and problems as to how the critic can sort out his own predilections from the actual 'meaning' of the text in hand. The hopeful search for 'decent feelings' corresponds to the working rule of *Milton's God*: that an author's 'intention' is inherently likely to be the best possible, the richest or most humanly responsive, construction we can place upon his work.

Empson's habits of reading have the noticeable effect (exactly contrary to Kenner's) of leaving the novel's form an open question, and so dissolving it into the normal continuity of human experience. In *Ulysses*, 'the situation is what we are to consider, and in real life, we may reflect, it sometimes turns out one way, sometimes another'. In one of his pre-war Japanese chronicles, Empson had noticed a similar indeterminacy, and the same truth to human experience, in the traditional drama of Japan. Many plays, he remarked, were put together from various sources, the doubt as to their outcome being a matter both of cultural expectation and general life-like experience.[45] In the case of *Ulysses*, the 'problematic' modern novel, this quality of open-endedness also represents an appeal to experience, to the balanced possibilities of how things might, in reality, work themselves out. Literary 'form' as such—a presumptive closure imposed upon the narrative by settled convention—is automatically thrown into question. The 'objective correlative', with all its adherents' various elaborations, remains an idea quite foreign to the experience which Empson discovers in *Ulysses*: the 'unearthly shocking surprise with which all the theorising of the book at last becomes solid, as an actual homely example, hard to know what to make of'.

In the play *Exiles*, Empson thinks Joyce's sexual obsessions rather 'depressing' and narrow-minded in themselves. But Joyce's play has a 'decisive saving quality'; the determination to 'work all its bothers into something eternal because universally true'. In Eliot's formulation, the literary work was an object yielded up by the unconscious mind and emphatically lacking any connection with the processes of will and conscious design. Empson, on the contrary, responds to what he finds of moral will and strength of purpose in Joyce's writing. Joyce was himself, Empson recalls, an 'intellectual type of critic'; and indeed, such claims of intellectual sympathy on the critic's part make him a kind of inward spokesman for the author and his problematic themes.

Joyce therefore wins understanding, or escapes from neurotic privacy, by working into dramatic form something 'eternally true'. Artistic truth is not *sui generis*, an aesthetic condition of literary forms, but an adequate responsiveness to human experience. Joyce's emotional conflicts are weighed against his need for rational self-understanding. In the same way, predicative logic—the theoretical stuff of *Complex Words*—cannot cover all the critical ground, any more than reason can hope to solve the intractable problems of human experience. It is, nevertheless, the minimal pattern of rational conviction upon which to rest one's hopes for mutual understanding. Susanne Langer, the aesthetic philosopher, describes the logical unit 'A = B' as a 'distinct, discursively-rendered concept', a 'structural characteristic of the feeling known as "logical conviction"'.[46] The experience of such convictions stands apart from the 'matrix of sense and emotion in which most of our mental acts are buried'. This is exactly the rationale of Complex Words, or of the use found for Bentley, the scholar-critic of Pastoral, whose 'absurd' rationality at least sometimes went to the heart of the matter.

So Empson's criticism is deeply imbued with the values of humanistic rationalism. He sees the modern critical consensus on Joyce, along with Donne and Coleridge, as symptomatic of a growing contempt for the philosophic outlook of the Enlightenment. His opponents might of course argue that Empson smuggles his rationalising, optimistic 'truths' out of his own philosophy into the texts he deals with. Empson would reply that he was merely responding reasonably, and with a decent degree of 'generosity', to the possibilities opened by those same texts. In the case of Joyce, I believe that Empson carries the argument, though without—in the nature of the quarrel—any possible final 'proof'. It does seem an unlikely, and a rather spoiling presumption, that Joyce means to caricature Stephen unmercifully throughout the *Portrait of an Artist*. Kenner, incidentally, makes a cardinal point of Stephen's apparent ignorance of the Aquinan aesthetic, a heterodox version of which he expounds in speculative mood. Kenner's own articles of faith coincide with those of Aqinas, treating Joyce's narrative as a closed, self-qualifying structure for ironic contemplation. Stephen offends by his overweening artistic ambition. His attitude oversteps the formalist belief in the radical discontinuity of the aesthetic, the moral and the religious spheres of value. Kenner thus applies, in a less conspicuous way, the same circular logic that typifies Cleanth Brooks's critical approach. Empson's is the opposite presumption, a belief in communicable truth and answerable motive, which declares literature an open field for moral interpretation.

The rationalising motive was deep in the origins of Ambiguity, or of verbal analysis as a modern concern of criticism. Robert Graves, recalling his own experiments in this field, describes how he cultivated the method 'partly to find relief from a war neurosis from which I still officially suffer'.[47] The technique of analysis was a kind of intellectual exorcism. Its most fruitful materials were phases of mental conflict, knotted meanings and 'deep' psychic disruptions. But the critic had to maintain, through all this disturbance, his basically 'normal' and rational responses. I shall later have cause to refer to Empson's several, somewhat contradictory statements on the 'poetry of conflict'. For the moment, these varied emphases may suggest a certain doubt, or perhaps a satisfying complexity, about the situation of the 'analytical' critic required to explicate—to make rational sense of—poems involving irrational conflicts of motive.

In the closing chapter of *Seven Types*, Empson finds the issue neatly stated in the preface to *Oxford Poetry, 1927*. There exists a 'logical conflict' between the 'denotatory and connotatory' sense of words; between 'an asceticism tending to kill language by stripping words of all associations' and 'a hedonism tending to kill language by dissipating their sense under a multiplicity of associations' (p. 234). The discussion then turns to a critique of formalism, with parallels from the theory of science which I have already remarked upon. The 'hedonistic' and 'ascetic' poles of language correspond to the two trends of development throughout *Seven Types*: the deepening psychology of conflict, hinging largely on complex and irrational kinds of association, and the compensating increase in rational reflection—the generalising activity—which makes the poetry available to sane understanding.

Empson was not alone in his philosophic passage from the 'new science' of Relativity to a humanistic principle of interpretation. Ortega Y Gasset, in *The Modern Theme* (1931), followed out much the same philosophic path. If subjectivity is the natural condition of all modern knowledge, we can best turn it to account by accepting the rich contrariety of possible views. There remain certain standards or norms of understanding, incapable of 'objective' formulation but evident enough in the way we are given to interpreting the world, our own and other people's. From these reflections, Ortega develops a philosophy of history which, in the place it assigns to *interpretation* as a regulative mode of understanding, resembles the view of literary history assumed in Empson's versions of Pastoral.

> The pleasure we derive from candour . . . includes a certain
> degree of disdain for the candid person. It is a benevolent
> enough disparagement. We enjoy the 'primitive' painter as
> we enjoy the soul of a child . . . Our vision is much ampler,
> more complete and more full of reservations.[48]

This complex of attitudes, including the hint of 'disparage-
ment' and slight consequent guilt—the ambiguous ethics of
'putting the complex into the simple'—associates readily with
Empson's definitions of pastoral.

This plainly allows the interpreter a certain licence of self-
expression, so far at least as reading past literature as it strikes a
contemporary. In his recent edition of Coleridge, Empson puts
the question quite squarely: if at one point the reader is dis-
gusted by the mariner's apparent tone of 'pious unction', then
he 'may *without serious falsification* regard Coleridge as writing
a parody of it' (p. 78; my italics). This suggestion hints at the
shift of attitude, and the kind of interpretative freedom, entailed
by the rationalising mood of Empson's criticism. It urges the
reader to actively reinterpret the poet's more orthodox symbolism, his deep-seated conflicts and wrestlings of conscience with
the Christian doctrine of unearned guilt.

The same questions arise with Empson's discursive or 'narrative' approach to Yeats's 'Byzantium' poems, where he comments
as if reassuringly that 'symbolic resistance is met only at a fairly
deep level'.[49] His meaning is clarified by the further remark that
such 'confusion at a deep level' is something 'inherent in
symbolist technique'. 'The Ancient Mariner' is another testing-
ground for any criticism which takes its stand on issues of
religious conscience. Among the New Critics, Robert Penn
Warren produces the customary symbolist props, with a perfectly
consistent reading of the poem as—at one level—a diatribe
against encroaching science (Sun) in defence of poetic imagination (Moon). Empson is much concerned in his Introduction to
show just how much contemporary science *did* in fact go into
the poem, from botany to the latest knowledge of electricity.
Some of his detailed suggestions are, I think, of doubtful relevance. In the mass, however, they help to shift the critical
emphasis away from the 'deep' regions of guilt-laden symbolism,

as explored by Warren, toward the rational and commonsense level at which we normally sort out the content of experience. Like the readings in *Seven Types*, Empson's analogies are sometimes far-fetched, but repay the carriage by appealing to the reader's unprejudiced sense of rational fitness. Empson does not wish, like Warren, to square his reading with a symbolist myth of total explanation.

Yet, despite his rejection of the Symbolist programme in general, Empson has concentrated a surprisingly large part of his critical thinking on poems which at least arguably belong to that tradition. He has also returned regularly to poetry of a Christian persuasion which, from the outset, seems to have revolted his moral conscience. He is fascinated by what he finds in Yeats: the 'deep confusion' engendered somewhere between the subterranean level of symbol and myth, and the rational level of poetic narrative. His interest in *Paradise Lost*, he remarks, is as much for 'the massive acceptance the poem has received' as for the possible civilising effect of a secular re-interpretation. In *Complex Words* also, he explores all the twisted reaches of paradox and covert implication, before eventually stating his faith in the ultimate sanity of language.

This brings us back to the equivocal position of the analytic critic, finding his most complex and rewarding subjects at a psychological depth far removed from his own rational convictions. Empson was therefore well advised, early in the progress of *Seven Types*, to warn the reader that his Ambiguities were ranged along no single scale of increasing complexity, and that 'psychological' and 'logical' degrees of disorder might not run parallel (p. 48). By the end of the book, these two scales of judgement stand in paradoxical relation. Pastoral provides an imaginative model of their reconciliation, incorporating 'the Critic' as an avatar of the 'complex' hero, rationalising the obscure sources of satisfaction in his 'simple' counterpart. Yet toward the end of *Some Versions*, with Lewis Carroll and the late nineteenth century, Empson detects a widening and in some ways less fruitful distance between the modern intellectual and his childlike delights. Child-cult is effectively the dead-end of Pastoral, 'less hopeful and more a return into oneself' (p. 205). Carroll remained a victim of his own curious obsessions, 'caught in the self-centred emotional life imposed by the detached intelli-gence' (p. 218).

Both here and in *Seven Types*, the progress of examples leads up to a point of extreme disunion between the intellectual and emotional qualities of involvement. Herbert's poem 'The Sacrifice', as the culminating instance of Ambiguity, throws a whole series of paradoxes into Empson's method. He is aware of its roots in traditional Christian doctrine, yet determined to show that it lifts that tradition into a larger, more questioning air of argument. Within one sentence of commentary, Empson describes the poem as having 'an assured and easy simplicity, a reliable and unassuming grandeur', and yet as showing 'successive fireworks of contradiction' and 'a mind jumping like a flea' (p. 226). This apparent contradiction is taken up and dramatised through the 'complex' and 'simple' variants of Pastoral, and again through the semantics of 'wit' and 'sense' which Empson explores in *Complex Words*. Ambiguity is unable to resolve the issue, which it poses inescapably by placing 'The Sacrifice' as its last, and in many ways most accomplished example. Sophisticated reason, on the one hand, finds a congenial, almost compulsive subject-matter in deep and irrational com-plexities—neurosis or religious paradox—on the other.

The element of self-expression in Empson's criticism comes out most strongly in the passages on 'The Sacrifice' and the *Alice* books. Perhaps, in juxtaposing themes of the deep un-conscious and the rationalising intellect, these chapters evoke a more general conflict in modern culture. E. H. Gombrich, in his masterly study of art and illusion, finds a similar union of oppo-sites in Cubist painting. Systematic distortion, or sophisticated effects of illusion, seem to compensate for a regressive choice of primitive subject-matter. Therefore the art-critic had better concern himself, not with the mythical sub-conscious of stored images, but with the fact that the artist 'found himself in a situation where his private conflicts acquired artistic relevance'.[50]

This catches precisely the mood of involvement, or the phase of rationalised response, that Empson most obviously values. It helps to explain his recent, otherwise surprising involvement in the scholarly work of establishing texts for the poems of Donne and Coleridge. His editorial methods impute 'intention' to that stage of the poem's genesis where 'private conflicts' acquire—from a commonsense viewpoint—generalised 'artistic relevance'. Empson has suggested that Eliot's theory of the 'objective correlative' can only have a useful application in cases like 'The Ancient Mariner', where 'an Inside needs to be related to an Outside, psychology to a history'.[51] Understanding is not a matter of divining some obscure private meaning from its adequately externalised form. The reader must be an interpreter, dealing to some extent with the poet's emotional conflicts as he himself—in the process of creative realisation—dealt with them. In his essays on Coleridge and Joyce, Empson's moral admiration goes out to the writer whose conflicts do not prevent him from expressing them in a valid, because humanly achieved, literary form.

I have tried, necessarily in somewhat roundabout fashion, to show how far Empson's outlook has opposed itself to the various orthodoxies in modern criticism. In the next chapter I discuss in more detail the concept of Pastoral and its place in Empson's developing outlook.

2

'Beyond Formalism':
Pastoral and the 'Subjective Correlative'

In his preface to *The Forlorn Demon*, Allen Tate describes and deprecates the yearning for 'eccentricity' in modern poetry. Empson is Tate's chief example, his early poems suggesting a kind of stylised despair and offbeat intellectualism which Tate thinks merely artificial.[1]

Tate's view has its counterpart in *Complex Words*, where Empson remarks (p. 244) that 'few writers have dared to make people as eccentric as they really are'. It may seem perverse to make eccentricity the norm in this way. But the word, in its root sense, stands for precisely that set of ideas about human nature, and hence about poetic form and meaning, which Empson had taken up in *Seven Types*. The 'juggling with contradictory impulses', the play of 'defences and equilibrium'—these incidental reflections signify an 'eccentric' or relativist attitude carried, as a matter of human fairness, into the practice of literary criticism. That this represents a 'democratic' attitude toward literature—a freedom of discourse, both for the critic and in the poetry he deals with—seems to be borne out by the arguments raised on the opposite side. Leavis, mistrusting the Joycian 'revolution of the word' and the kind of verbal criticism which goes with it, builds his own scheme of settled values on a framework of approval-terms, demanding assent and reinforced by constant repetition. John Casey finds the method reminiscent of religious and mystical injunctions—'God is good—His Knowledge is His Will.'[2] Casey believes, adopting his arguments from Wittgenstein, that such persuasive consistency of terms is the only evaluative 'proof' that criticism can hope to provide. Empson takes a very different line in *Complex Words*, where compacted doctrines (of the type 'might is right') are shown to be capable of a more discriminating logical analysis.

There is a certain affinity between Leavis's approach and the

Symbolist aesthetic, taking 'symbol' as opposed to 'discourse', as Frank Kermode uses those terms in his book *Romantic Image*. The Symbolist poem is opaque to rational explanations, and resists (as the New Critics argued of poetry in general) the presumption of paraphrase. Yet Kermode talks elsewhere of the 'later, semantic phase of Symbolist aesthetic, inagurated by Richards and established by Empson'.[3] This would seem to question the distinction I have drawn. Kermode goes on to make what might be seized upon as a reconciling judgement: Hulme's theory of Imagism is 'constricted by the sheer innocence of his semantics'. Which, one might think, distinguishes Hulme's case from that of the 'later semantic phase'. But Hulme's weakness in this department is charged to 'Symbolist aesthetics as a whole', and Empson is apparently not to be extricated from the general indictment.

It might be remembered, by way of background, that Kermode had recently taken issue with Empson over his chapter on Marvell in *Some Versions*. Kermode's arguments are enlarged upon in his own book *Pastoral Poetry* (1952), where he speaks of Empson's 'extraordinary analysis' of Marvell's 'The Garden' and comments elsewhere—his target fairly obvious—that Marvell 'is not good material for puzzle-solvers . . . the slipperiness of his meaning does not encourage the search for a complete solution'. Kermode has, I think, ignored a significant part of Empson's argument. The mood of Pastoral is, in itself, an implicit denial of the very possibility of 'complete solutions'. After much ingenious argument, the 'richness' of Marvell's poem is simply summarised as 'a readiness for argument not pursued' (*Some Versions*, p. 118). Its meanings are admitted to be almost inexhaustible, and criticism calls off its hunt for their 'logic' at the point of a willing suspension. Kermode has more recently raised such arguments into a full-scale philosophy of value. The meaning of a literary 'classic' is 'certainly, in some sense, indeterminate'; it lacks any 'clearly delineated semantic design' and rests in 'a system of potentialities beyond one's powers to actualise them'.[4]

Geoffrey Hartman, in his book *Beyond Formalism*, speaks of the natural tendency of Empson's Ambiguity to elude the structures of formalist reduction. 'Only Empson managed to escape it (the "shibboleth of form") by postulating types of ambiguity which showed how precarious the unity of form was, or how rebellious language was.'[5] Hartman's title expresses the growing dissatisfaction, among the more speculative theorists of literature, with the naïve objectivism and lack of epistemological tact in the New Critics. Empson and Kermode can both be found to express similar reservations.

There is perhaps some pretext in Empson's chapter on 'The Garden'—though not in its very open conclusion—for the quarrel which Kermode took up with it. Empson makes a rather abstract business of working out the 'hierarchies' of meaning, or the structures of implicated logic, which the poem's ambiguities yield. On this view, the poem would ultimately come to seem a complex unit of inter-related meanings, a structure conceived—on the best formalist terms—as a closed and inviolable object.

But Empsom qualifies this approach, and moves beyond the tenets of formalism, when he takes issue (in the same chapter) with James Smith's account of the 'metaphysical problem'. Of American critics, only William Van O'Connor has mentioned this essay from *Scrutiny*; but the relations he points to between Smith's ideas and those of the New Critics suggests a descent quite separate from anything in Empson's criticism. Through 'tension and structure', the terms of his title, O'Connor calls upon poetry to restore 'the living truth in truism'.[6] His stress on the inviolable structures of paradox leads to his treatment of the poem as, in Wimsatt's phrase, a 'verbal icon', a self-sufficient structure, offering itself only to passive contemplation and not (here Empson parts company) to actively reasoning argument. Some relevant questions were put to Cleanth Brooks, in 1949, by the philosopher Herbert Muller.[7] Muller opposed his 'relative' ideas to Brooks's 'absolute', and suggested that Brooks's method 'denies the critic the complex, ironic attitudes that he demands of the poem, and thereby betrays his own principle'. Muller detects in Brooks 'an arbitrary, totalitarian solution of our problems'; Brooks retorts against 'a muddled and finally irresponsible liberalism'. The implicit ideology of formalist criticism emerges clearly enough from this exchange. To cut the poem off from rational cross-questioning is to give it an absolute, 'iconic' status. It is also to deprive it of the consequential character whereby a rationalising criticism might work out its implications against the claims—ethical and aesthetic— of a dogmatic orthodoxy.

The connection is obvious in Brooks's recent essay on W. H. Auden as literary critic. Brooks approves the 'formalism', the demand for a poetic integration of opposites, in Auden's criticism. He likewise applauds Auden's 'sense of the limitations of art', a willingness 'to call it in final terms frivolous', preventing him from turning it into 'a kind of ersatz religion'.[8] It is just as typical that Empson, in reviewing *The Dyer's Hand*, found in Auden's 'parsonical' tone 'a tendency to twitter and look on the bright side'.[9]

The poetics of formalism were laid down clearly in James Smith's essay on the metaphysical conceit.[10] When Empson, in a recent article, thought back to his Cambridge days and youthful influences, it was Smith whom he associated particularly with T. S. Eliot and other 'early members of the neo-Christian movement'. This suggests an awareness, on Empson's part, of the link between Eliot's symbolist doctrines and the New Critical concepts of poetry as complex structure. Smith carries these to the full extent of their objectivistic logic. 'Once made, the figure does not disintegrate: it offers something unified and "solid" for our contemplation . . . tensions between the elements continues. . .' He seems to hesitate over 'solid', but asserts—what amounts to the same thing—that the proper stance of poetic understanding is that of disinterested 'contemplation'.

Empson, as we have seen, denies this passivity in the reader and demands his involvement in the process of actively recreating the poem's meaning. He differs from Smith on the same point that divides Muller and Brooks: the refusal, on Empson's side, to impose *a priori* notions of poetic structure which accommodate only a limited play of the reader's rational intelligence. His chapter on 'The Garden', open-ended for all its intricate logic, typifies the sceptical and self-qualifying habit of Empson's mind. He seems constantly on the verge of defining the complex implications, verbal or generic, which might satisfy, by somehow pinning down, his sense of the poem's richness. Yet he constantly relegates this purpose, detecting behind these provisional

structures a series of ironies and 'placing' attitudes which prevent their treatment as an integrating function of form. Within
Empson's reach, at this point, is a plausible logic of the Pastoral
complex of feelings, a theory of tempting neatness and explanatory power. Such is the Aristotelian 'staircase' of implications
which Empson discovers in the metaphysical puzzle about form
and content (p. 114). But Empson suddenly abandons this
approach. In terms of such an abstract logic 'there seems no way
of putting in a judgement of value' (p. 115). The conceit remains
effectively 'the vivid statement of a puzzle', and Empson realises
that 'in practice it is more'.

In this way, Empson habitually moves beyond what Kermode
identified in his survey as a secondary 'semantic' showing of the
Symbolist aesthetic. These questions of aesthetic doctrine have a
larger ethical bearing, as W. J. Ong has argued in his essays on
the New Criticism. Ong believes that the weight of ancient
heresies and refutations, once the preserve of theology, has now
been transferred to the work of art, in the guise of the various
'fallacies' erected by formalist criticism. The 'personalist' crisis
of biblical authority now takes a novel, apparently secularised
form, and the poem becomes 'the quiet pole that bears the weight
and moment of all'.[11] In his chapter 'Wit and Mystery', Ong
seems to endorse the New Critical canons of discontinuity and
closed poetic structure, which he claims explicitly as the substance of a theology. Word-play and paradox are equated with
the 'distinctive mysteries' of Christianity. Yet in another essay,
'The Jinnie in the Well-Wrought Urn', Ong seems to recognise
the human inevitability of personalist heresies. 'Each work of
art is not only an object but a kind of surrogate for a person.'

Perhaps, given his acute sense of the issues involved, Father
Ong finds comfort in certain modern theologies—for instance,
that of Martin Buber—which would make more room for
personalist interpretations. Brooks and Tate, however, in the
sanctions attaching to their critical doctrines, make no such
accommodating gestures. Their theology is more covert but less
flexible. Allen Tate, in his strictures on 'the Angelic Imagination', provides the most articulate version of what Empson
attacks in general as 'neo-Christian' doctrine. Tate argues that
in Romantic poetry, especially the productions of Poe, 'the

intellectual force is exhausted because in the end it has no real object. The human intellect cannot reach God as essence; only God as analogy.'[12] This repeats T. E. Hulme's repudiation of Romanticism in its intellectual or rationalising aspect. Michael Roberts in his early assessment of Hulme, and Graham Hough more recently, both attached their arguments for a revived Romanticism to a critique of Hulme's one-sided religion: its stress on discipline and self-limitation at the expense of— in Roberts's phrase—'the act of the intellect that is called faith'.[13]

The intellectual 'faith' of Empson's criticism is typified by his pursuit of Wordsworth's nature-doctrine, through three successive books and some twenty years' sustained examination. These passages make up a fine example of Empson's positive but essentially *provisional* habits of judgement. In *Seven Types* he is frankly mistrustful of Wordsworth's idealist turn of thought and language. In *Some Versions* he concludes, with a still nagging sense of unexplained mysteries, that Wordsworth's medium 'did not force him to make up his mind on these points' (p. 153). By the time of *Complex Words*, the language of *The Prelude* has become a standing challenge to Empson's powers of rational explanation. L. T. Lemon, in his book *The Partial Critics*, objected that Empson seemed to 'suffer no consternation' when his methods ran themselves into knots of contradiction over poetry he claimed to admire.[14] Clearly Lemon had read only the pages devoted to Wordsworth in *Seven Types*, and that without seeing their point. Empson's 'consternation', or more precisely his anxiety to do poetry justice by fully understanding its motives, is perhaps the most consistent principle in his criticism. Cleanth Brooks remarked of *Complex Words* that the 'bits of machinery' it offered might answer to some 'inner need' of Empson himself.[15] Certainly Empson has, and admits, such a need for rational understanding; but not the resulting sense, as Brooks further suggests, 'that the matter has been pegged down or tidied up'. Empson accepts the task of literary criticism as a willing but indefinite *approximation* to the goal of adequate understanding. This mood in *Seven Types* is expressed in a later Preface: '"final judgement" is a thing which must be indefinitely postponed' (p. xv). A degree of scepticism—in the positive sense of willing open-mindedness—weighs equally with the rationalist drive to understanding.

Rational scepticism of this kind was a part of the intellectual programme of *Experiment*, the Cambridge magazine which Empson co-edited and which published the earliest of his writings towards *Seven Types*. In an essay entitled 'Cynic or Sceptic', Max Black presented the case for 'enlightened scepticism' as 'the basis of a rational social attitude'. The principle of doubt, in this case, was not 'a defective vision of life', but a clear and honest view of 'the fundamental difficulties which beset the search for knowledge'. William Archer, in the same issue, sought to adjudicate the question of 'Poetry and Beliefs'. As Empson was later to do in *Complex Words*, Archer queries the pragmatic theory of poetic 'pseudo-statement' put forward by Richards in *Principles of Literary Criticism*. Straightforward assent to the poets' traditional beliefs may now be beyond rational reach, but one still needs the intellectual faith to differentiate 'objectified statement' ('O Rose, thou art sick'), partially objectified statement ('Love is a sickness') and unobjectified statement ('Beauty is Truth'). Empson's later classifications fall out differently, but he shares both the initial scepticism and the rationalising ambition of Archer's philosophy.[16]

The charge of merely seeking a satisfying intellectual 'machinery' seems more forceful when Empson turns it back, without conscious irony, upon Brooks himself. The poem's structure of inwrought paradox, whatever its demonstrable subtlety, cannot (Empson thinks) be used to determine 'whether the machine worked the right way'.[17] Empson's 'inner need', the very nature of which—in practice—is to remain unsatisfied, contrasts with Brooks's prescriptive desire to *account* for the poem; to match it with a notion of organised meaning which removes it from the informal context of a personal utterance. Empson seems aware of this background philosophy when he describes Brooks's search for 'the intellectual machinery of a fine and full statement'. Their mutual point of difference is that between Ambiguity, as the medium of human uncertainty and self-knowledge, and canonised Irony and Paradox as the principles, the iconic standards, of an orthodox critical method.

In reviewing *The Well-Wrought Urn*, Empson began to notice the dangers of what he feared might become, through critics like Brooks, a cramping set of conventions. Stuart Hampshire has lately remarked that pre-war philosophy, especially where involved in the sense-data controversy, seemed quite separate from politics at the time but now appears to have been 'indirectly linked to questions of freedom, and so to political progress'.[18] Such questions, I believe, are equally germane to the philosophy of *Complex Words*, and make the book partly a running critique of the current orthodoxies which Empson rejects. His arguments have the kind of philosophic force, not obvious at first impression, which Hampshire refers to. Empson presents such key-words as 'sense' and 'honest' as implicative structures which ratify a humanist—or, in Empson's usual terms, a 'renaissance'—view of human capacities and relations. And this, it becomes clear, is not simply a period-concept or a piece of localised cultural history. It takes up from *Seven Types* the cardinal ideas that understanding is an active process, that meanings imply their own, answerable logic and that poetry in its semantic aspect is accessible to reason and common human sympathies. Yet Empson refuses to erect his readings into abstract principle, to create putative 'rules' from his equations or push too far with his generalised theory of truth-conditions in poetry. In Pope's *Essay on Criticism*, he finds, the style comes to seem almost dialectical, with so cogent a sense of intra-verbal argument that 'the author partly fades out' (*Complex Words*, p. 98). 'Partly', however, is the crucial reservation, and one which operates throughout the book. Empson continually brings his 'bits of machinery' to the point of definition, of logical adequacy, only to lapse—as it seems—from a rationalised semantics into something more like the traditional style of 'appreciative' criticism.

Again, this seems to be partly the result of Empson's ingrained suspicion of anything resembling a hard-and-fast 'method' in literary criticism. If formalist theory deliberately excludes all account of an author's working intentions, then so might the machinery of Complex Words, when brought to the point of a self-sufficient logic. This would be to compromise the humanistic outlook which the book clearly intends. The problem is placed in a larger perspective by comparing *Complex Words* with the various uncollected essays which Empson published in the early fifties. In his extended debate with Dover Wilson, 'Hamlet When New', Empson remarks that he had discussed the play in *Complex Words* 'only in so far as suited the theme of the book (a theme which I am ignoring here). . .' Elsewhere he is firm that 'an ambiguity at this point . . . would only confuse the production'.[19] In general these essays on Shakespeare, Donne and Joyce stay clear of detailed verbal criticism and argue in the broadest commonsense terms that an author's 'intention' is always the first thing to be considered.

In *Seven Types* provision was made for such interests, but only as an adjunct or source of useful evidence for the main business—the verbal analysis—of Ambiguity. Of course, 'those who enjoy poems must in part be biographers', but Empson stresses that he is concerned less with 'the minds of poets' than with 'the mode of action of poetry' (p. 242). This priority stems from Empson's sense of the peculiar mysteries of poetic communication, and of the need in a sceptical and rationalist age for some 'intelligible process of interpretation' (p. 243). In the later essays, this search for 'intelligible' grounds of judgement more often gives way to a broadly psychologising style of criticism, militantly unconcerned with theory and not so much occupied with immediate verbal detail.

This avoidance of threatening regularities in the consequence of his own methods is, I think, deeply characteristic of Empson's criticism. Allen Tate perhaps helped to define the problem, from a less than sympathetic standpoint, when he remarked that 'the idea of infinite regression' was probably the 'subtlest fallacy' of humanistic beliefs.[20] Empson's mind cannot rest with any settled notion of literary form, any single rationale of Complex Words or full-blown theory of meaning. This amounts to a wholesale rejection of the various metaphysical sanctions which, as I have suggested, subtend the more orthodox critical canons of meaning and form. At one point in *Seven Types* Empson discovers in some lines of Shelley the disquieting implication that 'form' may be 'its own justification', that it 'sustains itself, like God, by the fact that it exists' (p. 161). This curious reaction seems linked with Empson's comments, later in the book, on

Pope's *Dunciad*, where he finds 'the indifference of God disgusting and the subservience of man unendurable' (p. 223). Again in
Milton's God, it is the idea of a *transcendent* deity—almighty in
the 'metaphysical sense' (p. 41)—that Empson has to hold at
bay before he can begin to put his reading of the poem on a
moral-humanist footing. So with the 'character' of Satan: if we
will but 'waive our metaphysical assumptions', the question of
motive will be seen to be 'complex as in human affairs' (p. 40).
Seizing upon Milton's denial of the Son's foreknowledge (p. 127),
or suggesting that foreknowledge is after all 'not remote from
common experience' (p. 115)—Empson is variously trying to
account for the poem's metaphysics, its 'official' doctrine,
through a rationale of accountable human motive.

The Christian-ontological critic, like Tate, has simply to
accept and make terms with that 'indifference of God' which
Empson finds so disgusting. He allows for the radical discontinuity
of the divine and the human, and sees no reason, in principle, to
justify the ways of God to man. Monroe K. Spears has commented, in a recent book, that 'metaphysical discontinuity is . . .
primarily a defence against naturalism and rationalism'.[21]
Empson likewise identifies the 'cult of Unnaturalism' with the
reactionary temper of Hulme, Eliot and their followers. By
drawing their dogmatic distinctions between aesthetics and
morality, the human and the divine, these critics were responsible
(in Empson's view) for a whole modern orthodoxy of frivolous
and wrong-headed judgement. The ethics of *Milton's God* is
entirely a matter of mutual human relations, whether of Adam
with Eve, Satan with God or the critic with the poet whose text
he is generously trying to interpret.

In *Complex Words* Empson is again anxious to insist that his
criteria are not 'metaphysical to the point of being useless'
(p. 46). As a literary label, the term 'metaphysical' is notoriously
vague; but Empson seems to describe, in the course of his writings, a definite change of attitude about the axis of the word's
ambiguity. The modern acceptance of 'metaphysical poetry'
was established and in the process of critical refinement during
the years of Empson's Cambridge apprenticeship. Jane Smith's
was a classic statement of the inbred logic of the metaphysical
conceit. In his account, the 'solidity' of a metaphor—its capacity

to remain in the mind, a tensive structure for renewed contemplation—holds out a distinct criterion of poetic value. *Seven Types* seems to carry, in certain of Empson's readings, an implicit appeal to some such structural standard. It is partly, and perhaps by initial design, a worked-out history of the metaphysical conceit, its historical rise and fall, understood on its own peculiar terms. Rhetorical effects in Pope and Peacock are explained by the collapse, or the partial failure, of what seems to be taken as the norm of a solid antithetical conceit (p. 22). Elsewhere, the oddity of Hood's use of language appears in his resorting to puns in order to 'back away' from the full 'echoes and implications of words' (p. 109). The decline—on this early view—is through Marvell and Vaughan to the pre-Romantics; the Augustans are treated mostly as exemplifying certain specialised and derivative devices, such as zeugma, 'never before handled with such neatness and consciousness'.

Leavis in his first, favourable review of *Seven Types*, found 'more of the history of English poetry in this book than any other'.[22] Indeed, Leavis's own book *Revaluation* (1936) builds to a large extent on the same critical standard and the same resultant view of poetic tradition. Like Empson, Leavis takes metaphysical 'wit' and its derivative forms as touchstones of quality, assimilating a part of the Augustan line—Pope, rather than Dryden—to this main tradition. And James Smith, writing in *Scrutiny*, could apply his 'metaphysical' standard to agree with Leavis that, in Shelley's poetry, 'reality, losing its complexity, gives place to a dream'.

In short, the doctrines of the American formalist critics had an earlier development, point for point, in the currency of Cambridge criticism around 1930. But Empson, even in *Seven Types*, never committed himself wholly to any such formalistic standards. If Peacock's or Hood's conceits fall short of the integral norm established by Donne or Herbert, the point of the comparison is not to devalue the lesser poet but to qualify criticism to deal with him on his own implied terms. Empson recognises that the queer evasiveness of Hood's habitual punning may be due to the sheer complexity of his social situation, requiring an almost heroic degree of displaced seriousness. Shelley, as I shall later make clear, is far from damned by Empson's critical approach. Like Wordsworth, he becomes a test-case or measure by which Empson takes new bearings for a broader-based, more generous practice of criticism.

Empson's attitude of mistrust toward the 'metaphysical' is discernible in his ambiguous use of the word in *Some Versions*. He has been discussing—in connection with Donne—the root metaphor of the Christian Incarnation, in terms of which 'the member of the class is the whole class, or its defining property' (p. 70). This leads straight on to the puzzles associated with God and goodness: 'though God is a person he and the good must be mutually independent; it was because Milton refused to play the tricks of the metaphysical and made God merely one of the persons of his story that Satan had so strong a case' (p. 71). The 'tricks of the metaphysical' here could be either those of the poets belonging to that school—Empson's immediate subject— or those of that 'transcendent' philosophy which he was later to play down in *Milton's God*. Probably the word contains something of both meanings, and the logic of the equation suggests the way in which Pastoral questions the background assumptions of both kinds of orthodoxy.

This all has much to do with the 'eccentricity' which Tate, from his own secure standpoint, deplores in Empson's writing. The heresies of Empson's critical outlook associate with the ideas which he holds about human motives and the ethics of 'generous' interpretation. In *Seven Types* he continually refers to those inherent 'limitations of the human condition' which make up the subject-matter of Pastoral. Poetic meaning is not so much a matter of achieved verbal 'point' as of an implicit recognition of the shifts and evasions by which human dignity sustains itself. 'This sort of contradiction is at once understood in literature, because the process of understanding one's friends must always be riddled with such indecisions and the machinery of such hypocrisy' (p. 44). Pronouncements like this might seem to give reason for Tate's limiting judgement. However, taking account of the larger background of argument, I would suggest that they signify something more seriously rooted in Empson's humanist outlook. He pursues the implications of poetry, not into their formal extension as properties of poetic structure, but into the human context of a rich and diverse experience to which—on his principled assumption—they ultimately appeal.

This amounts to a far-reaching difference of views as to the kind of experience which poetry ideally communicates. Graham Hough sees a model example of the creative experience in Empson's poem 'Missing Dates'.[23] He interprets the process of creation as a slow, painful working of the almost inarticulate— the background of despair—into something like a rational, and therefore communicable form. This tallies with Empson's critical outlook, and makes a notable contrast with the Symbolist idea of the poet passively waiting upon the creative event. Empson's 'despair', the subject of Tate's suspicions, is something very different from the mood of Eliot's *The Waste Land*. In an early review of Sherard Vines's volume of poems *Triforium*, Empson remarks that this poetry expresses despair, but 'only in a technical sense'; it is based 'not on renouncing anything', but on 'a solid and learned variety of gratification'.[24] Empson pointedly distinguishes such poetry—clearly after his own heart—from the 'fully digested despair', the 'Byronism of the scholar' which Eliot seemed to cultivate.

There is a plausible connection between *The Waste Land*, with its montage of dissociated images, and the idea and cultural consequences of Relativity-theory. Blackmur, in his *Primer of Ignorance*, goes even further. He thinks of the twenties as a time when 'we were learning a whole set of techniques for finding—even creating—trouble'.[25] More significantly, it is the 'law of uncertainty in mathematical physics'—the idea which figures in *Seven Types*—that Blackmur remembers as breaking down 'the last, healthy remnants of moral determinism'. Empson, in his poetry and criticism, showed exactly the opposite reaction to Relativity; a difference to be explained, perhaps, by the fully 'digested' attitude of despair encouraged on the one hand by the Symbolist aesthetic, and the kind of resistant *argumentation* enjoined by Empson's discursive poetics.

Blackmur thinks that modern man is in quest of a restored 'unity' which, with his new burden of knowledge, he can only come at by 'analogy and collateral form'. 'Collateral' implies the legacy of Hulme, the discontinuous levels of human and religious experience. Hence the radical closure of poetic form, precluding (for fear of personalist heresies) the incorporation of poetry into rational discourse. But Blackmur has yet another sense in mind for 'analogy'. He speaks of the 'passion for analogy in the creative sense . . . only in analogy are opposites identical'. In fact, his use of this term, like Empson's suspect 'metaphysical', translates with ease from the aesthetic (internal or structural) to the doctrinal level of argument. The poem—to recall Allen Tate—can comprehend the nature of divinity only by remaining at the disciplined remove of its own self-confessed limitations. The 'tricks of the metaphysical' are a calculated acceptance of the theological scheme of things.

HISTORY AND FORM IN PASTORAL: THE 'TIMELESS PRISON' OF SYMBOLISM

This comparison with formalist aesthetics can now be pursued into the *history* of Pastoral, which is after all what gives the book its organising shape and sequence. Spears suggests that the 'continuity' which Hulme really wished to repudiate was the nineteenth-century view of history as a continuing process of growth and understanding. Darwin and Marx are associated with the cultural emergence of 'naturalism and the "disappearance of God"'. Such is the now unfashionable, Wellsian view of history, the naturalistic humanism, which Empson has always been quick to defend. 'Naturalism' is what he takes up in *Complex Words* (p. 176) as 'a rationalistic view of man as most triumphant of the animals'. Upon the machinery of such words as Empson examines, 'you can start building yourself into a man'. Thus 'dog' becomes, absurdly enough, the substitute for 'God'; the biological *terminus a quo* of humanistic rationalism, as against the *terminus ad quem*—always inaccessible—of Christian teaching.

The 'disappearance of God' is likewise the starting-point of *Milton's God*: a secular reading, intended to rehabilitate the poem for people who can no longer accept the religious sanctions of orthodox belief. The philosophic mood of the book—certainly 'religious' in a more liberal sense—is contained in the reverence professed for the great and continuous intellectual development 'which has recently produced ourselves, who can describe it' (p. 131). This historical outlook, wherein the mind is considered capable of grasping and enlarging on its own pre-history, is perhaps the most important background idea in Empson's reading of Milton. Historical re-interpretation is an aspect of the secular freedom of conscience; it is an attitude on the critic's part which opens the poetry to rational understanding and fair-minded moral judgement. When Empson speaks of its theology as implying, at some indefinite end of time, God's 'abdication' as ruler and judge, this curious reading is entailed by the need to render the poem accountable to a secular framework of judgement. The angels, Empson imagines, might resist being absorbed into the Godhead 'like a peasantry under Communism trying to delay collectivisation' (p. 139). But at least God's intention to 'wither away', like the Marxist state, gives the religious myth a narrative dimension compatible with history and the politics of the imagination. Milton's own conflicts of political conscience, drawn parallel to some extent with the modern communist experience, once again exemplify the Pastoral quality of the socialised imagination. Empson comments in *Some Versions* that the writer under Communism 'might only exchange a sense of isolation for a sense of the waste of his powers' (p. 22).

The Pastoral tension between individual and society is just as important in *Milton's God*, where it offers a rationalising background of motive to replace the obscure metaphysics of Milton's theology. Empson works outward from the embattled politics of Milton's situation to the whole attendant history of liberal religious thought. He summarises the poem's argument as an attempt 'to cut out everything between the two ends of the large body of Western thought about God', and to 'stick to Moses except at the high points which anticipate Spinoza' (p. 143). It was the same rationalist conflict between personal and immanent conceptions of the Deity which led to the somewhat baffled discussion of Wordsworth in *Seven Types*. Here, as the general context of Milton's dramatic argument, it provides an adequate scale of human complication, a sense that the 'metaphysics' of the poem are really a matter of compromised moral heroism.

In this way, *Milton's God* is a manifestation of that spirit of 'naturalism' which Spears contrasts with the timeless, disengaged aesthetic of literary Symbolism. Kermode also speaks, in connection with the Symbolists, of their 'critical techniques... of the "timeless prison"'.[26] Kermode's intention, in *The Sense of an Ending*, is to qualify the modern insistence on the 'timeless', quasi-spatial aspects of form by stressing the degree to which meaning inheres in the chronology, the fictions of time and order, which largely define our readerly awareness. This dimension of time and change is suppressed by the formalist assumptions of poetic autonomy. For Empson also, the meaning of poetry is often qualified, in a way not easy to explain, by implicit tonings of time and change. In *Seven Types*, the subjective experience of time (in Swinburne, for instance, or the lines from Arthur Waley) suggests a source of poetic intensity beyond any obvious rhetorical account. In Swinburne's 'Laus Veneris', the juxtaposition of two time-scales, the mortal and the deathly-eternal, leads Empson's description into a vein of subjective response which belongs more to the style of 'appreciative' than of 'analytic' criticism. The poem's mood is fixed 'into an eternity outside the human order, in which tears are pointless, and the peace even of death unattainable' (p. 164). The apparent defeat of categorical distinctions—of 'analytic' criticism in the narrower sense—does not lead Empson to dismiss the poem, but on the contrary suggests a source of enjoyment beyond the confines of normal experience. In a sense it is the very 'disorder of memory' induced by Swinburne's technique which allows the poetry to pass its complications 'as a single unit into the reader's mind' (p. 165). This 'unit' is the result of a highly subjective synthesis of meanings, on a plane quite distinct from that envisaged by the formalist canons of poetic unity.

History and time thus impinge upon what Empson, unlike the rigorous formalist, can admit to recognising as the human, experiential context of poetic meaning. The changing forms of Pastoral are the nearest Empson comes to a critical formulation of these insights. Laurence Lerner, in a recent essay on Pastoral, works out his own definition of the *genre* and provides, at the same time, an interesting gloss on Empson's. He thinks it a sobering reflection 'on the human condition, or on the nineteenth century, or perhaps on both (there are moments when one is tempted to equate them)', that Pastoral in its traditional form should at length have given way to 'the land where the Jumblies live'.[27] When it comes to the late nineteenth century and writers like Lear and Dodgson, Empson is readier than Lerner to treat them as subject to the same queer complex of sentiments as the earlier heroes of the *genre*. In this sense Empson is more serious and consistent in making his equation between the nineteenth century—the age of Marx and Darwin, of history laying siege to human pretensions—and the 'human condition' at large. Dodgson and his creatures are faced with the same kinds of compromise, juggling the same contradictory impulses, as Empson had described in *Seven Types* as the typical condition of human life.

This complexity is very much at home with Dodgson and the late nineteenth century in general. Hugh Kenner ridiculed Empson by turning against him his own image of the White Knight in *Alice*, patiently labouring at his 'absurd' yet fruitful conceptions. Empson for his part would not, I think, disdain the comparison. History and knowledge, in this latest phase of Pastoral, outrun everything but those most tentative 'conceptions' of literary form which the modern critic can believe in. Alice, in a sense, becomes 'the critic' through her means of 'imaginative escape' (p. 221). Empson defends such attitudes in a note on one of his own poems, published in the second volume of 1940. 'This being over simple', he says (as it happens) of Leavis, 'is itself a way of escaping the complexity of the critic's problems'. Dodgson's eccentricity, and that of his fictional creatures, mirrors the critic's own situation as a highly specialised interpreter, isolated by the subtlety of his own intellectual equipment. The absurdities of the *Alice* books are a late but typical flowering of the Pastoral imagination. They concentrate the feelings of loss, the theme of history as a process of increasing isolation, which attach themselves to every stage of Empson's historical survey.

Elegy is indeed the dominant mood of *Some Versions*. The book opens with the famous discussion of Gray's poem, ostensibly on account of its 'latent politics', but also perhaps because the normal mood of elegy, the feelings engendered by time and change, connect in some fundamental way with the topic of

Pastoral. The likeliest connection is the fatalistic sense that 'we ought to accept the injustice of society as we do the inevitability of death' (p. 12). This sentiment picks up the occasional tone of *Seven Types*, expressed in the passage on Swinburne; the idea that certain disordered states of experience may convey some fundamental truth about the 'mode of apprehension' of poetry. Empson even ventures, at one point in *Seven Types*, the claim that poetic meaning frequently rests on 'a statement of the limitations of the human condition' (p. 73).

Geoffrey Hartman, in his book *Beyond Formalism*, goes so far as to suggest that 'elegy' may be, in terms of poetic meaning, the opposite of 'wit', of metaphysical 'point' and the associated virtues of formal complexity.[28] Elegy—as Empson implies in his comments on Swinburne—consists in a certain diffuseness of meaning, an appeal to orders of poetic experience beyond the working reach of verbal analysis as such. Hartman quotes Johnson's *Dictionary*, where 'elegy' is defined as 'a short poem without *points* or affected elegancies'. He goes on to argue that the poetics of formalism, based too narrowly on the seventeenth-century virtues of 'wit' and metaphysical 'point', define only one possibility of intensive poetic meaning. 'The history of style itself would seem to urge us beyond formalism by asking, What is the point of *point*?'[29]

Frank Kermode raises a similar argument, also with reference to Johnson, when he praises the typical Johnsonian sense that 'there was too much meaning for one's own perceptions, or anyone else's, to organise. . .'[30] Thus the quality in the literary 'classic' which Kermode calls its 'patience'—its availability to constant reinterpretation—is also that which eludes the prescriptive methods of formalistic criticism. The passage of time and the strain of elegy are again involved in this generalised philosophy of meaning. Kermode suggests, in a somewhat puzzling sentence, that the 'only certainty'—for the critic, presumably—is that the methods of criticism and the 'obscurer depths' of the classic both belong 'to a world that can end'. In effect he is joining his notion of the 'classic' to the arguments put forward in *The Sense of an Ending* for a criticism which would treat literature as a process in, and a pattern for, the meaningful experience of time.

The development of Empson's thought, from Ambiguity to Pastoral, provides something of a pattern in itself for these speculative ventures 'beyond formalism'. Metaphysical 'point', in *Some Versions*, is not so much the structural norm and defining property of poetry, but rather—as in Hartman's view—one possible extreme of its expressive range, held in a shifting balance with the opposite set of claims. The songs in Gay's *Beggar's Opera* 'can afford to be metaphysical poetry in spite of their date because they are intended to be comically "low"' (p. 180). The tricks of the metaphysical are treated here, not as an ultimate resource but as a particular *manner* of poetic thought, qualified and given its specific interest by its place in a changing history.

Pastoral may be seen, then, as a cover-term for the whole questioning process of moving 'beyond formalism' to reinstate somehow the various 'heresies'—the subjective element—proscribed by the New Critics. Perhaps such developments may be discerned even within the stronghold of orthodox formalist opinion. Murray Krieger has recalled that Tate, in an unpublished essay, contrived to work a passage 'from Brooks's scattered insights to an overall conception of the poem as metonymy and thus as what William Empson has defined as Pastoral'.[31] Blackmur likewise sees Tate as having 'raised' the Pastoral form, like Empson, to meet the requirements of a generalised poetic. He goes on, however, to speak of the 'ambiguous allegory of the pastoral' which suits the modern need for complicated meanings.[32] Such, for Tate, were the only means by which 'knowledge could enter poetry'. These are the terms of what yet remains, in Blackmur's implied acceptation, a Hulmian discontinuity of realms. The requirements of 'allegory', the idea of 'knowledge' as vouchsafed only by flashes of disciplined analogy—these conditions show how firmly the New Criticism was entrenched upon Hulme's aesthetic and moral foundations.

Empson's Pastoral is distinguished from Tate's, or from what Blackmur divines in it, by the willing inclusion of ironies not structurally *contained* but humanly *implicit* in poetry. Not only must the critic claim access to the poet's state of feeling—thus committing the 'intentional fallacy'—but also he needs to have experienced for himself, in his very calling as critic, something of the same ambiguities. This is to demand, like Muller against

Brooks, the prerogatives of irony and complicated motive for the critic as well as the poetry he encounters. In his note on the poem 'To an Old Lady', Empson refers to 'some body of people without fundamental beliefs as a basis for action' (*Collected Poems*, p. 98). And he qualifies this further: 'ridiculous to say "the present generation"'. Empson evidently sees man's tight-rope walk between impossible contraries, as Kermode sees the 'sense of an ending', as something inherent in human experience, a basis of ironic sympathy which has to be somehow included in the critical act of judgement.

For this reason, Empson's Pastoral is a focus for feelings which themselves demand a measure of 'generous' interpretation, a coming-to-terms with their complicated nature. In Empson's account, 'the pastoral figure is always ready to become the critic', and the imaginative writer, for his part, must sympathetically 'repeat the audience in himself' (p. 56). The critic is therefore bound up philosophically with all the ironies and shifts of attitude he tries to interpret. Arthur Mizener remarked, in his review of *Some Versions*, that Empson 'presents himself to his readers by a pastoral device', that of 'the revolutionary critic in the guise of a correspondent of the T.L.S.'.[33] The irony of the critic's situation is itself a version of Pastoral, increasingly in play (as we have seen) toward the end of the book. It consists largely in the delicate knowledge, on Empson's part, of the tact required to mediate between his own intellectual interests, or those of his age, and the claims of his text to a 'simple', straightforward interpretation.

This problem is raised more explicitly in *Milton's God*, where Empson demands that the critic 'should use his own moral judgement . . . as well as try to understand the author's', since that is 'the only way he can arrive at a "total reaction"' (p. 204). This, like so much of Empson's later writing, seems a flat and simplified statement of issues raised more tactfully and, as it were, *integrally* in his earlier criticism. His recent concerns have been strongly polemical; and in consequence he has come to mistrust the usual imputations of 'irony' by critics with a conformist or 'Neo-Christian' purpose in view. 'I would look rather ridiculous', he reflects at one point, 'if I presented myself (in judging Milton's Samson) as an indignant member of the bourgeoisie' (p. 212). But the tone in this case is frankly a matter of local tactics and offered in passing as a way to accommodate his own contradictory feelings. In *Some Versions* the ironies of critical involvement, of the 'complex' interpreter and his specialised satisfactions, are all a part of the framing metaphor of Pastoral itself.

These problems of critical tact and honesty exemplify the predicament of mankind in general, caught by his moral nature between the equivocal poles of egotism and self-denial. This comes out strongly in Empson's chapter on *The Beggar's Opera*, where the behaviour of Polly is described as having 'a claim to altruism' (although her sincerity in this 'would only be pathetic'). This mixture of attitudes can also find expression in the critic's ambiguous relations with literature. Tate, in his essay 'Is Literary Criticism Possible?', admits the inherently paradoxical element in criticism; the fact that it exists 'in the middle position between imagination and philosophy'.[34] Tate sees this middle-man dilemma as still upholding the doctrine of discontinuity, since he takes it to mean that criticism can never come fully to terms with poetry. From Tate's point of view, the remoteness of critical thought from the object of its attention is a state of acknowledged self-defeat, a condition which calls for the critic's disciplined humility. Empson, on the contrary, manages through the medium of Pastoral to project these problems of critical awareness into the very history of the *genre*. This is what makes it, in the end, such a pregnant and uniquely *inclusive* theory of literature.

Empson's concept of Pastoral is clearly open to the charge of pure subjectivism from anyone who can argue, in the name of personal experience, that life is not really like that at all. Such objections could be urged against any of those critics, like Kermode or Hartman, whose ventures beyond formalism have led them to introduce some less than self-evident ground of understanding. The Pastoral set of feelings is distilled into a few sentences of generalised reflection in Empson's first chapter. 'Some people are more delicate and complex than others', and if their preoccupations can only be kept from doing harm, then this is 'a good thing, though a small thing by comparison with our common humanity' (p. 23). This sense of moral compromise behind the claims of the intellectual—the component 'critic' of Pastoral—is thus connected with the whole 'machinery' of human virtues and limitations which Empson perceived in *Seven Types*. The strength of his apparently subjective arguments lies in the dramatic logic by which such sentiments appeal for constant re-interpretation in their various Pastoral forms. This history is defined by the changing vicissitudes of the 'complex' intelligence, continually adapting itself to social situations which call out its means of ironic self-protection.

The social mobility of Pastoral is a part of that rationalising play of intelligence which Empson counts as more important to an understanding of poetry than the rooted, illogical conflicts of canonised paradox. Pastoral lifts the subtleties of poetic argument into a larger, essentially social air, so that even a poem like Marvell's 'The Garden' comes to seem more remarkable for its delicate class-feelings than its witty metaphysics. Critics have tended to seize upon the differences which Empson himself points out between the Marxist and the Pastoral conceptions of literature, and to ignore the profound historicity which nevertheless permeates the *genre*.

Raymond Williams, for example, attacks the 'metaphysical' sanctions which lurk behind Empson's categories.[35] He calls for a firm distinction between Pastoral proper and a later, more cynical version which cuts away the received values of a basically aristocratic tradition. Straight 'pastoral', as Williams interprets it, makes a 'natural order' of the *status quo*, backed up by the standard devices and metaphors of a highly artificial tradition. For Empson, however, Pastoral *contains* all the latent ironies of its own historical undoing; most obvious in the process which leaves a character like Dodgson, the intellectual misfit, so barely in possession of his complicated meanings. It is a literature built upon conflict, social and individual, but not resigned to that situation in what Williams thinks of as a mode of reactionary sentiment. Like Empson's immediately pre-war poetry, Pastoral is a means of working the conflicts of political conscience, by way of ironic self-knowledge, into an achieved form of communal expression.

It is interesting to recall certain ideas which were current in Cambridge during this period, and which may have contributed to Empson's developing theories of Pastoral. The suggestion that language, and all forms of social communication, are based on modes of 'opposition' was advanced by C. K. Ogden in a book published in 1932. Empson was in Japan at the time, and the work of Ogden and Richards on Basic English was doubtless of interest to the young teacher abroad. Ogden's examples of 'creative' opposition include some conceptual pairs strikingly similar to those taken up into Pastoral. Of the classes 'town and country', 'learned and ignorant', he remarks: 'the oppositional definition may retain historical significance', yet 'new opposi-tions, such as "scientific" and "literary", have arrived and been superimposed on the old pair, which now have a literary rather than a scientific value'.[36]

It is no coincidence that this describes quite accurately the historical background of Empson's last chapter in *Some Versions*. Science and accelerating history, Darwin and social Darwinism, seem to outrun the artist and leave him isolated, compromised by his old habits of dependence—the pragmatic variations (in Ogden's terms) of 'town and country', 'learned and simple'. Ogden seems to imply, like Empson, that the very disappearance of certain traditional forms of conflict, brought about by the process of social levelling, may force the artist to invent new varieties of more or less specialised or private 'opposition'. Ogden's 'scientific' and 'literary' are precisely the poles of dis-sociated knowledge in Empson's account of the *Alice* books.

Poetry in its aspect of social dialogue—as something other than a timeless object—is therefore to be seen as depending in turn on the poet's inward conflicts of allegiance. Those states of productive opposition, discovered in Ambiguity and developed through Pastoral, suggest a philosophy of literary form far re-moved from the formalist equation of rhetorical structure with achieved poetic meaning. Empson's attitude emerges from a note to the second edition of *Seven Types*, where he recalls how 'imbecile' he had thought the reviewer who cited a line from his poem 'The Beautiful Train'—'And I a twister love what I abhor'—to show that such duplicity was a major fault in all Empson's work. Equivocations of this sort are of the very nature of Ambiguity and Pastoral. Empson's critic thinks him a self-condemned 'twister', as Tate called him 'eccentric', by a standard of integrity which simply misses the point of a good deal of his poetry and criticism.

The same misunderstanding is apparent when John Wain, in his famous 'reassessment' of Empson, looks to the poem 'The Teasers' for evidence of his formal shortcomings.[37] Wain first acclaims the 'brilliant discovery' of the verse-form, then deplores 'the uncertainty which keeps him swinging between unresolved possibilities'. Wain's analysis of the poem and its apparent disintegration oddly ignores the pointed relevance of form to theme; the way in which the uncertainties of metre and rhythm reflect in themselves the facing-about between impossible issues of choice. Empson rather disarmed further discussion by commenting later that so much had been cut out of the poem, for various personal reasons, that critics could hardly hope to understand it. The 'uncertainty' of Empson's poem—the irregularities of metre, the faltering break mid-stanza—are a part of its appropriate form, and call for a more circumspect reading. The poem is a series of indirections and virtual contradictions, barely brought to order. Form and self-expression are likewise exposed to all the complicating ironies of sceptical self-knowledge.

This example from Empson's poetry may help to explain (more by analogy than direct relation) the passage 'beyond formalism' in his critical writing. John Bayley, in a recent polemical essay, contrasted the 'forebearing simplicity of a dialogue'—his own poetic ideal—with what he called the 'null intimacy of formalism'. Bayley suggests that where the reader (or, more disturbingly, the poet) has been conditioned by formalist expectations, a poem will for him settle down in 'the most passive, least participatory' region of the mind.[38] This he brings about, poet or reader, by having the poem 'externalise itself', and by thus 'annihilating its subject'. Empson has been arguing a similar case for the role of active intelligence in poetry since his early comments in *Seven Types* on the 'fallacy' which regards the creative mind as a passive collector of impressions. Empson's criticism constantly implies that the 'dialogue' which Bayley describes—the intelligent *rapport* between poet and reader—is dependent upon another, enabling dialogue of the poet with his own conflicting motives.

A problem arises when these dialogues draw apart, as for

instance in the poetry of extreme and private conflict, where self-involvement seems to preclude effective communication. In an early review of George Barker's poems, Empson traced this 'misleading aesthetic' partly to the poet's 'taking poetry too seriously', and partly to his 'feeling too sure that it has no public'.[39] This was probably the reason for Empson's guarded and sometimes contradictory comments on the modern 'poetry of conflict'. His reservations appear in an interview with Christopher Ricks, where the notion of the poem as 'a kind of clinical object' is pursued into all manner of paradox. Such a poem 'is not addressed to any public', but has to be addressed to 'the audience within himself', since even its therapeutic function depends on the imagined purpose of communication.[40] I suggested in Chapter 1 that Empson's own poetry, in the period before he ceased publication, was perhaps threatened by a kind of dissociation between the private and the 'public' levels of dialogue. At this stage I am more interested in showing how Pastoral provided a root metaphor, a 'subjective correlative', for the complicated feelings which demanded expression in Empson's early writing.

Typical is the way in which Shakespeare's sonnets are referred to various dramatic situations in his later plays, using the hints of character and context to create an explanatory background far beyond the actual content of 'the words on the page'. 'Discoveries of language and feeling made from a personal situation may develop themselves so that they can be applied to quite different dramatic situations; but to know about these might tell one more about the original discoveries' (*Some Versions*, p. 86). This poses a challenge indeed to the formalist doctrines of textual autonomy. Empson's procedure is justified by the striking connections and echoes he discovers, and by the knotted complex of feelings which his chapter maps out convincingly onto local hints and details. Empson is asserting the critic's right to interpret beyond the artificial limits both of the isolated text and of literature conceived as something separable from the author's living interests and involvements. His openly biographical approach to Shakespeare is itself a part of the Pastoral attitude, its breadth and subjective generality.

Eliot's notion of the 'objective correlative' was the guarantee of a closed relation between poetry and experience—the remoteness, in Eliot's words, of 'the man who suffers' from 'the mind which creates'. To suggest, as I have, that Pastoral is a kind of 'subjective correlative' is not merely a perverse and trivial substitution of terms. The 'correlation' in this case is open-minded and interpersonal, and takes up—through its own play of metaphor—the articulate whole of the artist's creating and experiencing mind. Only by way of this mediating wholeness does Pastoral become, in a much expanded sense, the basis of a literary 'form'. Pastoral is a mode of imaginative order, rooted in the diverse and conflicting sources of 'complex' satisfaction. In Some Versions the genre is actively re-imagined, from the root materials of a mood and metaphor, through all the pragmatic variations it offers to the critic's own play of feelings.

A more recent philosopher of irony has argued that the ironist, if he is honest with himself, 'cannot be outside what he observes since what he observes is the predicament he and all men are in. . .'[41] Muecke ends a chapter on 'General Irony', his widest and most philosophic category, with a list of the curious anomalies, the problems and incompatibilities, which force the ironic observer into his coping position. He has to mediate 'between the individual and society, between reason and instinct, contemplation and action, the conscious and the unconscious. . .' All these antinomies enter into Empson's idea of Pastoral, the philosophic opposites emerging most clearly in the chapter on Marvell, where—as I shall try to show later—the problems of a reflective criticism find themselves mirrored in the poetry itself.

Muecke suggests that a similar range of ironies attach to the literary work, with all the puzzles of its form and mode of existence. It demands recognition both as an object, 'the thing communicated', and as the surrogate for a human subject, the poet who seeks to communicate.[42] Muecke discovers in this paradoxical status a further series of creative ironies. He would accept, as a broadening exercise of imagination, the tensions encountered by such critics as Ong, Hartman and Empson, between the impulse to move 'beyond formalism' and the ironic foreknowledge of the difficulties in their way.

The most important claim for Pastoral, I think, is that it works these problems and contradictions back into the fruitful complexities of an adequate critical vision. An example of this intimate exchange between form and meaning occurs in Empson's Pastoral reading of the Shakespeare sonnet 'They that have power to hurt and will do none'. Empson declares at the outset that the poem defies analysis: it is like 'a solid flute on which you can play a multitude of tunes, whose solidity no list of all possible tunes would go far to explain' (p. 77). The image is not used quite as one might have expected. Empson admits his incapacity to realise, not the sheer variety of meanings the poem may hold, but the *form* or structure which could possibly contain them, even when the meanings themselves—the 'tunes' of his analogy—seem possibly within grasp.

This is rather different from the attitude to multiple meaning which seems to have inspired *Seven Types*. Robert Graves's criticism first excited Empson because, as he said in a *Granta* review, one could feel 'this at any rate is complicated enough'; so many meanings could give the impression of richness—if only approximately—which one's feelings required. This attitude he seems to have adopted, quite deliberately, as a response to the modern predicament of criticism: the growth of knowledge with the loss of belief, and hence the inescapable relativity of all informed judgement. In 1928 he reviewed, for *Granta*, a book entitled *The Pre-War Mind in Britain*. Empson admired it, as he admired Graves's criticism, because 'one feels that nearly enough reasons are given, and that only reasons of this kind could make the thing intelligible at all'.[43]

By the time of *Some Versions* this intellectual mood has changed, and with it the attitude to questions of meaning and form. To revert to Empson's image: it is not the perhaps inexhaustible variety of 'tunes' or possible meanings which now tantalises the imagination, but the elusive, questionable form of the instrument which produces them. Empson's metaphor of the 'solid' flute seems hardly appropriate. A more equivocal use of 'solid' is found in his remark on a stanza of Marvell's 'The Garden': 'the paradoxes are still firmly maintained here, and the soul is as solid as the green thought' (p. 105). Throughout Empson's reading, the dilemmas of critical method are somehow anticipated by the poet's curious meditations on the theme and occasion of his own 'metaphysical' puzzlings. To talk in such terms need no longer seem the compound of presumptive 'fallacies' which the formalist critic would call it. The richness of Pastoral, its openness to creative interpretation, comes from the round of sympathetic ironies whereby the critic divines the common motives and shared situation of his own and the poet's habits of thought.

It is this that makes possible the deep continuity of human experience contained in Pastoral. Empson finds in the Shakespeare sonnets an implication of 'the condition for fullness of life; you cannot know beforehand what life will bring you if you open yourself to it' (pp. 80–1). This is true, not only of the poet's experience but also of the reader's reactions to poetry, in the way it creates and continually confounds his expectant responses. To shift Empson's reference a little: one cannot rest in any but a local and provisional idea of the poem's form, since too rigid a notion can only congeal its fluid potentialities. As Empson says in *Seven Types*, 'it does not even satisfy the understanding to stop living in order to understand' (p. 245). In Pastoral, this state of willing openness constantly chastens the impulse to formulate one's impressions.

Elsewhere in *Some Versions*, Empson offers an otherwise rather baffling commentary on Donne's 'The Exstasie'. ' "This Exstasie doth unperplex"/because it makes the disparate impulses of the human creature not merely open to the prying of the mind but prepared for its intrusion' (p. 111). Thus the poem, far from remaining an object for passive contemplation, takes on all the complexities and self-adapting subtlety of the critic as partner in mutual understanding. The supposed problems of literary from are hardly to be distinguished from the context of human relations and sympathies. The positive counterpart to these 'prying' doubts and insecurities lies in the generous domain of Pastoral irony. Between the feeling which 'combines breadth of sympathy with energy of judgement' (p. 57), and that which forces one into isolation 'by sheer strength of mind' (p. 171), there lies the entire subjective history of Pastoral. Form is inseparable from the matrix of human relations, whether of mutual dependence or the kind of ironic strength-through-isolation which marks the more adaptable creatures of Pastoral.

Modern criticism is much occupied with such elusive hermeneutic shadings between 'form' and 'content'. J. Hillis Miller has attempted, in a recent essay, to apply certain ideas of the French structuralist critics to Wordsworth's sonnet 'Composed upon Westminster Bridge'.[44] He argues expressly, where Empson had implied, that issues of poetic form impinge in various ways on our understanding of a poem's theme and occasion. Wordsworth oddly casts doubt, through certain inconsistencies of detail, on the reality of his remembered experience; while the form of the poem, in a similar way, seems to undermine its own substantial unity. Miller offers the analogy of a musical theme, repeating (doubtless unawares) the image Empson had used. 'Though the harmony is controlled, the linguistic "tones" finite in number, the compass small, the relation between the parts seems impossible to fix'. Miller's 'tones' have replaced Empson's more homely 'tunes'; Empson typically finds elements of independent sense in the component parts, whence his lively attempts at paraphrase. Miller takes on the structuralist principle of suspended meaning in all its rigour, and the result probably does more for his developing theory than for the understanding of Wordsworth's poem. Such could not be said of Empson, at least as the critic of Pastoral. His initiatives beyond formalism arise entirely from the practical encounter with poetry, without much burden of explicit theory.

Hartman merges his plea for literary history with the project of a phenomenology, or study of 'consciousness in its efforts to appear'.[45] Empson, I think, achieves this working relation in the nominal form of Pastoral. The possession of this 'subjective correlative' disengages the mind from its inveterate quest for form, and enables Empson to speak of *The Beggar's Opera*, for instance, as having a 'casualness and inclusiveness which allow it to collect into it things that had been floating in tradition' (p. 159). It was this productive looseness, apparently, which made Pastoral such a meeting-place and imaginative theatre for Empson's ideas at this stage in his thinking.

3

Complex Words
and the Grammar of Motives

If *Pastoral* supplied a ruling metaphor and imaginative frame for Empson's interests, it was in *Complex Words* that he set out its full implications for a theory of criticism. Its bearing can best be taken by setting it, to begin with, in the context of modern ideas about the meaning of literature and the proper aims of critical interpretation. In the terms of much current debate, this becomes a matter of hermeneutic principle, of the interpreter's relation to his text and to the whole project of historical understanding.

There are two main schools of thought to be distinguished. The one maintains a strict, factualistic approach; insists on the quest for an 'original' meaning, and so limits critical speculation to the task of establishing a credible range of meanings—a semantic 'horizon'—at the historical time in question. In current discussion, the thorough-going arguments of E. D. Hirsch[1] have freshly established the claims of this basically conservative principle.

The other school, somewhat in the tradition of modern theology, denies the possibility or, at any rate, the usefulness of such positivistic scholarship. Rather, the critic should admit the unbridgeable distance imposed by history between *his* world of experience, his conditioned understanding, and that of the author he is reading. Criticism has therefore to be conceived as a dialectical encounter between two distinct 'horizons'. This position involves a moderate degree of scepticism. We cannot positively *know* an author's intended meaning; but we can at least rely on structures of understanding, independent of time and change, which allow us to reconstitute the literary work with its new burden of significance. R. E. Palmer, in his book *Hermeneutics*,[2] has provided a useful survey of these (mainly German) currents of thought, and expressly opposed them to the ideas developed by Hirsch.

Once formulated, these questions present themselves with peculiar insistence to the reflective modern critic. The 'problem of knowledge' inserts the sceptical doubt as—precisely—one of those conditions of awareness which define the present intellectual horizon. Leavis's classic refusal to philosophise, his determinedly intuitive stance on questions of literary meaning and value—these amount to a definite position which he constantly re-states with all its deliberate lack of 'philosophical' support. Empson, it is true, has little sympathy with what he once described as the 'bother-headed' school of American critical theory. But, as I shall now try to show, Empson's criticism does have an inexplicit content of theory amounting, especially in *Complex Words*, to a highly articulate philosophy.

Critical theory, in this extended sense, is a constant reflection on the validity of its own attendant practice. Leavis avoids such issues by positing principles of intuitive or immediate response, and by treating literary language as a source of directly embodied meaning, yielding up its qualities more or less 'concretely' through sensuous apprehension. From the 'muscular enactment' of Keats to Shakespeare's 'metaphorical vitality' or Pope's varied effects of tone and cadence[3]—Leavis's appeal is mostly to the broadly *physical* properties of poetic language, rather than its complex semantic attributes.

With Empson, the mediations of theory take place almost entirely within, or in terms of, this semantic dimension. His progress from *Seven Types* to *Complex Words* is characterised by this development. As criticism discovers new areas of rational uncertainty, it sets about creating a new possible source of valid understanding. Georg Lukacs describes this function of critical 'mediation' in his book *History and Class Consciousness*.[4] 'Unmediated contemplation' leads finally to inert historicism, on the one hand, and to what he calls the 'indifference of form' —exemplified by the abstract Kantian tradition—on the other. Mediation is the virtue born of a necessity, the point at which the clear recognition of a problem becomes the condition of its defeat, the possibility of actively grasping its historical meaning.

Frederic Jameson, surveying these differences, observes how the New Critics by 'eternalising their touchstones', by 'fetishising language' and making it the source of an 'ahistorical plenitude', have managed to contain literature within 'purely ethical limits', without translating these into historical or social terms.[5] Where Empson differs from Leavis, Eliot or Cleanth Brooks, it is exactly this process of 'translation' that is often involved. *Complex Words* can be read in this light: as a commentary on the whole enlightened effort of humanist re-interpretation, given its cultural and semantic starting-point, the disappearance of God. Theory is not isolated, a matter of formal philosophy, or imported from some dubiously cognate discipline (as was, in effect, the New Critical doctrine through Eliot from F. H. Bradley). Theory is produced by the process of rational reflection, as scepticism comes to find its limits in the practical encounter of critic with text.

This internally-generated content of theory is clear enough in the sequence of Empson's books. *Seven Types* sets out with the basic faith of the verbal analyst: that if the poet is 'using the language properly', then it should be 'impossible to maintain' any distinction between the 'verbal' and the 'psychological' levels of meaning. Complexity of logical meaning 'ought to be based on complexities of thought' (p. 49). Empson's 'ought' begs the question, here, whether this is supposed to be an absolute or merely a desirable measure of poetic value. William Righter has complained (from a logical positivist standpoint) that Empson's arguments fail to meet this requirement. The increasing complexities at various levels—verbal, logical, psychological—do not run perfectly parallel or to a single, maximal end. The book's assymetrical argument denies what Empson apparently at one stage envisaged: the identity of a poem's 'meaning' with its rhetorical complexity, as assumed by formalist criticism. But Empson's books are often larger than the ideas they set out to prove. There is always the fruitful moment of encounter with the poem, when theory can only make a tactful advance toward adequate understanding. The pin-pointed ambiguities rarely cover the field; there is always some larger context of implication. Even where there is a 'pointed' logic, or (as in cases of the punning Fourth Type) a self-satisfied aptness of expression, Empson often senses that more obscure forces are in play. Typically this leads to his feeling that 'the stress of the situation absorbs them and they are felt to be natural under the circumstances' (p. 131). This was one of the directions in which Ambiguity opened into Pastoral. The sense of background 'circumstance', the pressure of social occasion, was a call to transform and supplement the resources of 'verbal' criticism. The distance between the surface categories and the genuine reach of Ambiguity—insights unobtainable on its own original terms—becomes the motive and generic basis of Pastoral.

This latter, as we have seen, is more a species of extended dramatic metaphor than a definite form or distinctive structure of meaning. Its prototypes are of the theatre, even in the case of lyrical poems, like Marvell's 'The Garden', which seem self-occupied to the point of solipsism. Empson's interpretations rest always on the complex interchange of feelings found most typically in a responsive theatre audience. His early drama criticism, published in *Granta*, gives some idea of the role which a generalised theory of drama was to play in his later thinking. Reviewing a production of *As You Like It*, he regrets the simplified style of presentation, the absence of 'the rather self-supporting dialectics which were so important a part of the Elizabethan attitude to poetry'.[6] The vague 'self-supporting' begs the question, for the moment, of whether or how these 'dialectics' are supposed to be 'in' the poetry itself. But one can see how these early reviews, for all their casual variety, helped Empson to formulate his ideas about literature; to state the difficulties of an adequate response and, in stating them, move some way toward a fruitful solution.

Empson was not alone, at the time, in sensing a certain question posed by literature, in its most complex modern forms, to the practical possibilities of drama. In another review he mentions, in passing, the book *Tragedy* by F. L. Lucas, published in 1927. Lucas had suggested that, in Empson's words, 'Proust has killed the drama'; that the modern novel, with all its psychological equipment and the narrative leisure to use it, had seemingly displaced the simple and limited forms of dramatic expression. However, knowing something of his future interests, one can find much more in Empson's comment than a blank pessimism about the prospects of drama. The modern premium on the novel results, he says, from the feeling that 'one thing to do with people is to take them at their flattest and then try to understand them'.[7] This statement has the distinct modality of Pastoral, whose central metaphor is precisely this of the 'flattest', or most apparently simple, becoming the foil of 'complex' interpretation. Pastoral is in part a conceptual rehabilitation of drama. In lyric poetry also the equivalent mood, that of ironic understatement, emerges from *Seven Types* in those passages which suggestively look forward to the later book. Already, in the context of Ambiguity, Empson observes that 'humility' and 'concentration' are allied to 'sincerity', and that these characteristics are evident especially in 'statements of the limitations of human life' (p. 60).

Yet *Seven Types*, as we have seen, gives no simple warrant for direct link between 'concentration' and 'sincerity', the structural and the psychological, as the formalist critic might equate them. I. A. Richards, in his early books, identified 'sincerity' with the range and balance of 'impulses' which the poem was able to satisfy in a competent reader. And the New Critics after him, although they eschewed his effective terminology, took over from Richards that assured and easy commerce between the poem's and the poet's integrity which gives formalist criticism its main basis of value-judgement. In Empson's account their relation is more problematic and less open to moralising dogma. Yet Empson says quite plainly, in the closing pages of *Seven Types*, that the modern reader needs some 'machinery', at least putative, for judging a poet's 'sincerity'; that many modern poets are manifest 'charlatans', and that this makes the problem of the critic's credibility all the more urgent.

In *Seven Types*, Empson is already coming to feel that literary works should be accepted as 'things rich in their interpretations rather than their meaning' (p. 120). The poetry in question is a passage from Herbert describing what Empson calls 'a flat and as it were pastoral exchange of gifts'. The word 'pastoral', tentatively used, has something of its later pragmatic implications. Criticism seems to find its working example in a hint of the poem's dramatic background and its style of social reserve. 'Interpretation' must exceed the sum, no matter how subtly defined, of clear-cut, isolated 'meanings'. It is in the same spirit that Empson, casting about in *Complex Words* for a handy definition of metaphor, chooses the suggestive idea of a 'double structure of pregnancy' (p. 343), rather than any formal theory based on logical schemes of identity. Instancing a possible emendation in Shakespeare, deriving from arguments by complex analogy, Empson objects that 'you lose the effect not only of richness but of breadth, or even of simplicity' (p. 346). These attributes, with the hint of a critical paradox resolved, lead metaphor back to Pastoral, where indeed—in Empson's developing thought—it is most at home.

Thus drama is at the root both of Pastoral and of the way in which Empson came to conceive of literary forms in general. It is significant that drama should have struck him at the time as problematic medium, threatened by the new-found capabilities of the novel. Empson's comments on Proust are few and casual. But an essay on Virginia Woolf, published just after *Seven Types*, re-states the issue with a somewhat altered emphasis.[8] Empson finds in *Mrs. Dalloway* the same generic strengths of the modern novel: its ability, over long stretches of narrative, to store up memories, impressions and images, similar in their workings to poetic language or to 'what would be given by an annotated edition'. However, Empson now expresses reservations which amount to a shrewd critique of the stream-of-consciousness style. A novelist's 'wit', he remarks, is 'likely to carry its own setting and explanation', but his 'personal poetry' (the subconscious stream of his imagery) is not likely to be so 'reliable'.

Empson had read *Ulysses* with excitement, and had helped to edit the magazine *Experiment* which published, along with his own material, some early portions of Joyce's *Work in Progress*. He had himself written (apparently influenced by Gertrude Stein) the curious prose-poem 'About a Ball in the Nineteenth Century', which exploits verbal associations to the point of surrealist extravagance. It must therefore have been a considered and decisive reaction which led him to make these remarks on Virginia Woolf's novelistic technique. The essay was published in 1931, when the earlier studies of Pastoral were under way. What Empson came to miss in surrealistic or subjective prose, that 'setting and comparison' provided only by the conscious mind, proved itself capable of all the requisite subtleties in the *genre* of Pastoral.

In one of his reviews for *Granta*, Empson speaks of the modern distaste for overtly 'dramatic' behaviour, and of the much greater interest to be found in the 'subdued complexity of the normal'.[9] In his film reviews especially, it is obvious that this complexity is a matter of interpretation, not of meaning, as these are distinguished in *Seven Types*. Empson remarks in one case that any too-obvious insistence on dramatic 'point', or on meanings too forcefully driven home, will soon seem as naïve as the old 'objective' realism of Victorian theatre. In short, these early assignments regularly fastened Empson's attention onto problems of literary form and receptive attitude which later found their way back into his criticism. This piece in particular closes with the pertinent question: 'would you find that distinction in the text, I wonder?' Film and theatre gave ample room and tentative shape to these elusive reflections on form and meaning.

Above all, they revealed the difficulty of reaching even a provisional notion of what, for the sensitive critic, was legitimately 'in' the text. In *Seven Types*, Empson's readings are constantly qualified by a sense of dramatic contexts which lie beyond reach of constituent analysis. Such, for instance, is the suggestive background, the retreat from immediate verbal detail, in Empson's elusive but telling remarks on a song from *Measure for Measure*. 'It is these two contradictions . . . which convey the ambivalence of her feeling for him. (And yet, after all, it is no use calling this a serious contradiction; we know what her total feelings are well enough . . .)' (p. 181). A footnote to the 1961 edition joins onto these reflections and shows their importance in Empson's sequence of thought. The song still appears to him to turn the clash of feelings 'into poetry', although it must to some extent be regarded as 'inherently a dramatic one'. In his Preface for the new edition, Empson had reprinted some remarks from a previous review of the book by James Smith, the main point of which had been to question the bearing of 'dramatic' upon 'poetic' cases of Ambiguity. Dramatic situations, Smith thought, were matters of contingent circumstance, and could only be 'ambiguous' in a manner quite distinct from the pointed, intentional ambiguities of poetic language. Poems, according to Smith, were 'noumenal' objects—products of creative will—and therefore stood apart from the promiscuous contexts of Empson's Ambiguity.

Again, it seems to be the peculiar quality of Empson's criticism, like the feelings of Shakespeare's song, to thrive in the space of a theoretical near-contradiction. One would after all expect Empson, with his express approval of arguments from 'intention', to agree with Smith in calling the poem a 'noumenon', or product of achieved creative will. Instead he offers, in reply to Smith, two basic arguments: firstly, that the poet may mean more than he knows, and secondly, that no critical judgement can ever hope to have the final word. I have already recalled, in Chapter 2, that Smith had developed a critical theory similar, in many respects, to those of the American New Critics. To call the poem 'noumenal', from their viewpoint, is not to make the poet's intention available to reasoned enquiry. On the contrary, it is all the more firmly closed off within its own aesthetic limits, being the property—in effect—of the poet's own private world of experience. By meeting Smith's arguments in his Preface, and apparently taking them up at various points in his footnotes, Empson is making an important point about literary communication in general.

When he came to prepare *Seven Types* for this 1961 edition, Empson's arguments had doubtless gained confidence from his interim researches into the nature of Complex Words. The Preface contains a useful statement of his case against James Smith's critical assumptions. 'As I understand it, there is always in great poetry a feeling of generalisation from a case which has been presented . . . an appeal to a background of human experience, which is all the more present when it cannot be named' (p. xv). This idea of 'generalisation' is very important to Empson. It operates in the two dimensions of meaning which he tries to reconcile as the working province of valid critical judgement. He speaks elsewhere of the 'reality (that is, the transferability)' of the poet's lyrical experience (p. 254). The question of 'sincerity' therefore comes down to the basic *condition* of achieved poetic meaning. And again, the language of generalised 'sense'—as defined in practice throughout *Complex Words*— can provide a measure of linguistic sanity and normative usage by which to judge the more extraordinary feats of poetic style.

As Empson puts the case in his reply to Smith, this normative idea is closely bound up with the vaguer sense of dramatic 'background' discovered in 'all great poetry'.

Empson was later prepared to claim, in a correspondence over *Milton's God*, that 'some general view of life' could be found behind a good poet's every turn of language and style.[10] Empson's criticism thus contains, implicitly at first but overtly in *Complex Words*, what might be called (after Wittgenstein) the search for a 'generality notation'. Wittgenstein remarks in his *Notebooks* that generality, in the field of human understanding, 'makes its appearance like an argument'.[11] Empson also, in *Complex Words*, treats the truth-conditions of language, not as a matter of factual or empirical statement—on which view, as I. A. Richards had shown, poetry could only have 'emotive' truth—but rather as a logic of semantic equations, bearing its own internal claims to validity. 'Generalisation', in this sense, becomes the logic of poetic language and the source of any possible validation for critical judgement.

I shall have more to say later about the rational 'machinery' of *Complex Words*, and the way in which it opens the question of individual 'style', at least in its cognitive-semantic aspect, to a generalised theory of language. Empson offers the term 'head meaning', for the sense of a word 'in the air' at a given time, and 'chief meaning' for what an author's style and immediate intention try to push into prominence. These form the basic logical framework of his interpretations in *Complex Words*. However, Empson's 'literary' chapters go far beyond the limits of this simple dualism, handling whole contexts of associative meaning by what amounts to a cumulative proof of the book's main argument: that such dialectics are the basis of all communication in language, whatever the superimposed subtleties of individual styles.

Hirsch makes the point that 'interpretation' in criticism must take its bearings from Kantian ethics, which he finds to consist in the general rule that the text is not a *means* but a self-sufficient *end* of interpretive enquiry.[12] Being in effect the author's surrogate voice, his writing demands of the critic a due deference and respect for its 'proper' signification, identified as far as possible with his original intention. So far as it goes, this principle cannot be faulted, and Empson would be the last to question its validity. However, it contains no definite idea or practicable theory as to how, exactly, such a rule is to be followed in the business of detailed criticism. Empson has come at the problem by a more roundabout philosophic route, but his work seems to answer the more urgent need of displaying the machinery of such judgements in an intimate relation with the very workings of poetic language.

This all pre-supposes a distinction which Roman Jakobson has recently made more explicit: that the literary critic is not a 'cryptanalyst', assembling meanings from scratch in some alien code, but a privileged interpreter who works within the more or less familiar limits of his own culture and language.[13] The rational semantics of *Complex Words* are a practical affirmation of Jakobson's argument. In *Seven Types*, Empson had been concerned mainly with the 'vertical' reaches of association, or what Saussure calls the 'paradigmatic' dimension; the meanings called out by a word's associative properties, without any clear or decisive controls of context. As opposed to this vertical dimension of meaning, Saussure mentions also a 'grammatical' aspect, a realm of 'structural rules', which tends to incorporate and restrain 'the unmotivated sign'.[14] These need not be the rules of 'grammar' in the usual, restricted sense. They may represent a context of semantics, but one which is ordered on the 'syntagmatic' plane, the horizontal and not the vertical. Saussure insists that the vertical sets are relatively unmotivated; that 'terms in an associative family occur neither in fixed numbers nor in a definite order', whereas those of the syntagm 'immediately suggest an order of succession'.

This is the background of Empson's theoretical advance in *Complex Words*. Meanings are articulate, accountable in terms of an ordered 'grammar', and above all an evidence of 'motivation'. Such is the operative level of 'intention' in *Complex Words*. In *Seven Types*, the workings of Ambiguity are felt to occupy a more private, less answerable region of the poet's mind; so that questions of intention come down usually to the complaint of Empson's critics that he has foisted his own ingenious puzzles onto the poet's self-evident meaning. *Seven Types* never quite comes to terms with this problem of essential credibility.

Since most of its examples are nonce-associations, or 'witty' connections of some kind or other, it is difficult to see how Ambiguity fits into the 'generalising' case, the search for a normative machinery, which Empson hopes to prove. For instance, there is a puzzling passage (pp. 104–5) which discusses the workings of certain overtly 'etymological' puns. If these are 'too completely justified by their derivation', then the effect of poetic wit, or ingenious 'point', would seem to be lost. How can the poet's intentions bear—or be *appreciated* as bearing—on the mere facts of language, however pointed or relevant, which he happens to exploit? Between the private and historical dimensions of language, the act of association and its ready resources, there is as yet no available connection which avoids the obvious problems of creative choice and originality.

Empson's advance in *Complex Words* could well be described as a new and individual use of the dictionary. Hugh Kenner thought him rather old-fashioned and naïve in his reverence for the O.E.D.[15] But Kenner had failed to appreciate, I think, the sheer originality of Empson's lexical resources. A large and articulate background of language, organised into families of associative meaning, now becomes the working rationale of each of Empson's chapters. He adds the components of a linguistic theory, a broad-based semantic and lexical framework, to his previously rather ad hoc and piecemeal use of the dictionary's resources. Criticism becomes a threefold process of interpretation. The poet's language at first defines its relevant semantic regions and, within broad limits, the range of its thematic implications. Then the dictionary, having filled out the historical context, allows the critic to familiarise himself actively with the likely equations of logic and feeling which the state of the language made possible. *Seven Types* set out to show 'how a properly-qualified mind works' when reading poetry; and thus, by extension, 'how those properly qualified minds have worked which have not at all understood their own working' (p. 248). But it is not until *Complex Words* that Empson arrives at a normative conception of language which would make this more than a hopeful plan of approach.

'It is possible', he suggests in *Seven Types*, 'that there are some writers who write very largely with this sense of a language as such, so that their effects would be almost out of reach of analysis' (p. 6). Most likely this latent resource 'could not be explained in intelligible terms'. *Complex Words* thus marks a notable extension of the limits to what may be 'intelligible' as soundly-based criticism. It brings a degree of theoretical clarity both to the concept of style, as an author's linguistic quiddity, and to the idea of literary language as entailing its own specific rules of intelligibility. Hirsch has pointed out that the 'repudiation of theory in favour of common sense' itself implies a theoretical position, and that 'the commonalty of common sense' should naturally lead to some agreement on its terms and premises.[16] Empson's later criticism includes precisely the theory, or implicit rational grounds, of commonsense judgement.

An interesting test of these ideas on style and attitude is the poet Rochester, whose case Empson discussed in a review of 1953.[17] He finds in Rochester a standing example of the insufficiency of formalist methods in criticism. Rochester's jaunty style only 'comes off', Empson suggests, if one realises—against all the orthodox bans—the 'philosophy' manifest in the poet's life. One has to 'believe' Rochester, to take him on trust and see the implications of his desperate libertine ethic, if the poems are to seem at all serious. The style is deceptive and calls for circumspect reading. Thus 'this absolute duty to display ease . . . has to be considered before it seems sensible to call the lyrics of Rochester very deep'. In his own poem 'Reflections from Rochester', Empson pursues the theme of rakish egotism to a darker conclusion: competition tooth-and-claw, social Darwinism and the arms race. But in this review, and in *Complex Words*, he ventures the more hopeful idea that egotism—or enlightened self-interest—may be the one reliable basis for mutual understanding. This moral outlook is also present in the essays on 'theories of value' which form an Appendix to *Complex Words*. As well as supporting his general argument, that judgements of value may be rational and not merely 'emotive', these chapters define the ethic of mutuality—or of commonsense social interest —which so often colours the interpretative viewpoint in *Complex Words*. Questions of 'style' are inseparable in the long run from a cluster of attitudes which the poet Rochester, by forcing them to a paradoxical conclusion, helps to isolate and define.

Empson's critical assumptions have frequently taken colour from his dealings with eighteenth-century poetry. Already in *Seven Types* an ethic of rational mutuality permits an appeal to what he calls 'the normal habits of the human mind' (p. 215). Typically he moves on from Crashaw's perverse ecstasies (in the 'Hymn to Saint Teresa') to Dryden's more public, though not less complicated sexual word-play. Common to both is the paradoxical union of love and death in a single equivocal thought. But Dryden implies also (in Empson's paraphrase) the sense that 'nothing is to be valued more than mutual forebearance' (p. 220). This suggests a recognition of the rich, often compromised variety of human satisfactions. As with Rochester, it is necessary to bear in mind the whole ironic story of man's limitations, his partial self-knowledge and contradictory treatment of himself and others. It is eighteenth-century usage which provides Empson, in *Complex Words*, with the clearest examples of this mutual ethic which raises the question of style into a touchstone of human generosity.

It is Pope who gives Empson the opportunity, in *Complex Words*, for his most inwardly revealing and qualified piece of practical criticism. Pope manages to erect the 'contradictions of his self-contempt and self-justification' into 'a solid and intelligent humility before the triumphs and social usefulness possible to his art' (p. 97). The tact and sureness of Empson's reading perhaps tend to obscure, by so completely *expressing*, the poem's implications for critical theory. Pope's brilliant performance with 'wit', as a matter of verbal strategy, mirrors exactly the use and limitations of critical ingenuity in seeking out the sources of Pope's impressive balance of judgement. As defined reflexively by Pope's semantics, 'wit' must eventually give way to 'sense'; or, in the rational scheme of things, to that broader provision of 'generous' judgement demanded in turn of Pope's attentive reader. The semantic function of 'sense' in the poem's dialectics is to offer 'a steady bass note in contrast to the high gyrations of *wit*' (p. 99). The meaning of the *Essay* thus acts out the very conditions of its being adequately understood.

This permits Empson to define as it were in the formal mode of *Complex Words* what he had first described more impressionistically in the context of Pastoral. In *Some Versions* he had spoken of the 'play of irony and judgement' which could shelter behind the 'impersonal dignified form' of Augustan poetry (p. 167). This feeling that 'form', however subtly one defines it, never quite matches the range of poetic meaning, was—I have suggested—the deepest motive behind Empson's creative re-discovery of Pastoral. This goes with a certain shift of emphasis, in Empson's thinking, from the characteristic 'metaphysical' virtues of 'point' and self-contained argument, to the broadly 'Augustan' poetic rules of good sense and rational argument. In *Seven Types* Empson is already given to reflect that the Augustans would have regarded Ambiguity sometimes as a 'grace', sometimes as a 'generalisation' (p. 68). This is in effect the argument which emerges, with far greater clarity and point, from Empson's treatment of the *Essay on Criticism*. The virtue of Pope's pointed style is precisely its unforced *generalising* quality, the inner dialectic by which 'wit' moves over to accommodate the sheer magnanimity of 'sense'.

In *Seven Types*, Empson judges the Augustans (especially Johnson) as often having triumphed, in some obscure way, by failing to achieve the 'compactness and polish' (p. 70) identified with the Metaphysicals. Pastoral goes some way toward making this a constituent mood of certain kinds of poetry, properly understood. And *Complex Words*, with its central example from Pope, shows explicitly the native limitations of 'wit', or of purely self-supporting dialectics, compared with the steadier, more rational mediations of 'sense'.

In one of Empson's earliest reviews for *Granta* he objects that the novels of Thornton Wilder are 'continually exploiting his style to make an escape from his subject'.[18] Subsequently he was to say much the same thing about Henry James's late style, and of R. P. Blackmur's more Jamesian convolutions.[19] This notion of a style somehow 'exploited' implies that style is regarded as essentially normative, or at least as containing its own implicit limits of useful development. *Complex Words* can be seen to offer a workable theory, in semantic terms, of literary style in its relation to language at large. Such is the object-lesson provided by Pope's *Essay*: a running critique of the pretensions of 'wit' against the background of commonsense judgement. From Pope's semantics Empson derives both a period style and a generalised ethic of interpretation. The larger message is what Hirsch vaguely outlines as a 'general agreement' on the 'commonalty of sense'. Empson's critical faith is that 'generosity' will, at some point, coincide with 'generality'; that, for a certain liberal breadth of interpretative judgement, there may exist an equivalent structure of rational assent which in some sense guarantees the right-minded process of 'generous' interpretation. In his Appendices on 'Theories of Value', Empson re-states what the book as a whole is meant to demonstrate: that understanding stems from mutual regard, and that 'intellectuality' is a sufficient and reliable basis for both. For this one could substitute 'generality' or simply 'sense', as the word is defined by its ramifications and associative logic in *Complex Words*.

DRAMATIC 'CHARACTER' AND THE COMMONSENSE ETHIC

Empson sets out to show that this ethic of mutuality—historically at its strongest in the English eighteenth century—may convincingly be joined to a general theory of language and interpretation. But the commonsense ethic is also, unmistakably, a period concept; and Empson's turn of argument, in the practical chapters of *Complex Words*, needs to be seen in the light of his rationalist sympathies. The result is most often an ironic undermining of the sense of values—especially 'tragic' values—upheld by the opposing ethic of Christian self-renunciation. Words like 'fool' and 'honest' have a down-to-earth quality of healthy scepticism which, Empson argues, permits their users to build up a trust in human nature based on a shared knowledge of its needs and attendant weaknesses. 'Dog' is the most cynical of the family, a rock-bottom term of mutual disillusion, yet at the same time a 'hearty' recognition of mankind's common predicament.

There is not much room in this rationalist outlook for anything in the nature of a 'tragic' philosophy of values. It is interesting to notice how Empson's readings of Shakespeare, in particular the chapter on *Othello*, tend to play down the metaphysical meaning of tragedy, while concentrating on the verbal 'machinery' of Shakespeare's text. Empson lays the ground for his reading of *Othello* with a previous chapter on the normative senses of 'honest', the way in which it enabled a certain mutual irony to cut away the sanctions of official morality and substitute an unillusioned sense of mutual fallibility. Then, in Shakespeare's deviant uses of the word, he traces the pathology of its possible semantic distortions. 'The confusion of moral theory in the audience' is latent also in 'the confusion of the word' (p. 235). Nineteenth-century audiences took Iago 'as an abstract term "evil"'; whereas in Empson's reading he becomes 'a critique on an unconscious pun'. Othello and Iago carry on an intensive dialogue with the play's verbal resources, just as the play itself, on a larger view, works out a sub-set of the rational structure of 'honest'.

The effect of Empson's semantic priorities can best be seen by comparing his reading with the celebrated essay of Leavis.[20] The essence of Leavis's interpretation is the argument that Othello, with his manifest taste for grandiloquent self-assertion, fails to live up to the renunciatory ethic of tragedy in general. This philosophy associates in turn with Leavis's belief in the primacy of the poetic 'medium'—the unselfconscious naturalness of language—over anything pertaining to the poet's verbal ingenuity. Such, as I have pointed out already, was the root of Leavis's early quarrel with Empson's methods of criticism. When applied to *Othello*, it leads on naturally to his judgement that the hero's eloquence is a species of face-saving 'rhetoric', and that therefore his character is gravely flawed and open from the outset to Iago's insinuating wiles. This seems to Leavis to compromise his stature as a tragic hero, by breaking down his claims to moral self-possession and integrity. Empson takes a quite different view. He finds Othello all the more plausible for his contradictory motives, and is happy to allow 'a certain wilful heightening to be expected of a man of honour' (p. 245).

Empson's understanding of Iago's character carries the same appeal to a rationalising judgement of motives. For Empson, evil 'has no unity' (p. 231). If nineteenth-century audiences could regard Iago as 'pure Evil', their response no longer seems adequate to an age more aware of the hidden complications of character and motive. Helen Gardner has recently argued that tragedy, with its delicate economies of guilt and retribution, can scarcely survive the Freudian enlightenment as to matters of motive and responsibility.[21] Possibly this was one cause for Empson (in his own reminiscence) having 'always' been troubled by the findings of psychoanalysis. But the cultural *fact* of Freud's modern influence becomes an inescapable part of the complex of attitudes found in a present-day audience. Whilst watching *Othello*, the Victorians (Empson reflects) could not recognise the virtues of being 'frank to yourself about your own desires' (p. 235). From some points of view, as apparently from Helen Gardner's, the modern condition of willing self-knowledge may bring a painful or disabling kind of clarity. For Empson, it seems to have fallen square with his own temperament and—despite his comment on Freud—to have enriched the sources of his criticism.

Empson thus pursues the implications of language into the 'character' of Othello, just as he followed the twists of Pastoral irony into Gay's Polly Peachum. More a complicated figment than a 'character' of Pastoral, Polly's ambiguities tease Empson's judgement beyond any possibility of moral conclusions. Conventional distinctions between 'conscious' and 'unconscious' motives no longer seem to apply: she is 'less impeded than we are' (*Some Versions*, p. 194), and her 'intentions' are consequently anyone's guess. She seems by turns pathetic, ingenuous, scheming and sinister; but how much of this is actually 'in' the character, or even—at a liberal estimate—'in' the text? At this point the question of critical fidelity joins on to the problems of generously allowing for the range and varieties of human motivation. Polly is not a 'character' held up for moralising judgement, or inviting the kind of simplified response which Empson imputes to a Victorian audience. Neither does she exist in the play, as Othello seems to exist for Leavis's purpose, as an obvious candidate for stern moral judgement. Her character is traversed by the ironies, the intrigues and patent contradictions which make up the Pastoral *genre* as a whole. In *Seven Types* Empson had commented that human life is 'so much a matter of juggling with contradictory impulses' that such behaviour often proves people to possess 'the right number of impulses', and so to have 'a fair title to humanity' (p. 197).

Empson's reading of *Othello* thus tries to rehabilitate the hero's character by showing him to possess, in terms of the play's semantic implications, a 'fair title to humanity'. The rationalising approach through Complex Words carries with it a certain generosity of feeling, an ethic of forebearing mutuality, which sets to one side the more inhuman demands of a 'tragic' philosophy. The book deals, as Empson says, with a special class of 'vague rich intimate words' (p. 158). It interprets meanings which have somehow freed themselves from the high religious sanctions, or 'official' morality, of Christian tradition. Consequently, as Empson shows, language has to build upon those relations, sympathies, minimal grounds of trust and understanding which commonsense offers to the rational mind. Thus the developed Restoration use of 'dog' shows its 'humour of mutuality' (p. 162), carried over from what Empson had earlier described as the distinctive *Beggar's Opera* set of ironies. These words are 'complex', not by virtue of their plenary meaning, their depth or symbolic content, but by reason of the scope they offer to a process of humanistic re-interpretation. They present themselves rather like blank cheques, the value of which depends almost entirely on the currencies of language and communal feeling. Implicit in their flatness, their vague and colloquial nature, is a constant appeal to *interpretation* in the sense which Empson envisages.

The background politics of Pastoral can thus be seen as the essential pre-history of the period-semantics which Empson explores in *Complex Words*. I have already touched briefly on that shift of historical sympathies by which Crashaw's obscure sexual punning, in the context of Ambiguity, was held up to view in the commonsense light of Dryden's more 'public' variations on a similar theme. Polly is the subject of much the same process in *Some Versions*. Her language constantly associates the ideas of love and death, both of which radiate from the play's recurrent use of the ambiguous verb 'to die'. But Empson shows how these hints of perverse satisfaction are lifted into a larger air of communal ironies and chastened self-understanding. In the same manner, the cases of aberrant usage in *Complex Words*—'honest' in *Othello*, or 'dog' in *Timon of Athens*—are at once interpreted and critically placed by Empson's demonstration of their larger, more 'normal' contexts of application. The communicative power of this language

depends entirely on its appeal to a 'democratic' mood of understanding. This mood is defined both in historical terms, as the
practical result of Restoration politics, and in terms of a rationalised secular faith which Empson presents as the basic resource
of 'complex' understanding.

As a matter of immediate history, this background is made
clear enough in *Some Versions*. The Augustan 'heroic' tradition
had of course been Tory and Royalist in spirit. For this combination 'the King's divine right made the best magical symbol'
(p. 163). Later events, however, destroyed this symbolic security,
so that now the old conventions were turned on their head.
Pastoral replaced the hero with his inverted likeness, the rogue;
and so 'the only romance to be extracted from the Whig govern-
ment was to satirise it'. Authority, and the source of an established symbolism, are both cut away by the rise of opposing
attitudes. In consequence, there occurs a change in the structures
of belief and, behind these, the linguistic conventions of society
at large.

'Vague' and 'rich'—these are the qualities of language
which most often attract Empson's attention in *Complex Words*.
'Rich' exactly in proportion with their vagueness; offering a
hidden complexity of meaning which formed what Empson calls
a 'half-secret rival' to the official values of Christian society.
The adjectives are associated in *Complex Words*, and also on one
occasion in *Some Versions*, where Empson detects in a speech of
Gay's Polly 'a vague rich memory of the blood of the sacrament'
(p. 198). Here, however, the symbolic overtones are curiously
qualified by Empson's interpretation. The dramatic incident in
question is vaguely 'a symbol or analysis of something universal'.
But through the workings of a Pastoral double irony, this impression 'both refutes itself and insists on its point more suggestively'.
It finally appeals to 'analysis, not symbol'. The argumentation
here is subtle, almost tortuous but it does clearly show the
rationalising motive at work in Empson's criticism. He interprets
Polly's veiled reference as depending upon 'analysis'—or a covert
process of argument—rather than the subterranean depths of
Symbol. Human motives, however sinister, are at least open to
rational interpretation. They are not conceived as deriving some
ultimate sanction from symbolic or religious realms of value.

One finds the same attitude at work in *Milton's God*. The characters of *Paradise Lost* no longer bear the primal, undifferentiated guilt of their parts in the original myth. Empson allows them the balanced understanding and variety of possible motive which, as we have seen, animates the characters of *Pastoral*. Against this generous background of allowance, the Christian economies of Grace and Original Sin seem elements of another, unjust and unaccountable plot of divine intrigue. 'In ordinary moral terms, God behaves disgracefully' (p. 192). It is a precondition of Empson's demythologising approach that he represent the myth as an intellectual subject of debate, played out and realised within the principal actors' minds. Theology is not an absolute system of values with its own symbolic sanctions, cut off from interference by the rationalising mind. It is the drama of conscience and intellectual motive in Milton's characters and, by implication, in Milton himself. The poem has no proper (or communicable) interest part from this internal dialogue of motives.

Religious myth has this much in common with the predisposed ethic of Leavis's 'tragedy'. It appeals to a sense of the human condition which places the values of passive submission to authority above those of human fulfilment and self-realisation. These doctrines are the opposite of that 'mutual' or 'hearty' sense of open possibilities which Empson discovers in his Complex Words. The ethos of tragedy, as a matter of philosophic principle, is something foreign to the general semantics of humanistic rationalism. So also are the reaches of 'deep' symbolic value which support the structures of myth and religious paradox. Ambiguity and Pastoral are both oddly prone, by their equivocal nature, to draw out paradoxes of a perverse or irrational sort which Empson seems almost embarrassed to handle. Even the 'equations' of *Complex Words* may seem serviceable, at face value, to a study of the pathology of literary meaning. Colin Clarke in his book on Lawrence, *River of Dissolution*,[22] claims that 'the idiom of Empson insists on its appropriateness' to his own purpose. Lawrence's 'equations' are the deep obsessive symbols which, according to Clarke, allowed him to erect a whole metaphysics on the basis of his own psychic conflicts.

It is interesting, in this regard, that Empson should have recently taken issue with John Sparrow's moralising indictment of *Lady Chatterley's Lover*.[23] Empson argues that the sexual practices Lawrence hints at were meant as a kind of restorative therapy, a cure for the woman's frigidity. The point here is that Empson would refuse Clarke's arguments from his major 'equation' (defined as the link between 'dissolution as sublimation and dissolution as corruption'). *Seven Types* had indeed shown that Ambiguity, coupled with the knowledge of Freud, could lead the critic into similar regions; as for instance in the passage on Crashaw's sexual and fecal imagery (pp. 222–4). There Empson finds it a 'violent and deeply-rooted ambivalence'. But he still thinks the violence somehow tempered by reflective irony: it is, after all, 'an extreme exercise of humility' and one is driven to consider 'what his public thought when they read it' (p. 224). The imagery is lifted away from its dark private origins into the larger, more sociable air of emergent Pastoral.

One could multiply examples of the way Empson's methods have been kidnapped, divorced from their rationalistic background and applied to illustrate some darker psychological theme. Thus Conor Cruise O'Brien, in his book *Maria Cross* (a study of the Catholic imagination) suggests that 'the method . . . is well suited to the highly-charged, obsessed and "amphibological" writings of Bloy'.[25] By the time of *Complex Words*, Empson was definitely of the opinion that matters of psychopathology should not—or, if he chooses, need not—be a main concern of the literary critic. Reflexive words like 'sense' and 'honest' reveal in themselves the structures of their richest and, at the same time, their most natural or *normative* meaning. The critic, as opposed to the analyst of irrational ideas, need not abandon the commonsense grammar of 'sensible' implications. If Wordsworth constructs a paradoxical or deviant semantic background for 'sense', then this should be considered 'a question for Wordsworth and not for his exegetist' (p. 320). Interpretation can show just where and how the poet appears to deviate from the grammar of normal usage. It cannot, however, assume the same community of shared understanding if it tries, beyond this, to justify the logic of a private system of equations.

Empson reserves his fourth type of equation for cases like that of Wordsworth, where the poetry carries conviction but the derived arguments of the analyst strike bedrock in the form of irrational or paradoxical assertions. At one point he takes issue with Middleton Murray, preferring to ascribe a fourth-type equation than to introduce talk of 'metaphysics' (p. 349). The only metaphysical ideas which need to be mentioned are those which were (on a reasonable supposition) 'in the mind of the author'. To the extent that they pre-empt the logic of his language, demanding a specialised rhetoric, rather than remaining a matter of theme and idea, such issues (in Empson's opinion) cannot engage the critic's intelligence at a level of useful activity.

Hugh Kenner, as so often, provides the definitive opposite view and demonstrates the logic of Empson's theory. The method of *Complex Words*, he objects, 'simply locks poet, poem, language and reader inside a "communicative situation" and explores the intricacies of that'.[25] Empson has deliberately chosen 'blank' words and phrases which derive their only possible significance from 'context and tone'. His methods would be exercised in vain upon those meanings 'too profound for atomisation', typified for Kenner by some images from Eliot's poetry. Only 'a real city or actual death' could fully exhaust the significance of Eliot's symbols.

This should have classic status: a perfect case of critical disagreement on the clearest terms of opposed interest. Empson does indeed refer literary meaning to the 'communicative situation' of poem and reader. And it is the sense of this energising context, its constraints and possibilities, which allows Empson to disregard the claims of that private repleteness of symbolic meaning described by Kenner. Empson's 'vague rich intimate' words are a locus for the kind of humanistic feeling which Kenner—in what Empson calls the 'neo-Christian' fashion—rejects out of hand. Kenner's is basically a Symbolist aesthetic, treating the sources of poetic meaning as a matter of deep subconscious origin, cut off entirely from the rational play of intelligence. It was against this notion that Empson insisted, in the first essay published toward *Complex Words*, that 'emotions well handled in art are somehow absorbed into the structure; their expression is also made to express where and why they are valid'.[26] This amounts to an argument against Symbolist and 'emotive' doctrines alike, since it holds that poetry exists in a human context of deducible reasons and motives. So it may be merely a needful generosity, on the critic's part, to realise the full situation—personal and social—out of which a poet is writing when he expresses certain feelings.

This principle is at work in Empson's occasional dealings (several book reviews and a passage in *Complex Words*) with the poetry of A. E. Housman. Empson finds this poetry 'musical' and 'absorbing'; yet has to recognise the logical weakness and the undigested philosophy of Housman's gloomy outlook. Its apparent power of conviction cannot, Empson thinks, be merely the product of a harmlessly 'emotive' use of language. It must be rather 'the active false logic of persecution mania' (*Complex Words*, p. 13). Yet this, surely, would make it bad poetry. Empson concludes that we must understand and interpret it as being—quite conceivably—the language of a reasonable man in a certain *imagined* set of circumstances. Reviewing Housman's poems on another occasion, Empson remarks that 'the foundations of all this narrow and haunting poetry seem to me very solid'.[27] For all their 'narrowness', then, the poems open up into a larger realm of sufficiently familiar experience.

Swinburne's poetry seems to have carried Empson through a similar process of accommodating argument. In *Seven Types* the passages on Swinburne are mostly confined to local comment on the poet's 'synaesthetic' effects and the presence (which Empson tries to define) of a diffuse and languorous 'sadistic' tone. This latter quality, 'whether or not it is particularly realistic', is at least supplied by the poet with some credible background of ideas; to the point, Empson thinks, where they seem to amount to a 'perfectly solid metaphysical conceit' (p. 165). This, however, begs all the questions of moral and rational accountability in poetry. Regarded in this way—as 'solidly' presenting its own peculiar logic—the poem is effectively sealed off from any larger appeal to human experience in general. In *Complex Words* the enquiry is extended on two critical fronts. It shows Swinburne's sadism 'adequately absorbed or dramatised into a story' (p. 78). And the 'dramatic' context, in this sense, is shown to consist in a certain wilful slanting of verbal implications which can only be interpreted, in turn, by an appeal to the normative 'equations' which it parodies. On the strength of such arguments Empson can now say with confidence (in a recent published correspondence) that 'one can appreciate the poetry without sharing the mental disease'.[28]

These examples may help to explain the curious division, in *Complex Words*, between the approach of its essays in period semantics and the claim for a generalised theory which seems to lie behind them. The problem is posed most acutely by the humanistic bias which tends to discount, or at least actively to re-interpret, the tragic element in literature. With Housman and Swinburne, it is likewise a matter of rejecting a quiescent or passive attitude to experience, and seeing what exactly are the rational motives which cause human feelings to assume paradoxical forms. This procedure amounts to a definite ethic of interpretation. It is a theory of intelligible meaning, on the one hand, and a morality of critical judgement on the other. In this way, despite its rather puzzling construction, *Complex Words* has a deep coherence of argument and purpose. The opening chapters of theory join on to the practical criticism—or the best of it—exactly in so far as the reader is able to assent to them in this responsive and paradigmatic fashion.

It seems to me that the less impressive chapters, those which fail in their particular undertaking, fail also in this constitutive relation with the argument of the book as a whole. One such case is the essay on Milton's use of the word 'all' in *Paradise Lost*. Empson includes this tentative example as a test-case and possible limit to his theory. He gives good grounds for, but rejects on principle, the view of Milton's 'all' as a kind of 'Freudian symbol' (p. 104). Logical equations might, he thinks, make some headway with its intractable sense, though perhaps only by showing 'the different depths of consciousness' involved in anything like an adequate explanation. A footnote at the end of the chapter actually pre-figures the entire basic argument of *Milton's God* in a few dense sentences. However, the note runs into obvious difficulties, or at least disharmony with the rest of Empson's book, when it has to explain Milton's language as evidence of his being 'so intensely self-assured that he hardly criticised his work—it had only to suit his feelings' (p. 104).

This cuts against the whole grain of argument in *Complex Words*. It gives the appeal to 'feelings' an independent status, and so cuts off Milton's 'deeper' motives from their adequate expression in what he actually wrote.

The problem about this chapter is diagnosed more exactly in a prescient passage from *Seven Types*. Empson is in the process of considering, and rejecting as inadequate, Richards's separate designations of poetic Sense, Feeling, Tone and Intention. He remarks that such handy distinctions might well be 'excellent as psychology', but that this would not be literary criticism; they would, as Empson understands it, 'start much further back' (p. 238). Milton's 'all' is a deliberate trial of method, apparently intended to determine where precisely the distinction falls between questions of semantic implication and doubts as to the 'depths of unconsciousness which are being tapped' (p. 104). Empson has to admit that Milton's use of 'all' is in places so indefinite, so powerfully emotive, that it becomes a kind of encompassing symbol.

The essay on Milton was written specifically for the book—not reprinted—so perhaps it was meant as a fair indication of the possible problems involved. From now on, as in his review of Christopher Ricks's *Milton's Grand Style*, Empson was to insist that verbal analysis in itself was insufficient as a critical approach to Milton's poem.[29] *Milton's God* continues in the rationalising vein of *Complex Words*, although it has more to do with questions of narrative cause and effect than with local details of semantic implication. Empson delivers the poem from theology by recounting it as straightforward narrative; turning Christian paradox into an issue of moral injustice, not simply a symbolic institution; and thus presenting the poem to the secular tribunal of plain common sense. In this matter of basic attitude, the two books are very similar. In *Milton's God*, however, Empson's interest shifts from the semantic to the moral and doctrinal plane. He is still concerned with the bearings of paradox on a rational grammar of assent, but now with Christianity —and its humanistic opposite—as the definite centre of debate.

4

Semantics and Historical Method: the Phenomenology of Meaning

I have so far made a rather unwieldy complex of Empson's ideas on language and criticism. This seemed the best way to show how his thinking has developed simultaneously in several directions, while preserving the kind of deep continuity observable between Pastoral and Complex Words. I have tried to suggest how the elements of theory in Empson's thinking have fed back constantly into his practical criticism, and also how their limits have been tested, in certain cases, against the teasing complexities of a largely intuitive response. What I propose to do now is to follow the lead of *Complex Words* into a somewhat more specialised region of linguistic and philosophic enquiry. The attempt is worthwhile because Empson's book, although it deals only fitfully with questions of theory, does lay claim to a number of important truths about the workings of language and the generalised nature of interpretation.

We can best begin by comparing Empson's doctrine of verbal 'equations' with the context-theory of meaning espoused by I. A. Richards in *The Philosophy of Rhetoric* (1936) and subsequent books. Empson believes that decisive 'patches' of compressed argument are often carried (and retained) in individual words, rather than being spread through some extended passage of language which then becomes the control, or context, which defines their relevant senses. On this latter view, the word would lose its assertive independence, its force of compacted argument; it would simply adjust pragmatically to whatever dominant set of meanings formed its immediate context. Empson speaks of his Complex Words as being able, like people, to seize their occasion and influence opinion; of 'dog', for instance, as 'ready for the chance it took' at the Restoration (p. 167). Such words articulate the juncture of some specific meaning with the general currency of usage. They possess an intellectual or moral identity, a self-sufficient quality which makes them the surrogates of an author's intention. Empson makes the same assumption, incidentally, about the characters of Pastoral and Milton's protagonists. They retain a complex independence of motive, a resistance to simple explanation which allows them—in *Milton's God*—to question the levelling moral regime of religious myth.

Semantic 'grammar' is the crux of *Complex Words*, and also —by a typical twist of implication—an instance of its own compacted meaning. 'Grammar' may be understood either as a normative (rule-making) science or a merely descriptive process of classification. Richards had listed examples to show how the word 'grammar', in various contexts of argument, took colour from their background assumptions. Empson argues, on the contrary, that the word as properly used contains *both* meanings, although usually with a strong priority of one or the other. This, he believes, explains its apparent argumentative force, and thus shows something significant about the very grammar of 'grammar'. William Hotopf, in his book *Language, Thought and Comprehension*, argues that Empson misunderstood the position of Richards in raising this issue of practical semantics.[1] Empson took him to be saying that the sense of the word was suspended between two alternative meanings; and so (thinks Hotopf) he brought in his own rival theory of 'equations' and compacted doctrines. In one respect Hotopf is quite right. Richards adopts, in his later books, a thorough-going theory of contextual semantics which would totally discount the articulate inner logic of Empson's Complex Words. But Hotopf cannot, as he seems to believe, collapse the operative difference between the two theories simply by demonstrating Empson's *parti pris*. Indeed, his attempted mediation shows how radically different are the two critics' basic conceptions of language. For Richards, 'grammar' as word *or* concept is defined entirely by particular contexts of usage. It carries in itself no inherent grammar of suggested applications, no semantic logic to make its complicated meaning plain. For Empson, there exists a conceptual means of following the word's inherent logic; a structure of intelligible usage, like that which articulates the logic of 'sense' or allows him to work out the implicated ironies of 'honest'.

These words, like 'grammar', both denote and semantically *enact* the rational means of their own interpretation.

Complex meanings therefore reflect a grammar of answerable motive. The words which Empson examines are balanced between the implications of context and a definite purpose of utterance. Empson shows Johnson (p. 170) manoeuvring to avoid the hearty, raffish sense of 'dog', and Jane Austen (p. 303) neatly side-stepping the more embarrassing implications of 'sense'. The grammar of such volitional structures cannot be rule-bound, as in the prescriptive sense of the word. Rather it represents, for author and reader alike, a nexus of implications which a context may try to impose but which verbal tact, for reasons private or social, may contrive to avoid. In such semantic strategies the critic may fairly claim to detect the workings of authorial intention.

In this sense Empson's linguistic researches are a kind of literary phenomenology. Richards effectively denied such an approach when, together with Ogden in *The Meaning of Meaning*, he gave short shrift to the language-philosophy of Edmund Husserl.[2] Richards is completely at odds with Husserl's philosophy of meaning. He dismisses as mere 'metaphysics' the claim of the phenomenologist that language, like all forms of experience, offers itself to reasoned interpretation through communal structures of awareness. Richards adhered, in his early books, to a behaviourist philosophy of language which denied the validity of any such 'subjective' or 'transcendental' account of meaning. His idea of the 'sign-situation', based on a purely reflex model of verbal reference, entailed the view that poetry—since it made no factual claims to truth—must be a separate 'emotive' species of statement. Empson's reply will seem philosophically more coherent if we recognise that it stands very much in line with Husserl's critique of the naïve and self-defeating assumptions of positivism.

Empson remarks in *Complex Words* that it is 'because the historical background is so rich and still so much alive . . . that one can fairly do what seems absurdly unhistorical, make a set of equations from first principles' (p. 269). This statement effectively closes the gap which appears to exist between the period-semantics and the generalised theory of Complex Words. It also answers exactly to Husserl's philosophical project for the recovery of meaning from a history which can always be re-appropriated by the rational imagination. Husserl provides a working critique of the 'emotive' theory of language. Understanding demands 'not a sense to be "postulated" as such and such (or even to be "interpreted" in order to reconcile the interests of the understanding and the emotions), but a sense to be explicated in the first place, and with primary originality, out of experience itself'.[3] This may remind us of that curious passage, in *Complex Words*, where Empson admits the claims of the 'emotive' as an aspect of creative psychology, but insists that the critic's proper concern is with the rational workings of a poet's language.

Logic, according to Husserl, is incomplete without a full account of the authenticating experience forming its background. And yet—he is equally emphatic—that experience has to be referred to logic; the 'intentionality of experience' is inseparably bound up with the 'intentionality of predicative judgement'.[4] Empson likewise points out (*Complex Words*, p. 46) that the simple sentence, with its subject, verb and predicate, mirrors in itself the generalised process of communication. Hence the importance for Empson's theory of arguments effectively contained *within single words*. Such units of meaning are, in a double sense, 'articulate'; they communicate by virtue of a self-contained structure of intelligible sense.

Empson's position is already taken up, if not with full conceptual clarity, in *Seven Types*. For instance, in a passage on Pope, Empson declares himself confident that he is basically 'describing the mind of Pope', but remarks that his criticism would still achieve its object 'if it described the attitude only of the majority of his readers' (p. 127). This faith in the common basis of understanding, as between an author's mind and his reader's normal responses, answers very closely to Husserl's conception of communicable meaning. Empson also finds a particular interest in 'the contrast between the stock response and the response demanded by the author' (p. 127). This moves a considerable distance toward the grammar of motives in *Complex Words*. It is interesting that a series of examples from Pope should have led Ambiguity up to this new stage of logical order. It was Empson's chapter on the *Essay on Criticism*, in the later book, which fruitfully pursued this finding-out of meaning through the logical implications of an author's turns of style. In *Seven Types* the object is more generally to locate the sources of that ironic 'magnanimity' which Empson feels behind the obvious jabs of Pope's satirical contempt.

It should now be evident why Empson found an historical locus for *Complex Words* in the Restoration and Augustan periods. These authors call for *interpretation*, rather than mere explication; their complexity is a matter of social nuance, of tactful understatement and ironic self-regard. Ambiguity tended, as it were, to lay siege to man the conscious or *intending* subject of language. It drew either deeply, on the poet's private conflicts and associations, or more superficially on the stock resources of the language at large. *Complex Words*, with its wider and later historical focus, finds language a more answerable medium, capable of holding within it the articulate grammars of motive which allow the interpreter to set about deducing an author's commitments of style. Donald Davie, in his study of the changing relations between 'science' and 'poetry', has likewise expressed a certain rational preference for the Augustan poetic and its truthfulness to reason. Can we, he asks, be perfectly sure, when reading the seventeenth-century poets, that our minds are not 'trapped by the multiple ambiguities . . . into envisaging an identity' when rational sense 'will countenance only a comparison or analogy'?[5] Empson asks the same basic question in *Complex Words*; and the result is a marked shift forward in history, from the seventeenth-century poets who figured so largely in *Seven Types* to the age of rationalism and social propriety.

Davie further suggests that 'the whole enormous question of the relation between science and literature' is something best referred to the literary critic in his province of historical semantics. Davie's arguments are useful here since they imply the cognitive circularity, the kind of verbal-historical reprise, which Empson's criticism achieves in *Complex Words*. Science, or one of its essential disciplines—predicative logic—is taken to have some definite, though historically variable, place in poetic language. The seventeenth-century poets, Davie suggests, exhibited a naïve 'literalism' in their metaphors, whereas the

Augustans were usually more rational and circumspect. This means in turn that criticism, in its generalising capacity, must also to some degree have incorporated the logical assumptions of 'science', or applied commonsense reason. Criticism thus rests its judgements on what is *articulate* (or rationally self-evident) in the language of poetry. Richards, at the opposite extreme, excludes the logic of factual statement from the understanding of poetry, and so confines criticism to an assessment of emotional states—or of the poem's pragmatic benefits—with no pretence to rational validity.

Of course the charge of circular argument may still be brought against a criticism, like Empson's, which tends to single out words and works reflecting his own main interests and sympathies. It is no coincidence that 'wit', 'sense' and 'grammar' all carry the logic of their own justification in Empson's ingenious treatment. Davie is also frankly partisan in wishing to restore the Augustan canons of rational decorum to the working centre of a modern poetics. As a practising poet he sees a way beyond the current Imagist fashion through a renewed awareness of poetic syntax as 'intellectual physiognomy'.[6]

Empson, however, makes larger claims from the critical point of view. He is not merely attempting a local or polemical rehabilitation of the Augustan norms. His approach in *Complex Words*, like the equations it deals with, is nothing if not generally valid. The Augustan conventions are central to his argument, but serve as focal points of demonstration, and not as mere examples of a more or less congenial period style. Again, this emerges most clearly from 'grammar', that crucial topic-word in Empson's semantics. He discovers in 'our ordinary mixed idea of grammar' the notions both of 'codifying how people *do* talk' and of 'telling people how they *ought* to talk' (p. 318). Pope's *Essay* is used, not simply to state the claims of Augustan rhetoric —of 'wit' and its relatives—but to enact them semantically and make out the case for their generalised validity. 'Wit' is shown to represent 'a fairly complete parody of the Augustan critical position' (p. 88). But the *Essay* appeals finally to 'sense', which brings in a context of critical judgement far wider than the rather 'conceited', self-supporting dialectics of 'wit'. It can therefore register as a kind of 'parody', where a less circumspect or qualified criticism—with the methods, perhaps, of *Seven Types*—would treat its idiolect as building up into a solid critical position behind the claims of 'wit'.

This is the basic difference between Empson's and Davie's use of the Augustans as poetic exemplars. Indeed, when he came to review Davie's *Purity of Diction in English Verse* (1952), Empson did object that it seemed 'at least premature' to erect a whole theory of poetic language on what happened to be the current movement of reaction.[7] Empson must have found himself in general agreement with Davie; but here, as with the American New Critics, the hint of an emergent orthodoxy causes him to reserve his sympathies. In this case he counters Davie's prescriptions with the idea that 'urbanity' of style is a matter of 'being able to assume any form of cultivation in an audience'. This overcomes the rule-making element in Davie's poetics by throwing it open to interpretation; the broader context of mutual feeling which defines itself, in *Complex Words*, as the background of all effective communication.

It is this additional resource in Empson's criticism—his allowing the poem to imply the terms of its own acceptance—which effectively redeems *Complex Words* from purely circular argument. Empson's amounts to what I have already defined, in contrast to formalist assumptions, as a 'continuity-principle' in criticism. We can talk intelligently about poetry, even paraphrase its meaning with a fair claim to accuracy, because it shares with prose discourse the fundamental logic common to all articulate thought. And if this justification still seems circular, there is evidence of a more dogmatic circularity, *mutatis mutandis*, in the doctrines of formalist criticism. Cleanth Brooks, as we have seen, rejects the continuity-principle. He asserts that the poem is a closed, self-authenticating structure of meanings, and that paraphrase can therefore be only a vague and illegitimate means of critical approach. Brooks says of Wordsworth's 'Intimations of Mortality', in this connection, that it is 'not only a poem, but . . . a parable about poetry'.[8] 'Parable' here has a quite specific meaning. A parable brings home its point and relevance in virtual isolation from the contingent spheres of 'original' meaning and authorial 'intention'. It is a piece of self-contained moral argument, conceived for a certain suasive purpose ideally unaffected by changes of time and circumstance. It is therefore best served by a habit of reading which discounts the possibility of direct appeal to an author's intentions, and relies instead on the hermeneutic rules of an orthodox rhetoric. The parable therefore has no commerce with interpretation, in the sense of the word suggested here. It overrides the usual doubts and ambiguities of human understanding, and thus manages without the interpretative machinery required if one is to sort them into some kind of rational order. In this sense it rejects the phenomenological process by which—as I have suggested—Empson moves over from Ambiguity to Complex Words.

These characteristics of the parable correspond to Brooks's requirements of poetry and criticism. So far as it makes terms with us at all, the poem makes them largely prohibitive and intransitive. Brooks uses the example of Wordsworth's 'Ode' as an argument for the indispensability of paradox to the poet's imagination. Wordsworth chooses 'ambiguity and paradox' rather than 'plain, discursive simplicity' because his creative insight demands that he do more than 'analyse his experience as the scientist does, breaking it up into parts . . . classifying the various parts'. Poetry is therefore a unique and extra-logical realm of discourse. The imagery of light in Wordsworth's poem serves as a symbol for 'aspects of man's vision which seem mutually incompatible—intuition and analytic reason'.

Brooks's arguments depend on certain assumptions about the nature of human experience—its division into distinct mental compartments of reason and intuition—which Empson would find both unnecessary and misleading. The circularity of his doctrine differs in one essential point from that of *Complex Words*. Empson's assumptions, if at all valid, are proven by the fact that we, as readers, can repeat for ourselves and actively assent to the kinds of semantic operation he discovers in Pope or Shakespeare. Nothing is confirmed beyond argument, although much (we may agree) is refined and pointed up beyond reasonable doubt. On Brooks's side, the argument from Wordsworth against the 'heresy of paraphrase' clearly runs premise directly into conclusion. The critic *must* not talk about 'intention' or prose-sense equivalents because—on Brooks's formalist assumptions—he simply *cannot.* Empson works on the opposite, more hopeful assumption: that the possibility of paraphrase, of under-standing a poet's motives and the bearing of his intention, needs only an act of rational faith to justify the attempt.

For this reason the limits of criticism are also the limits of common sense or ordinary logic. Kenner's 'actual death' and 'real city'—intensive private symbols, intuitively grasped but scarcely explainable—fall outside these commonsense limits. Stanley Cavell makes the same point about 'ordinary language' philosophy. Specialised terms, private references and symbols— these must elude the clarifying 'grammar' of ordinary usage. So, according to Cavell, 'you will not find out what "number" or "neurosis" or "mass-society" mean if you only listen for our ordinary uses of these terms'.[9] The examples Kenner offers are evocative symbols; we understand them, more or less, through their curious resonance, the weight and multiplicity of their associations. They afford in themselves no control or guarantee of what the reader, with his own private stock of such con-nections, is likely to make of them. Like a musical chord struck in isolation, they hold a wealth of indefinite meaning but noth-ing to identify by its discursive part in a larger context of argu-ment.

The comparison holds for *Complex Words*, where Empson shows (for example) 'sense' and 'honest', with their varied structures of implication, running through Shakespeare's plays like harmonic progressions in a work of music. In fact Empson comments in *Seven Types* that this sort of complex intelligibility is more "like" music than are the releasing effects of open vowels which are usually given that praise' (p. 120). It is worth noticing that Empson appeals to this vaguer variety of word-music in the rather blank and unsuccessful chapter ' "All" in *Paradise Lost*'. Milton is 'drawing on the vowel for part of the resonance of a feeling he must not express more plainly' (*Com-plex Words*, p. 101–2). This chapter gravitates toward the private and symbolic, as opposed to the social and contextual, plane of meaning.

Cavell looks to Wittgenstein for the terms upon which the philosopher can properly ignore such private reaches of expres-sion. 'To see that ordinary language is natural is to see that

(perhaps even see why) it is normative for what can be said.'[10]
This form of reasoning (so the claim runs) can 'coax the mind
down from self-assertion—subjective assertion and private
definition—and lead it back, through the community, home'.
Criticism cannot 'coax the mind down' in precisely this way. It
can, however, point to the specialised rhetorics, the deviant
semantics and strains of illogic, in styles which elude the
commonsense norm. This presumably is what Empson means
when he says, rather oddly, that his reading of Yeats (in a recent
essay) meets 'symbolic resistance' only at a 'fairly deep level'.[11]
The level would seem to be that of the 'profound' literary
symbol, as presented by Kenner. Empson's virtual rejection of
all such meanings, especially in his later essays, cannot possibly
be reconciled with Kenner's point of view.

Empson went to the root of the matter in some remarks on the
topic of 'intuition' which appeared in the course of an early
review for *Granta*. Taking his cue from Middleton Murry,
Empson left the puzzle very much as he found it: an impossible
paradox.

> If intuition, in the sense of arriving rapidly at a judgement
> without conscious process, is to be made a part of 'intelli-
> gence', the nature of whose division from the other parts can
> only be made clear by further understanding of the problem
> of consciousness . . . then, pending such understanding, there
> does not seem much to say.[12]

This has the familiar early-Empson tone: the rational juggling
with various possibilities, if only to sort them provisionally into
some kind of satisfying order. It is this attitude, rather than the
final sense of blankness, which makes an answer to the claims of
pure 'intuition'. Empson's sequence of argument, with its
elaborately self-supporting logic, seems to express the confidence
that rational debate can at least be clear about the issues involved.

There is the same broad claim behind the rationalising arguments of *Complex Words*. To bank too heavily on 'emotive'
theories of language is the same evasion of reasoned argument
that Empson objects to in the direct appeal to 'intuition'. His
own philosophy is set out most explicitly in the chapter 'Feelings

in Words'. Emotive uses of language, he suggests, are 'ordinarily felt to be trivial and separate from the straightforward uses' (*Complex Words*, p. 33). 'Straightforward' contains the normative argument for a grammar of rational semantics. For this reason, he continues, 'there is no ground for supposing that the same [emotive] trick is really at work on a large scale without our knowing it' (p. 33). Such 'straightforward' uses of language gain both point and credibility—like Pope's masterly 'sense'—by insisting on, and making fully articulate, their semantic implications. 'Emotive' uses, on the contrary, exploit a careful blurring of logical structure to achieve their rhetorical effect.

Cavell situates 'philosophy' at the point where 'you already know what the dictionary can teach you; where, for some reason . . . you are forced into philosophising'.[13] Empson's disclaimers make it hard to accuse him of 'philosophising' in any abstract or purely theoretical way. But it is I think important to notice how *Complex Words* enters the realm of philosophical linguistics at precisely the point identified by Cavell. This, indeed, is what sets his criticism apart from the kind of positivistic literary scholarship proposed by Hirsch as a model of interpretative method. Empson discerns two basic dimensions in the understanding of a Complex Word: the informing background of historical context and the implications *of* and *for* the semantic grammar of its usage. This latter is the ground of 'philosophic' criticism in Cavell's sense of the word, as developed also by Wittgenstein in his later writings. Wittgenstein mentions his particular interest in 'the grammar of those words which describe what are called "mental activities"'. Most of the perennial problems of philosophy could, he thinks, be reduced to 'phrases describing sense-data'.[14] Like Complex Words, the most interesting and revealing 'grammars' are those which possess a reflexive or self-analysing character; which seem to specify in themselves something of the responsive equipment required to interpret them.

Empson discovers just such a grammar in the intentional structure of inter-related meanings surrounding the word 'sense' and its various cognates. His chapter 'Sense and Sensibility' sets out what amounts to an operative model of the act of 'sensible' and 'sensitive' interpretation, mediated by the actual meanings of the word. Empson finds two main arguments present: that 'good judgement is inherent in a normal use of the senses' and that 'delicacy of feeling is inherent in a high power of using the senses' (p. 267). These, he admits, have to take the emotion/ judgement dualism for granted, which seems to contradict the book's main thesis; but some such convention (as with his puzzlings over critical 'intuition') has to be the starting-point of reasoned analysis. Most importantly, Empson is able to claim both that 'these notions would arise naturally from the words' and that the implicit arguments are in themselves 'fairly true' (p. 268). Thus the problem of sense is fundamentally the problem of 'sense'. Empson sees, like Wittgenstein, that our philosophies of mind, our attitude to experience and the passage from 'reception' to 'reaction'—the problems, in short, of all inter-pretation—have their natural 'grammars' which are manifest in the logic of commonsense usage.

STRUCTURES AND MEANING: THE LIMITS OF EXPLANATION

In his *Notebooks* of 1914–16, one can see how Wittgenstein's earlier ideas of meaning and reference held him back from a veritable theory of Complex Words. The propositional statement and the 'complex sign' are taken to be equivalent. However, this 'sign' still seems to be envisaged in a picturing or spatial order of reference, just as logic was supposed to 'picture' the world, by a kind of projective geometry, in Wittgenstein's early *Tractatus*. Thus 'a single word cannot be true or false'; it can only enter a logical framework as part of some larger context of statement. The orders of 'complex' to which Wittgenstein refers are evidently conceived as *intensional* or analytic structures, based entirely on the sui-referential form of logical statements. Their validity cannot be a matter of generalised 'truth' since, as Wittgenstein observes, 'the agreement of two complexes is obviously internal, and for that reason can only be shown'.[15] This distinction between the explanatory and the 'showing', or exhibitive, function of philosophy is one which Wittgenstein later erected into a general rule. I mention it at this point, in summary fashion, because it seems to indicate a certain constitutive limit in the process of reasoning out the logic of complex statement. Empson meets the same basic problem in his own researches, but typically moves off in a different direction which helps to clarify the working method of *Complex Words*.

There is a point of connection between Wittgenstein's argu-ments and the assumptions which support both the Imagist aesthetic and the formalist canons of poetic meaning and struc-ture. Formalist criticism likewise stresses the 'showing', or purely intuitable aspect of poetic communication, while pointing up the 'intensional' (or internally- ordered) play of meaning. Wittgenstein appears to be searching for a model of metaphor, rather than straightforward reference, as he tries to square his propositional logic with a generalised notion of 'truth'. He is still thinking in terms of spatial correspondence, on a kind of image-theory, when he suggests that a 'correlation of relations' must be the condition of logical truth. The proposition is seen as a structure projected onto reality by some form of geometric pattern.

Empson's chapter on 'Metaphor', in *Complex Words*, tries out the logic of just such a theory. Empson takes this at its subtlest in the idea of 'proportion-schemes', where various lines of meta-phorical comparison—apart from those directly implied—come into play as qualifying parts of a referential structure. He describes (on pp. 336–8) a typically complicated structural gloss, ultimately based on imagist assumptions, of the metaphor involved in 'rooting out' one's faults and vices. Such explana-tions in the formal mode very much resemble Wittgenstein's spatialised conception of the logic of statement. Empson rejects them as leading in the end, through the narrowness of their logic, to a largely emotive view of metaphor. He concludes (p. 343) that the idea of a 'double structure of pregnancy' might provide a more flexible and ultimately more *rational* approach to the problems of metaphor. As I have tried to show, this appeal to the background complexity of language, interpretable though not readily defined, makes up a large part of the philosophic argument in *Complex Words*. Cavell sees it as the main implica-tion of 'pregnancy', on Empson's terms, that any conceivable paraphrase would be 'indefinitely long and elaborate'.[16] It rests on the process of *interpretation*, which Empson shows to be essentially normative but incapable of precise definition.

Empson's chief example in his chapter on 'Pregnancy' is again a double-edged, reflexive usage. He takes the word 'man' in Hamlet's terse lines of tribute to his father:

> He was a man, take him for all in all,
> I shall not look upon his like again.
>
> (*Complex Words*, p. 321)

Obviously, the 'appreciative pregnancy' of 'man'—the force of its understatement—relies to a large extent on our providing the required stock of associative values. This need not perhaps be a matter of humanist conviction, but it does demand a responsive sense of the word's humane liberality. All the more important Complex Words are 'pregnant' in this humanly-appealing way. They tend to build up, like 'man', from rock-bottom animal attributes to a full predication of sympathetic human qualities. In fact, Empson's notion of Pregnancy embodies precisely what Hugh Kenner dislikes about *Complex Words*: the assumption 'that words are more the property of speakers than of things'. His objection encapsulates the theory of reference which characterises Symbolist aesthetics as a whole, and which also has much to do with formalist rhetorics of metaphor.

Empson's reading for *Complex Words* included Scott Buchanan's book *Symbolic Distance*.[17] This turns out to be a treatment of logic and the rhetoric of metaphor on thorough-going visual-projective lines. Empson found it 'so suggestive that it no longer suggested anything' (p. 341). The proposed schemata seemed to Empson to occupy an uncertain and probably fictitious region of the deep 'unconscious'—a resort he was trying to avoid—and the whole attempt to formalise metaphor struck him as misguided and restrictive. Empson substitutes the idea of Pregnancy, which he intends to convey both a 'feeling of rich-ness' about metaphoric meaning and a 'source of advice on how to think about the matter' (p. 341). These remarks are fairly vague and hardly definitive, but they bear out the thesis of *Complex Words*: that the richest uses of literary language possess an implicit structure of meanings which cannot be reduced to the formal properties of a worked-out rhetoric.

So, when Empson rests metaphor on Pregnancy rather than the machinery of proportion-schemes, his choice points up some crucial topics in *Complex Words*. A certain mistrust of visual analogies, or imagistic theories of meaning, seems to have been strong with Empson from the outset. Bertrand Russell gave cause for suspicion in a *Granta* review. ' "I see no difficulty in saying that eternal truths form a part of God's nature from all eternity" means merely "At no particular time does the problem force itself upon my attention as a sort of picture".'[18] This seems to register the same kind of problem with Russell's theory as presents itself in Wittgenstein's logic. Empson resists this picture-theory just as he resists the irrational tendencies of literary Imagism. And there is indeed a likeness between the critical outlook of T. E. Hulme and the earlier reasonings of Wittgenstein. For Hulme, thought is 'prior to language' and consists in 'the simultaneous presentation to the mind of two different images'.[19] Empson has pointed out the absurd in-sufficiency of this as a description even of our everyday and practical, let alone our more imaginative, thought-processes. His reaction to Russell clarifies and deepens this point of disagreement. No kind of visualised logical projection, whatever its subtleties of form, can attain to the richness of felt implication which occupies the critic and (properly) the philosopher of language.

ORDINARY LANGUAGE AND SEMANTIC HISTORY

The idea of Pregnancy therefore carries a broad-based appeal for interpretation in the place of formal explication. So, finally, the theory and method of *Complex Words* are inseparable from the attitudes, the social and moral background, of the period which the book makes its main home territory. 'Ordinary language' cannot be the province of a neutral methodology. It takes colour and definition from the rational confidence which opposes commonsense to dogma in the history of human thought. Naturally the approach has its strongest hold in a period when such beliefs were current and frequently expressed. In Johnson especially, Empson notices how the hints of a secular philosophy are carried not by the 'official verbal machinery' but by casual and colloquial phrases which Johnson—'on grounds of dignity' —would never have noticed, let alone analysed. This is not an appeal to Johnson's 'subconscious' or to fugitive motives in his deduced psychological make-up. It is more a matter of what Cavell calls 'finding-out-what-a-word-really-means'. In such cases, the intentionality of language is entirely bound up with the inexplicit sanctions of ordinary usage. The language of Augustan humanism is apt to Empson's critical purpose because —as he demonstrates from Pope—it builds upon the humanly-conditioned possibilities of 'pregnant' meaning.

Dr Johnson's opinions and his historical situation are almost emblematic in this respect. *The Lives of the Poets*, with their touch of disdain for metaphysical 'wit' on grounds of Augustan taste and good sense, project a foreshortened version of the change of attitudes found between *Seven Types* and *Complex Words*. Johnson's particular turns of usage, also, are a constant control for Empson's semantic speculations. At one point, as Empson convincingly shows, Johnson 'has to use a synonym for "honesty" and to put "horse" beside "dog" to prevent the slang senses from rising at him' (p. 173). Johnson is likewise an occasional mentor, mostly on matters of moral judgement, for Empson's chapters on Shakespeare.

This topical centrality of the Augustan age, its hard-put rationalism and commonsense ethic, gives *Complex Words* a basic historical bearing. Above all, the idea of a certain set of shared assumptions—a condition of mutual intelligibility—saves criticism from nagging puzzles about an author's 'private' or unavowed meanings. This gives Empson his critical handle for judging what must have been the verbal tactics behind Johnson's strategic avoidance of certain implications. Empson, I think, is more in mind of this background than of anything in the poet's 'unconscious' when he remarks elsewhere of Dylan Thomas: 'you do begin to wonder whether he meant something more than he knew'. Cavell's philosophy constantly returns to the same question, as contained in the title of his book: *Must We Mean What We Say?* His answer lies in the province of ordinary language, at the point where (in his sense of the word) we begin to 'philosophise'. Assuming the normative status of ordinary language, we may find even that deviant uses begin to *mean* more when viewed against the implicit norm.

Such has been Empson's experience with the poetry of Wordsworth. The poet's characteristic 'equations' are baffling to a certain point, but eventually near enough to the paradigms of reason to be grasped by commonsense intelligence. Empson's chapter on *The Prelude* is an exercise in critical reading which, by a subtle adjustment of expectations, turns the critic's embarrassment (the fact that he disapproves intellectually of poetry which his feelings admire) into a rich and positive source of understanding. In *Seven Types* Empson had come up against Wordsworth's metaphysics—his pantheistic doctrine—and frankly jibbed at the evasiveness of his logic. In *Complex Words*, he can allow that the metaphysics are 'a deduction only'; Wordsworth is seen to be experimenting with complex and *communicable* structures of meaning which effectively redeem his semantics from the charge of sophistry or self-deception. Empson is now mainly interested, not in any 'theory in Wordsworth's mind about the word', but in the 'manipulative feeling' of its various uses, or the sense of what the poet 'could make it do' (p. 293).

In *Seven Types* it was 'Tintern Abbey' which called out Empson's habit of resistance. In the later book his attention is turned to *The Prelude*, and the change of subject is marked—or perhaps partly motivated—by a change in critical approach. The difference amounts to a less definite or 'technical' use of the highly paradoxical senses of 'sense' explored in the earlier poetry. In so far as he tends to welcome this change, Empson is clearly at odds with formalist critics like Brooks, who place such value on Wordsworth's paradoxical leanings. Empson further argues that it is a 'social difference' in the language which 'makes it hard to pin down the difference between the words in general' (p. 301). The words in question are 'feeling' and 'sense', distinguished by what Empson believes to be the stronger 'technical' conviction achieved and expressed by 'feeling'. Wordsworth had perhaps used this word more frequently in 'Tintern Abbey' because at that time he was writing 'with more direct conviction'. Substituting 'sense' for 'feeling' in a passage from *The Prelude* (as Empson does by way of experiment), the context of argument seems too settled and the word too heavily weighted to carry its normal implications. Empson borrows from Samuel Butler the observation that, when people begin to 'feel', they are usually 'taking what seems to them the more worldly course'. This leaves them prepared, he infers, to 'act in a way that might seem against their principles' (p. 301). 'Feeling' therefore occupies a realm of private conviction which inclines to disregard, or impatiently set aside, the normative judgement of 'sense'.

Empson imputes a measure of self-conscious irony—even of social reserve—to Wordsworth's more developed semantics of 'sense'. Irony and 'ordinary language' are indeed the major themes of *Complex Words*, and it remains for me to demonstrate their logic of mutual reinforcement. The most obvious connection lies in that 'humour of mutuality' which Empson discovers in the basic workings of many of the words he examines. 'Fool' is perhaps the most striking example. In its richest and most natural application—so the argument runs—'fool' connotes the genial range of ironies and sympathies which Erasmus derived from it. Fooled as well as fooling, the benign monitor of mankind's common condition—'fool' has a mutual or reflexive dimension as part of its inherent structure. The word is complex only by virtue of its openness to ironic inflections. Its meaning is the product of a whole human background of reciprocal ironies and recognitions. Only the familiar structures of humanistic sentiment could fill it out to complexity.

Other critics, of course, have followed the logic of 'fool' into very different regions. Enid Welsford, in her classic study, found a predominance of just the opposite set of ideas. 'To those who do not repudiate the religious insight . . . the human spirit is uneasy in this world because it is at home elsewhere'. On this reasoning, 'the fool is wiser than the humanist'.[20] For Empson, on the contrary, 'fool' expresses precisely the complication of motive, the wry humour and generous irony, which characterise the humanist position.

To this extent, Empson's critical stance comes down to a set of moral premises. It is, however, a matter of commonsense reflection that such words as 'fool', in their richest and in some sense their *normal* application, possess a moral-semantic symmetry which implies an imaginative 'truth' about human affairs. Pastoral irony has the same general claim to validity. The 'fooler fooled' is both spokesman and scapegoat, ironically in command of life's little ironies. Thomas Hardy comes to mind here as an author characteristically off-centre by Empson's interpretative standard. 'What is so disgusting about Hardy's Spirit Ironical is that nobody has a chance to call it Fool' (p. 155). By comparison, the God or gods in *King Lear* are involved with mankind, caught up in the universal foolery of purposes mistook. Empson treats their apparent dethronement as a reason for interpreting their part in the play—through various baffled allusions to them—as an element in the interlocking structure of ironies. God as supreme disposer, exempt from the trials and reversals of human motivation, can only seem monstrously remote and unimaginable. In this sense the essay clearly looks forward to the humanised theology of *Milton's God*.

The ethical bearings of Empson's criticism are confirmed, in a negative but revealing way, by what seems to be his failure to come to terms with Swift's *Gulliver's Travels*. Swift is the kind of cynical ironist furthest removed from the Erasmic tone of genial candour. He represents, like Hardy's Spirit Ironical, a break in the communicative circuit of generous feelings. Empson's reading of the last chapter of *Gulliver*, in *Complex Words*, is curiously at odds with the book's apparent meaning. Swift's 'ideal animal' is, he thinks, the 'pointless "calculating horse"' of the book's final chapter. Empson refuses to accept that Swift may be satirising this 'ideal' rationality; indeed he has remarked elsewhere that such an interpretation, by making Swift repudiate every last ideal, amounts to a thoroughly cynical misreading.[21] However, he still sees Swift as offending against the ethic of humane understanding. Hence his comment that 'the horse as generous has a point . . . but not the horse as Cold Reason' (p. 169). This seems a real case of conflict between Empson's rationalising bias (the need to make sense of Swift's complications) and his idea of humanistic 'sense'. If Swift is to be credited with a complex play of feeling, his techniques come to seem too narrow and contradictory; his satire apparently trapped by its own desperate devices.

Swift has always been something of a test-case for Empson's criticism. In *Some Versions*, he had devoted some rather puzzling pages to the element of obsessional word-play in Swift's sexual language. 'Sense', 'spirit' and other ambiguities, hovering between the religious and the grossly physical, conjure up for Swift the inherent disgusting compromise of the human condition. The immediate point was that these were essentially *private* obsessions, fostered in (and perhaps caused by) a certain contempt of the writer's audience. Swift's case comes up in the chapter 'Double Plots' (pp. 54–6), the arguments of which serve to shift attention from the deeper levels of Freudian psychology to the kind of socialised and animate awareness which Empson attributes to an ideal theatre audience. Against this articulate background, the obsessive puns of Swift are seen to be narrowly self-occupied, exploiting language only by ignoring the commonsense dimensions of meaning. This throws some light on the difficulties with Swift in *Complex Words*. Swift's peculiarities are there pitched against the humanist ideal, the standard of 'generous' irony, which to some extent takes over the rationalising function which attaches to the idea of an audience in *Some Versions*. In the later book, Empson describes Swift's style as insinuating its horrors all the more powerfully for the implicit comparison with 'the amiable complex of Erasmus' (p. 110).

A part of the creepiness of Swift's obsessive punning comes from its appeal to obscure etymologies, whether factual or false. The sense of 'profundity' behind such meanings is beyond the rational account of Empson's phenomenology. They carry, as often as not, a hint of irrational doctrine which appeals to an inbred logic of paradox, and eludes the normative structures of equation. In *Seven Types*, there was no such obvious difficulty in saying that Ambiguities were based on, or justified by, arguments from derivation. As with Milton's latinic echoes, the hint of a support from etymology gives added weight and resonance to a poet's language. For *Complex Words*, the question is more problematic. Indeed, Empson has to insist, at one point, that the 'ordinary equation process has nothing to do with etymology' (p. 81). Archbishop Trench had argued from the Latin *poena* that 'pain' and 'punishment' were derived from the same source, and that therefore 'in the heart of man' the two were implicitly connected. Empson of course finds this idea repulsive. The problem is aggravated by the fact that Complex Words, unlike Ambiguities, carry 'compacted doctrines' and involve definite truth-claims. They therefore possess more consequence as a factor in moral debate.

It is vital for this reason that words maintain, on Empson's view, a certain self-directing character, released from their supposed immemorial sanctions and answering rather to the social and humanising process which has taken them up. Empson describes this change most strikingly in the case of 'dog'. The word became a kind of accommodating blank which allowed a redeeming sense of 'hearty' mutual feeling to overlay its uses for plain insult. Like 'man', it illustrates the workings of 'appreciative pregnancy', which in this case builds on a totally unillusioned, but shared and therefore trustful view of human nature. 'Dog' is therefore 'God's opposite'—not a word replete with meaning, but a piece of unassuming verbal currency which takes up the humours of man the social animal. Trench's etymology makes a pointed appeal to Original Sin, so the religious parallels here are by no means forced or remote. C. S. Lewis's *Studies in Words* is a full-scale example of the same covert doctrine as supports the arguments of Trench. Lewis constantly refers to 'linguistic pre-history', and sets out to show 'the independent efforts of our language to provide itself with necessary tools of thought'.[22] His methods have to be distinguished, finely but firmly, from those of Empson. Lewis makes 'our language' as independent as possible from 'us', its manipulative users. He wants to concede nothing to 'individual semantic agility' which can feasibly be referred back to linguistic pre-history (usually identified by Lewis with Greek and Latin origins). Lewis's classicism therefore represents a traditionalist or conservative attitude to language, and a certain unwillingness to connect its development with the active machinations of human intelligence. Empson, on the contrary, tries to demonstrate in *Complex Words* that the subtleties of usage, in words like 'sense', depend very largely on the intentional acts, the sensitive verbal resources, of individual speakers and writers.

As we have seen already, the problem of etymology was present in Ambiguities of the Third Type. It was not so much forced upon Empson's attention simply because *Seven Types* was philosophically a less searching account of language. The question remained a matter of skilful adjustment: how to credit the poet with 'wit' and originality if his puns could be largely accounted for by derivation. Empson admits it as a valid objection that 'in so far as an ambiguity is justified, it is moved upwards or downwards on my scale out of the third type' (p. 102). Puns will tend to seem trivial if they lack the resonance of a supporting etymology. However, 'from the point of view of verbal ingenuity' (p. 105), such a direct appeal to origins would diminish our sense of a poet's creative independence.

Yet of all the seven Types, it was here, in the Third, that Empson took the lead for *Complex Words*. Ambiguities of this order occur 'when two ideas . . . can be given in one word simultaneously' (*Seven Types*, p. 102). More than any of Empson's summary definitions, this looks forward to the later idea of 'statements in words'. But there is no provision within Ambiguity for the working balance between language and style which Empson was to recognise in the later book. In so far as it generates these problems, the Third Type of Ambiguity throws a paradox into Empson's early style of verbal criticism. The Fourth Type moves away from this difficult region, but without providing anything like a workable answer. Its examples are 'less conscious, because more completely accepted, or fitted into a larger unit' (p. 131). They possess, in other words, the kind of contextual spread—as opposed to the structure of meanings in a single decisive word—which Empson was later to reject in I. A. Richards's theory of 'grammar'.

This question of etymology brings out the difference between Empson's researches in *Complex Words* and the studies of historical semanticists like Lewis and Leo Spitzer. The difference is important, since it bears on the question of linguistic *intentionality* which, as I have argued, lies at the centre of philosophic interest in Empson's book. Spitzer, like Lewis, writes what amounts to a theocentric history of language.[23] Where Empson harks back to the humanist enlightenment, taking his interpretative aims and bearings from secular values, Spitzer on the contrary regards it as something of a disaster, a 'dislocation' of semantic fields which had hitherto enshrined a stable representative order. Spitzer continually makes the appeal to etymology which Empson, for good reason, tries to avoid. He seeks out the characterising 'etymon', the root meaning and its line of descent, whence to divine some salient point of semantic distinction.

It is natural, with his concern for this kind of semantic validation, that Spitzer should regret the scepticism and the fragmentation of age-old cultural values which he finds in the language of secular Enlightenment. In an essay on *Don Quixote*, Spitzer discusses the 'perspectivism' of Cervantes' language; its sheer multiplicity of synonyms and rival meanings, all pointing up above the confusion to the one source of truth—God the Creator. 'It was possible for many etymons to be proposed for the same word, since God may have deposited different meanings in a single term'.[24] God is the supreme 'entendedor' of language. Spitzer borrows this word from Cervantes himself, and it helps to define by contrast the *absence* of any such supreme 'intender' in Empson's secular semantics.

It is perhaps a consequence of Spitzer's philosophical views that he has written more or less separately in the two main fields of his semantic research. *Linguistics and Literary History* (1948) is mainly devoted to individual authors, their styles and characterising figures of language. *Essays in Historical Semantics* (published in the same year) deals more generally with the history of language as a branch of philological enquiry. Spitzer himself distinguishes *Stilsprachen* (where language as a whole subsumes the variety of styles) and *Sprachstile* (where styles make expressive capital of language). Spitzer's criticism does not attain to the internal balance, the combined interest in style and usage, which Empson achieves in *Complex Words*. Perhaps this would be foreign to Spitzer's purpose; certainly it would entail a change in his theoretical focus and, consequently, his historical bearings. Empson interprets the 'enlightenment' or humanistic habits of language by himself enacting their inward logic. He rehearses and justifies the theory of his book by an immanent critique of the language of secular rationalism. Criticism of this kind—an active *recreation* of language in its formative moment —yields an ethics of interpretation far removed from the nostalgic traditionalism of a scholar like Spitzer.

Empson shares at least Spitzer's basic premise, the rational faith that 'there is a power vested in the human mind of investigating the human mind'. I would argue, however, that Empson takes this idea much further towards its fulfilment—the critical practice it warrants—than Spitzer would allow. Empson makes criticism a more answerable, because more rationally confident, phenomenology of meaning. One cannot discount the profoundly different, at times even mystical orientation of Spitzer's philology. I should call Empson's the finer achievement of critical reason; Spitzer's, perhaps, the more accountable prelude to a history of ideas.

COMPLEX WORDS AND THE 'RENAISSANCE' VIEW OF MAN

Empson and Spitzer enact, between them, the cultural rift which they both discern in the history of language, but differently interpret: the shift from 'medieval' to 'renaissance' patterns of thought. Spitzer looks back regretfully to the medieval harmonies of faith and received wisdom. Empson attaches much more importance to the independent processes of thought by which language managed to free itself from all such bonds of authority. The same point is at stake, on more general terms, when Empson defends his readings of Donne and Herbert in *Seven Types* from the scholarly strictures of Rosamund Tuve.[25] His opponent had argued that these poets, when they appeared most ingenious and original, were mostly drawing on a stock of religious conceits and rhetorical tropes which existed already in the main tradition of medieval thought. Empson takes just the opposite line of approach. It is fairer to the poet, or it is more conducive to a generous understanding of his poetry, if we assume him to have worked out for himself the more striking implications of his subject. Empson treats Donne as a 'renaissance' figure: a rational sceptic, questioning old ideas and values, and so (most importantly) creating a new basis for received conventions. Donne is the individual genius who *transforms* the materials of an outworn tradition. The same applies to *Complex Words*: usage and 'wit' are equally dependent on an active recreation of verbal resources through the workings of creative mentality.

The 'renaissance' character of Empson's criticism is likewise evident in his approach to Shakespearian drama. In 1953 he published an essay on the 'character' of Falstaff, provoked in part by Dover Wilson's interpretation, and also—more generally —by the orthodox critical ban on such topics of discussion.[26]

Wilson saw *Henry V* as a vestige of the old medieval morality-plays, and Falstaff as a descendant of the tempting Satan, the farcical stage-devil of the same tradition. Empson urges the opposite, or broadly 'renaissance' view, with Falstaff as a complex and largely sympathetic character, worthy of a more generous reading. Empson is not throwing in a flippant aside when he remarks that, if critics are to call Falstaff's treatment 'calculated degradation', then 'I do not know what we expect our own old age to be like'.[27] Critics have mostly been either embarrassed or (like W. W. Robson) amused and condescending about these personal irruptions in Empson's writing.[28] They are most frequent and self-searching in *Milton's God*, where the defence of Satan proceeds along much the same lines as Empson's championship of Falstaff. Can the critic morally *afford* to despise Milton's Satan, given the remotest understanding of the poem's background politics? 'My own life has turned out pretty easy so far, but if . . .' (p. 89). The readiness for moral self-involvement goes with the sense of a natural complexity about human motives, and also with the belief—as applied to Falstaff or Satan—that no grim doctrine of divine retribution can account for their inherent variety.

To this extent, the issue between Empson and Dover Wilson turns upon the question of interpretative faith. Empson follows out the insight of *Complex Words*: that where 'the stage effect is . . . crude and as it were mythical', the interpretation called for is all the more 'complex' (p. 141). Empson's general notions of human 'character' were set out clearly in *Seven Types*, where he constantly refers to the contradictions, vaccilations and sheer social 'hypocrisy' involved in all human dealings. In the essay on Falstaff, more than twenty years later, he still lays it down as a useful rule that 'one should accept all theories, however contradictory, which add to the total effect'. This attitude supports the 'renaissance' view of Falstaff, the assumption that he is a creature of rich and varied motive, demanding the proper allowance of basic human sympathy.

This stress on conflicts of motive as an aspect of dramatic 'character' is parallelled by the importance Empson attaches to the inward conflicts of language. The strategies of motive in Shakespeare's characters resemble those in his more complicated

uses of key-words like 'sense' and 'fool'. *King Lear,* in Empson's
reading, takes place in a world where 'good intentions get painfully and farcically twisted by one's own character and by unexpected events' (p. 154). This broad-minded sympathy with
the characters' personal situation is matched by the methods of
semantic exploration attempted in *Complex Words*. The contortions wrought upon the patient logic of 'honest' and 'fool' are
much like those 'farcical' twists of motive which still cannot
obscure the larger, more hopeful meaning of experience held out
to a generous interpreter.

   Philip Hobsbaum thinks it 'strange' that Empson should
attribute Lear's dying exaltation to his deluded belief in
Cordelia's revival, and yet still make this 'something far more
pessimistic than those critics who would reject that view'.[29]
But Empson's reaction here is in keeping with the whole rationalistic tenor of *Complex Words*. Lear's state of delusion, despite
his private raptures, remains a melancholy spectacle to the
reasoning mind. A similar question arises with Lear's grief-
stricken reference to the dead Cordelia as his 'fool'. Instead of
pursuing this into the realm of mystical equations, Empson
thinks we should take it as a dramatic sign that Lear 'must be
utterly crazy to call one by the name of the other' (p. 152).
More recently Empson has taken issue with Maynard Mack over
the same problem in *Lear*: the invitation (which Mack seems
happy to accept) to exalt Lear's tragic delusion into a form of
wholesale mysticism.[30] Empson admits the force of Lear's vision-
ary ravings, but insists that it works mainly by a heightening
of pathos, an effect which still appeals to an audience's sense of
realities. It is for this reason also that the logic of 'fool', in
Complex Words, is not anchored solely in the crowning series
of paradoxes which mark Lear's escape into insanity. The word
retains its commonsense basis, and is never entirely beyond reach
of the 'amiable complex' of Erasmus.

   'Fool' is perhaps the best example of the balance achieved in
Complex Words between the rhetoric of an individual style—in
this case a singular dramatic experience—and the normative
background of usage. The balance is found, furthermore, in
appealing to a state of civilised expectation which Empson can
identify for the purpose with Shakespeare's audience, but which

also implies a generalised 'ethic of mutuality'. Such is the 'renaissance' quality of feeling which characterises *Complex Words*. Empson is interested in the 'state of language and feeling' which 'gave a writer peculiar opportunities to make full use of this group of ideas' (p. 114). In such periods of communal exchange, there is no firm distinction to be drawn between individual 'style' and the existing potential of the language. Even the apparent conflict between etymology and a rationalising semantics—the ground of Empson's difference with Lewis—disappears in the case of 'fool'. Empson anticipates the objection that Erasmus, after all, wrote in Latin, and that 'he probably never thought in English at all' (p. 111). He denies nonetheless that the question is merely one of possible 'influence', and argues instead that 'a complexity of feeling of this sort can be put into classical Latin or any other language with a general word for *fool*' (p. 112).

This is, I think, a significant point of theoretical reprise in *Complex Words*. It defines the philosophic spirit, the ironic temper and the moment of many-levelled historical sympathy which characterise Empson's finest criticism. Yet throughout this chapter, he resists the methodological temptation to make a clear-cut structural 'conceit' of the ironies in 'fool'. He even reflects (p. 113) that the symmetry of the word, as used for effects of mutual comparison, seems to assert 'a particularly firm belief in the false identity'. The equations in question are those of Empson's 'Type IV', the reversible collocation of two head senses, the ambitiousness of which (and their resistance to rational criticism) Empson elsewhere discovers in Wordsworth's mystical language. It is clear, however, that this extreme case of 'fool' is on the same general footing, and appeals to the same complex of feelings, as the primary Erasmic sense. The double-equation structure, Empson concludes, is possible only because 'this rather peculiar state of feeling treats them as two examples of a general truth, and in this way it can be classed as an effect of mutual metaphor' (p. 113).

As Empson explains it, the 'peculiar state of feeling' is still to be interpreted on terms of mutual understanding. The more extreme cases of 'fool', whether cynical or mysteriously elevated, like those which occur in *Lear*, have to be set against this standard of extended human sympathies which defines the word's central range of meaning. Perhaps it was this logic of reciprocal feeling which Empson meant in *Seven Types* when he spoke rather uncertainly of 'meanings latent in the mode of action of language' (p. 7). *Complex Words* achieves a remarkable and delicate adjustment between the claims of reason and those of expressive freedom. John Crowe Ranson has reasonably pointed out that any adequate 'logic of poetic figure' would still be a logical anomaly, meaning in effect a 'logic of logical aberrations, applicable to the conventions of poetic language'.[31] Empson's critical path between the provinces of equation and mutual metaphor comprises the real 'theoretical' content of *Complex Words*. It is an achievement of mediating reason far beyond the *ad hoc* mechanics of a 'logic' of poetry represented by his table of equations.

It was largely this character of logical explicitness which Ransom mistrusted in Empson's criticism. He spoke of 'the reading of the poet's muddled mind by some later, freer and more self-conscious mind'. Cleanth Brooks likewise wants to legislate that 'the principles of criticism define the area relevant to criticism; they do not constitute a method for carrying it out'.[32] The formalist critic naturally wishes to preserve poetry from the meddling intellect which seems to challenge the supposed autonomy of form. Ransom's essay therefore discriminates between the local perceptions which he finds so valuable in Empson's work, and the rationalising bias which he rejects as irrelevant to the specialised 'logic' of poetic figure.

What Ransom objects to is, in effect, the whole developing philosophy of Empson's criticism. It is the background of generalised awareness which has kept him, at least since *Seven Types*, from implying a poetics apart from the workings of ordinary language. Empson's reasons for this check on his own incipient method are obvious in a comment (made in 1963) on George Herbert and his treatment in *Seven Types*. It struck Empson, in reading the old passages through, 'that my attitude was what I have come to call Neo-Christian; happy to find such an extravagant specimen, I slapped the author on the back and egged him on to be even nastier'.[33] Empson now feels that the usual need for metaphysical wit ('though seldom its conscious purpose') was to keep the paradoxes of religion at a comfortable distance.

Empson's revised estimate of Herbert suggests the more qualified account of poetic mentality which informs *Complex Words* and the later criticism. It is this reading-back of rational resistance into the poet's own mind, rather than the charge of misapplied 'ingenuity', which rouses Ransom's defences against Empson's critical approach. I have tried to show how this principle works as a means of approaching the poet's *intention*, in the widest sense, through the 'intentionality', or complex semantics, of his language. This is really nothing more than a drawing-out in detail of the ideas implicit in *Complex Words*. With these in mind, one can look back over Empson's criticism as a whole, and appreciate the depth and consistency of the arguments it offers for a generously rational approach to literature.

5

'Other Minds':
the Morality of Knowledge

In *Seven Types*, Empson suggested that his methods might seem less questionable 'to a mind trained by dividing the word of God in the pulpit' (p. 184). To the extent that this echoes T. S. Eliot's interest in Lancelot Andrewes, Eliot may indeed be called—a title which he declined—the father of the modern practice of 'verbal' criticism. Empson's casual comparison bears, in retrospect, a certain weight of irony. The critics most open to his influence were those for whom verbal analysis, in one guise or another, was a useful adjunct to theology.

In *Seven Types*, Empson's choice of main examples was often such as to underline and sharpen this methodological tension. In the lines from Wordsworth's 'Tintern Abbey', and in Herbert's 'The Sacrifice'—two of Empson's more controversial subjects—other commentators in various fields have discovered a warrant for isolating certain theological uses of language, and thus preserving them from rational enquiry. The philosopher John Wisdom offers the same lines from Wordsworth in his well-known essay 'Gods'.[1] He argues, briefly, that statements of faith elude the strict process of logical reasoning; that such assertions are rather persuasive than definitive, offering not a chain of logical argument but the deep configuration of a man's beliefs, comprehensible only to those prepared to sympathise with its claims.

From a different angle of approach, but to much the same effect, comes an essay by Thomas F. Merrill on Herbert's 'The Sacrifice'.[2] Merrill thinks Empson's arguments sound in themselves but somewhat beside the point. Devotional poetry, he suggests, reveals a structure of meaning unique in its power to express and sustain the logical anomalies of religious faith. Merrill takes up Ian Ramsey's distinction, made to a similar purpose, between the 'model' (or logically-adequate example) and the 'qualifier' (or shift to the super-rational) as elements of religious language.[3] Thus, according to Merrill, the poem celebrates, at this higher level of meaning, the 'hypostatic union' of Christ and the poet's grammatical First Person. Furthermore, the poetry is 'successful'—rhetorically and theologically persuasive—in so far as it leaves these mysteries 'intact' and preserves their problematic character. Merrill is here applying, for reasons more explicitly doctrinal, the standards of poetic 'integrity' which I have identified with the American New Critics.

Wisdom's and Ramsey's ideas show the modern *rapprochement* between theology and logical philosophy, a good-willed parcelling-out of territories which seems to have replaced their earlier quarrels. Empson is left very much out on a limb. Even I. A. Richards, contributing in 1950 to a symposium on 'Religion and the Intellectuals', denied that the Verification Principle had any bearing on questions of religious belief, and went on to suggest that theologians should concern themselves with 'plausibilities rather than necessities'.[4] Richards's attitude connects easily enough with the philosophic dualism behind his 'emotive' theory of poetic language. Poetry and religion are both to be saved by a doctrine which sidesteps the onward march of scientific knowledge. Empson clearly had many and complicated reasons for his difference with Richards in *Complex Words*.

If, like Richards, the positivist philosopher has to admit and accommodate his liking for poetry, then of course this conflict of priorities will prevent (or at least embarrass) a reasoning approach to literary meaning. Richards's books contain little in the way of fully-worked examples of critical method. Such excursions usually revert to the question of reader-psychology, or the theory of satisfied 'impulse' which alone—by the dubious virtue of solipsism—provides a refuge from the strictures of positivist logic. The same movement of thought can be identified in A. J. Ayers' glances at aesthetics in *Language, Truth and Logic*. Since aesthetic (and ethical) terms of judgement are merely suasive, and not intended as logical propositions, the only argument properly derived from such judgements is 'information about our own mental and physical make-up'.[5]

Empson, unlike Richards, is concerned with poetic language, its meanings and modes of statement, and not with the supposed

psychology of an ideal reader. Empson also disagrees, as we have
seen, with the selective use made of Richards by the later formalist critics—the transfer of all such complexities from an affective
to a purely rhetorical plane. In place of this he develops a more
qualified, philosophic and ultimately *phenomenological* account
of literary meaning. In his early defence of Richards against
John Sparrow, Empson conceded the likely objection that, in
Richards's affective criticism, the idea of psychic 'self-completion'
could tend to obscure 'the element of objectivity' in critical
judgement.[6] Indeed, by a strange twist in its logic, the positivist
description of poetry excludes the poetic 'object' itself from any
but the most superficial account.

It is useful at this point to recall the slogan 'subjective correlative' in suggesting the nature of Empson's achievement in
reconciling these two philosophies, each self-defeating on its own
narrow terms—the 'subjective' and 'objective' views of literature. The phrase possesses its own logic of justification. So far as
one can point convincingly to the correlating details, the
interpretative logic of what one finds in a text, this response
will be validated as 'objectively' as its nature permits. Only a
slight change of emphasis, albeit a crucial one, distinguishes this
from the logic implicit in Eliot's notion of the 'objective correlative'. Yet there is, behind this difference of terms, a whole
connected theory of perception and interpretation at stake.
Eliot's philosophical grounding was in the Idealism of F. H.
Bradley, the subject of his early Harvard dissertation, lately
published in book form.[7] In Empson's case the aptest comparison,
as I have already suggested, is with the phenomenology of
Husserl and his various disciples.

Eliot, in his work on Bradley, shows the apparent closeness
and the ultimate radical difference between these two philosophical outlooks. At one point he expounds an almost
Husserlian concept of 'intention'. Reality is analysable into
'intended objects (qualities) and the intention (or moment of
objectification)'.[8] But it is not the human perceiver's 'intending', or the logic of his perceptions, which Bradley thinks of as
adequate to this task. 'Reality is simply that which is intended
and the ideal is that which intends'.[9] Hence perhaps Eliot's
theory of the 'objective correlative': the literary product of a

mysterious and always inaccessible process of creation, cut off effectively from any kind of rational self-inspection. Eliot makes much of Bradley's concept of Transcendence, of 'a leap which science cannot take and metaphysics can take'. He concludes, with Bradley, that 'the idea, and its predication of reality, may exist previous to the articulation of language'. Such were Eliot's idealistic supports in removing the meaning of poetry beyond the explanatory grasp of unaided human reason. The metaphysical 'leap' which he expounds from Bradley is very much in line with Wisdom's and Ramsey's descriptions of religious language.

From the phenomenological point of view, these idealistic doctrines can be reversed to place man, the intelligent perceiver, at the creative centre of his own reality. Philosophy can only justify itself by a principled return to the groundings of experience in individual judgements and perceptions. But—most importantly—this phenomenological 'reduction' does not entail, like Richards's psychologism, a loss of rational confidence in the objective grounds of experience. Husserl distinguishes 'intention' from 'empty intuition'; the intended object is the end-result of a receptive process which has fully to *realise* its meaning and implications. Transferred from the realm of sensuous perception to that of language and signification, Husserl's philosophy indicates a confident answer to the problem of literary 'intention'. The entire rationale of *Complex Words* is comprehended in Husserl's belief that the 'intentionality of predicative judgements' leads back ultimately to the 'intentionality of experience'.[10] Husserl holds that logic in itself is not primary or self-sufficient, and that it needs a theory of expression in which to ground its—otherwise naïve—quest for certitude. But this subjective appeal, far from supporting an emotivist outlook, opens the way to what Husserl calls 'an intersubjective cognitive community' of meaning, with its own proven logic and sources of conviction.

This relates signally to Empson's belief, expressed in *Seven Types*, that all good poetry requires an active effort of intellectual sympathy on the reader's part; and that poetry hardly exists, in its rightful condition, without such engagement. Robert Graves made the same point in his book *Poetic Unreason*, which

Empson recollects was an influence on the writing of *Seven Types*.[11] Graves proposed to examine the 'phase of mental conflict' which lay behind the *reader's* immediate response; and then to work back from this to the author and his own apparent conflicts. It seems indeed that the idea of intentionality, or of the reader's constitutive role in poetry, is inseparable from that of Ambiguity and multiple meaning.

Some arguments of Merleau-Ponty, the later exponent of Husserl's ideas, provide an interesting parallel. He distinguishes what he calls 'monocular' imagery, that which is purely objective and not yet a product of active interpretation, from 'binocular' images, 'all collected together, by the last of their number, into the ipseity of the thing'.[12] He is referring mainly to the process of optical adjustment by which we make sense of visual objects. But the same argument could be used to explain how Ambiguity, as a qualitative feature of poetry, becomes the basis of creative self-discovery through language. Ambiguous perceptions, according to Merleau-Ponty, are those to which 'we ourselves give a significance through the attitude which we take up'.[13]

The place of the poet's 'attitudes', in relation to the ambiguities of his language, is the point at which Empson parts company with the formalist critics. The difference is put most strikingly in his remarks on George Herbert which I quoted at the close of Chapter 4. Herbert's paradoxes are not to be thought of as making up some unique and self-supporting system of beliefs. They are part of the poet's intelligent effort to reconcile reason with the beguiling false logic of religious metaphor. The question of the poem's formal status, as an object for passive contemplation or a stimulus to rational enquiry, thus comes to seem identical with the question of poetic 'intention'. The engagement with Wordsworth in *Seven Types* is a splendid example of the way Empson's criticism tests itself creatively against the philosophic puzzles involved. John Wisdom, as we have seen, accepts the claims of Wordsworth's idealism simply by positing a 'logic of interpretation' which extends a special licence to imaginative uses of language. And Muriel Bradbrook, in a review of *Seven Types*, criticised Empson for his needless logical fussing, since Wordsworth's poetry rested (to quote

Empson's answering footnote) on a total 'transcendence of the subject-object relationship' (p. 153n).

It is precisely this early surrender to mysticism that Empson refuses to make in *Seven Types*, and goes on refusing through his chapter on Wordsworth in *Complex Words*. His readings frequently insist on questions of critical method *and* of the moral attitudes which underlie them. One possible interpretation, man 'has a spirit immanent in nature in the same way as is the spirit of God, and is decently independent from him'. In the second version Wordsworth's implications are 'less fortunate'; if God is himself the whole of nature, then man is at once subject to 'determinism and predestination' (*Seven Types*, p. 153). Empson is not merely tilting at Wordsworth's lofty rhetoric. Reviewing an edition of the poems of Thomas Hardy in 1940, he found himself irritated by the sheer complacency of a poet who made no real attempt to reconcile the patent contradictions of his own philosophy. Such, he reflected, is the evasive outlook of most people 'who are admired for unpretentious integrity'.[14] This mistrust of 'integrity', in its root sense— single-minded commitment to principle—corresponds to the view of Ambiguity which makes it more a matter of unresolved complexities than a clear-cut acceptance of paradox.

One can feel these problems and implications of Empson's method piling up, as it were, against the intractable sense of Wordsworth's lines. There is room still for involuntary admiration of the poetry, a feeling which Empson would not deny: 'I must protest again that I enjoy these lines very much' (p. 154). But even this divided reaction signifies, not a nonplussed objection on principle, but the whole spirit of open-minded reasonableness in which that objection is raised. What Empson misses in the poetry is some sign that the poet's intelligence compassed the kinds of logical problem which the critic has to deal with. Wordsworth's topic, the imaginative fusing of subject and object, inevitably calls out the associated puzzles about poetic form and meaning. If the critic, like Bradbrook, forecloses the problem by allowing the poetry to 'transcend' all such difficulties, then poet and critic are both denied that dialogue of reason, the measure of mutual intelligence, which makes Ambiguity the medium of rational understanding.

Empson's experience with Wordsworth resembles the critique of intuition, or the process of logical 'reduction', which Husserl set out as the first requirement of all philosophy. Merleau-Ponty begins with the same objective. He describes the tendency of perceptions to organise random data; and finds that *ambiguous* perceptual sets 'reveal more effectively the presence within us of spontaneous evaluation'.[15] His consequent statement that there is 'no unity without unification' is also the implicit message of Empson's Ambiguity. The point emerges from a rather be-wildered passage describing Shakespeare's Cressida and the variety of motives—or dramatic 'selves'—which she seems to contain. The puzzle here, says Empson, is 'the assumption of difference within a term dedicated to unity' (p. 179). 'Integrity' as a standard of moral judgement would clearly be inappropriate in this case. The paradox extends to the whole questionable notion of literary 'form', as affected by the idea of Ambiguity. Paul Deman has remarked of the New Criticism that, for all its specifications of unitary form, it finally became 'a criticism of ambiguity, an ironic reflection of the absence of the unity it had postulated'.[16]

Deman's rather recondite thesis, in his book *Blindness and Insight*, is that one critic's 'blindness' to such implications, arising from some brilliant but unrealised perception, can itself be the prelude to another's more circumspect and qualified 'insight'. In Empson's case this formula has to be modified. His criticism derives its richness and subtlety from the simultaneous presence of perception and reflection, immediate response and a certain intellectual reserve. Empson's passage on Wordsworth, like his later (Pastoral) chapter on Marvell, interrogates its sub-ject with such tact and self-involvement on the critic's part, that the poem as a topic of meditation comes to *include* inescapably the problems posed by its own deceiving form.

It is this decisive play of attitudes which sets Empson's criti-cism apart from the formalist assumptions of poetic 'unity'. Hugh Kenner provides an interesting example of the turn taken by Ambiguity when a full-blown rhetoric is required of it. In his study of G. K. Chesterton, Kenner connects the modern Christian emphasis on paradox with the revival by T. S. Eliot of seventeenth-century poetry. He mounts a religious doctrine on his verbal demonstrations by observing that, since man is a creature of paradoxical needs and aspirations, so 'he is comforted only by paradoxes; every suffering man repeats the suffering of God'.[17] In Empson's, no less than in Kenner's explications, the logic of pun and paradox culminates very often in the two main articles of Christian belief, the mystery of Incarnation and the suffering of Christ. The latter predominates in *Seven Types*, with its last and most fruitful example in Herbert's 'The Sacrifice'. The theme of Incarnation is more prominent in *Some Versions*, where it provides the root ideas of the one-and-the-many, the victim as hero, and more remotely the child-as-critic.

Ogden and Richards had noticed, in *The Meaning of Meaning*, how often such tricks of verbal logic were the source of religious and theosophical doctrines. The mystique of Yoga they took to depend on 'a hypostatisation of verbal entities combined with a belief in ascending planes of reality where these entities reside'.[18] Empson's essay on 'The Garden' admits the appeal of such heady abstractions, exploring at length the implications of a conceit 'on which one can build a hierarchy of values' (*Some Versions*, p. 117). This is unmistakably the inbred logic of paradox. But Empson enters an important reservation when he describes Marvell's wit and levity as 'more convincing' than Wordsworth's grander and less *arguable* version of the same ideas. Empson pictures Marvell, from one stanza to the next, as 'enjoying in a receptive state the exhilaration which an exercise of wit has produced' (p. 108). The 'wit' of the poem seems to coexist, in a momentary way, with the 'receptive' faculty which the critic should also attain to, if he is inward enough with the poet's rapt state of mind.

It is helpful to recall, at this stage, the contention of phenomenology that awareness is many-levelled, that consciousness cannot entirely coincide with its object or (by pure intuition) with itself. The play of intelligence finds its scope in the space opened up by the multiple layers of constituted meaning. Ambiguity is not aimed, like the reasonings of theology, at the final restitution of single, transcendent meaning. On the contrary, it firmly resists such absolutes, and maintains its ambiguous nature by always assuming, beyond the structures of its own witty logic, the further complications of a 'placing' attitude, more or less serious, on the poet's part. Thus Empson sees a connection between Marvell's wire-drawn arguments and the genial brand of 'idealism' used—with more zest than commitment—in Shakespeare's 'The Phoenix and the Turtle'.

Empson's doubts about Ambiguity as a full-scale philosophy of meaning, the hallmark of all 'great poetry', are made clear in the 1961 preface to *Seven Types*. Reviewers had taken examples from Dante and Wordsworth to make the point that 'real' ambiguity was a much larger, more deeply-rooted feature of poetry than the 'superficial and finicking' varieties which Empson had uncovered. Empson agrees vaguely but seems to avoid the issue. Great poetry, he concedes, has always a 'feeling of generalisation' from its appeal to a background of 'human experience'. But this, as I have argued, looks forward more directly to the commonsense logic of *Complex Words* than to any universal metaphysics of poetic Ambiguity.

Empson is not concerned with the wholesale metaphysics of ambiguity proposed by the philosopher of language, W. M. Urban. Such structures of meaning cannot, according to Urban, be reduced to analysis 'without a remainder'. They refer, not to local contexts of language, but to whole 'universes of discourse'. Their truths are metaphysical, the criteria being 'not coercive but persuasive', and ultimately 'self-authenticating' for the believer.[19] Cleanth Brooks calls upon Urban for philosophical support in *The Well-Wrought Urn*.[20] He wants his privileged figures of paradox and irony to carry the same self-authenticating value as Urban's meta-linguistic ambiguity. Empson seems anxious to avoid such wholesale philosophic sanctions. He typically insists that the poet's creative intelligence sees round and beyond the self-supporting logic of his verbal games. Thus Shakespeare, in 'The Phoenix and the Turtle', makes his playful metaphysics seem 'an engagingly simple-minded piece of idealism' (*Some Versions*, p. 114). To which Empson adds, in a downright way: 'this seems to me intentional'. The poet's 'intention' is located precisely in the knowing play of attitude, ironic and self-critical, which keeps both poet and reader from an unreflecting state of immersion in the poem's metaphysical conceits. With Shakespeare's half-serious logic, 'once you cease to impose a staircase the thing shifts from heroic to mock-pastoral' (p. 115).

Comparing Marvell and Wordsworth, Empson concludes that the main point of difference is something in the earlier poet's language—a quality of wit, of tactful and intelligent humility—which is of the essence of Pastoral. Marvell's style of wit is partly a matter of plain good sense, of standing somewhat apart from the intricate logic of his own conceits. 'Sense' in effect runs the whole gamut of meanings established for it in *Complex Words*. The poet's physical senses, at one end of the scale, are translated —by his witty logic and detached state of entrancement—onto the highest plane of mystic-contemplative 'sense'. It is this quality of conscious self-possession, made possible but not *pre-occupied* by its own metaphysics, which gives Marvell the decided advantage—in Empson's opinion—over Wordsworth's philosophy of nature.

His chapter on 'The Garden' is remarkably subtle and elusive. Talking ostensibly about themes and ideas in the poem, Empson also hints at puzzles of critical approach which seem hardly distinct—so deft and reflexive is the commentary—from the poem's thematic content. The basic contrast of ideas is between 'powers inherent (in the mind) and powers worked out in prac-tice' (p. 102). This is the running topic of Pastoral, the theme first raised in connection with Gray's 'Elegy'. The contrast is underlined, in Marvell's poem, by the 'unruly impulses' of ran-dom thought and the workings of an intellect which paradoxically cannot 'employ' them without somehow distorting their nature. Involved in Empson's reading is the poet's all too pressing sense of his real-life situation, idling and equivocating his way through the Civil War period. '"Unemployment" is too painful and normal even in the fullest life for such a theme to be trivial' (p. 102). This reflection has the tone of slightly offbeat practical wisdom which has often seemed 'eccentric' to readers of Empson's more recent criticism. It is, however, very much a part of the Pastoral complex of feelings. In Empson's statement, the poet's sense of compromise merges with the recurrent burden of Pastoral ('the waste even in a fortunate life, the isolation even of a life rich in intimacy'—p. 12), and this in turn finds an echo in the moody paradox about mental processes. Marvell's pre-carious wit finds an answer to these antinomies, without pre-tending to have simply 'transcended' them in thought. The compromise still makes itself felt through the half-serious logic of Marvell's case for withdrawing into the 'contemplative' life. And at the level of pure reason, consciousness 'no longer makes an important distinction'; its workings may, with sufficient subtlety, balance the 'impulses' of unimpeded instinct without, in the process, cutting them off from their natural source.

In *Complex Words*, we have already seen how Empson comes to terms with Wordsworth's philosophy, explaining it—as far as he can—by the compact semantics of 'sense'. Wordsworth, like Marvell, connects the basic process of sensory perception with 'the supreme act of imagination'. But Wordsworth tends to 'jump over' the middle range of meanings implicit in the phrase 'good sense'. When Wordsworth adopts his prophetic strain, 'he will not allow any mediating process to have occurred' (*Complex Words*, p. 304). This 'mediating process', lacking in Wordsworth, is the locus of wit and self-possessed intelligence in Marvell's more tempered mysticism. It warrants the appeal to poetic 'intention', in the fullest sense; that reserved and articulate play of meanings which, according to Husserl, leads us back to the *intentionality* of experience itself.

Empson was later to demonstrate how Pope's *Essay on Criticism* could provide a working model of critical method by enacting in its own semantics the movements of thought on which practical judgement depends. There is a vast claim being made for the method in general when Empson finds Pope successfully moving over from 'sense=prose meaning' to 'sense=imagination', all within the governing terms of 'the good humour of a reasonable man' (*Complex Words*, p. 99). Marvell does the same, although more by force of implicit ideas than by exemplary semantics. Marvell's unimpeded impulses 'let themselves be known because they are not altered by being known, because their principle of indeterminacy no longer acts' (*Some Versions*, p. 103). This 'principle', drawn from contemporary science, was the focus in *Seven Types* for all those paradoxes which Empson found attaching to the idea of literary form. In 'The Garden', Marvell's turns of argument modulate so easily into a witty and unforced background of feelings that the problem of critical method—or of intelligence up against the paradoxes of imagination—all but disappears. Marvell's main themes are central to Pastoral because the hero of that *genre* 'is always ready to be the critic; he not only includes everything but may in some unexpected way know it' (p. 103).

The word 'know', in this context, has a paradoxical air which suggests that it opens into complicated questions of knowledge and self-awareness. In Pastoral, these are contained and expressed by the metaphor, and the more conscious critical business, of 'putting the complex into the simple'. This provides, as in Marvell's poem, an imaginative drama which absorbs and justifies the methodological tension between intuitive and intellectual habits of response. The idea that such conflicts *can* be somehow contained, so that criticism becomes a normal and 'unimpeded' activity of judgement, emerges again in the practical chapters of *Complex Words*. It is among the background suggestions of 'honest', as Empson interprets the word. So far as a man 'satisfies his own nature' and is 'honest to himself', he may reasonably be expected 'to have generous feelings' which arise from 'his own unobstructed nature' and not from rule or principle (p. 216). This is essentially what Empson identifies in Pope as 'the "common sense" which is to become adequate to the task of criticism' (p. 100). It involves a notion of creative intelligence on the poet's side, and receptive awareness on the critic's, which amounts to a definite and tested philosophy of mind.

In the last chapter of *Seven Types*, which already begins to generalise away from the theme of Ambiguity, Empson remarks that it would often be 'unprofitable' to insist on the ambiguities in Pope, because he 'expected his readers to prune their minds of any early disorder' (p. 241). This seems an alarming concession, surprisingly unnoticed by Empson's critical opponents. It admits in effect that Ambiguity is largely a matter of logical 'disorder', and that now his interests—well on the road to *Complex Words* —are not to be wholly identified with what has gone before. The seventeenth-century poets provide the most fruitful examples of Ambiguity because, as Empson recognises, their tastes were less inhibited by conscious scruple than those of their Augustan successors. Pastoral finds a typically pragmatic way of drawing out the relevant ideas in Donne, Marvell and Shakespeare, and presenting them as it were in the rationalising image of the

Pastoral poet-as-critic. This entails, as a matter of philosophic viewpoint, a very different account of literary history from that which Eliot encoded in the phrase 'dissociation of sensibility'. Eliot believed that the seventeenth-century poets exhibited a fusion of 'thought' and 'emotion' which was subsequently lost for reasons (it seems) jointly social and religious.[21] For Empson, the myth of a 'unified' sensibility is less appealing, or less available to rational demonstration, than the complex of attitudes which sought to overcome the inherent divisions of human mentality and to work them into some kind of logical order. It is this shift of outlook which leads, in *Some Versions*, to Empson's deliberately qualified—almost evasive—treatment of metaphysical 'wit'. The indirections of a poet's argument are the evidence of a largeness of creative mentality which actively explores its own paradoxical nature.

Pastoral thus *contains* the mood of eighteenth-century rationalism, not only as the product of that particular period but as an enduring, always available and often indispensable habit of thought. The oblique approach to Milton through his editors, Pearce and Bentley, is to some extent an ironic reflection on the rationalising character of 'the critic'. But it also puts forward the serious contention (looking forward to *Milton's God*) that this is nonetheless 'a fit state of mind to appreciate poetry' (p. 126). The idea of Pastoral does of course carry a note of generalised nostalgia, and this can be felt most strongly in Empson's remarks on Milton and the 'golden age' of Classical mythology which the poet had to repudiate. But the mediations of reason—even in the 'absurd' form of Bentley and his reductive arguments—forestall the development of a wholesale myth of 'dissociated' faculties, such as Eliot sought to promote.

MILTON'S GOD AND THE 'QUESTION OF INTENTION'

On the face of it, there is little in common between *Milton's God* and these earlier interests of Empson's criticism. It is a frankly polemical book, intended mainly as a moral rejoinder to what Empson sees as the 'Neo-Christian' tendency in modern criticism. Yet the book takes on a more impressive unity of argument if one sees it as a further, more insistent attempt to mark off the *intentional* character of poetry from the regions of myth and religious paradox. Empson arraigns God's conduct in the poem by comparing him with a human father who—so the argument runs—'should judge an act of disobedience *in the light of its intention*' (p. 161; italics mine). There is an odd but inescapable chain of moral and interpretative logic to be followed here. With the drama thus naturalised, God stands trial for his intentions—the indefinite punishment of all mankind for one trivial misdeed—precisely insofar as he ignored or misconstrued the intentions of Adam and Eve. And Milton's poem must in turn be understood in the light of the poet's intentions, which for Empson involve a whole range of complicating factors. Milton is treated, like Donne or Marvell, as possessing the natural intelligence to recognise the problems of the myth he is trying to defend and therefore to question it with at least a part of his mind. This state of inward division is what Empson discovered, on a wittier level of argument, in Marvell's 'The Garden'. It is bound up with the humanist philosophy which places most value on the poet's independence of received ideas and tradition. Milton's 'intentions' are there to interpret where they divided his mind against its own more orthodox side, and so allowed him somewhat to civilise the doctrines he set up to defend.

Empson therefore demands of Milton, and likewise of his God, the same basic virtues of sane and generous judgement that he finds necessary in the mundane business of literary criticism. This common standard is evident when, at one point, he states the condition: 'if God is good, that is, if he is the kind of teacher who wants to produce an independent-minded student' (p. 160). Empson attaches equal importance to these two considerations of 'intention' and moral 'independence'. The bitter polemic of his final chapter ('Christianity') is balanced elsewhere by what appears movingly in the chapter on Milton's Eve: a faith in the native generosity of human impulse, untouched by the moral contortions of religious paradox. 'The independence of our feelings from our will' was for Saint Augustine 'the essence of being fallen'. For Empson it remains a basic safeguard against 'the lethal convictions which so often capture our brains' (p. 169).

Empson sets up 'unaided reason and normal sentiment' (p. 252) as arbiters of Milton's poetry. In this can be recognised the hard-won conclusion of *Complex Words*, that some kind of natural morality—a logic of mutual feeling—must attach to the normal uses of language. Against this proven background, Empson pits all varieties of paradox and dogma, including those of Christian mysticism, subsumed under the category 'A is B'. He is nevertheless able to show that these depend, for what suasive effect they possess, on the natural resources of trust and confidence built up around the language of rational statement. Richard Sleight's was an oddly misjudged reaction—in an otherwise perceptive review—when he spoke of the 'horrifying vistas of stupidity, arrogance and malice' brought out by Empson's 'ruthless rationalism'.[22] From the meanings evoked by 'honest', Sleight could conclude only that 'most of us are fools and liars as well as being amazingly self-centred'. This all seems strangely off the point. Empson certainly presents some cynical and even brutal uses of honest', especially in Iago's rhetoric of tempting ambiguities. But behind these perversions of its meaning, the word stands basically for the unillusioned, the minimal but solid grounds of human trust and self-respect. Sleight seems to have missed, for some reason, the ironic but compassionate tone which Empson lends to his final paraphrase of 'honest':

> I am sorry for you, fool that you are, when I see you forced, as all humanity is forced, to reconcile in yourself these shifting and contradictory virtues. But by the same token you cannot cheat me. (*Complex Words*, p. 202)

This is not, as Sleight supposes, a cynical double-thrust, but a hopeful expression of disabused mutual reliance.

In his footnote on Orwell's 1984 (p. 83), Empson faces the apparent liability of language to encode through paradox the kind of insane 'doublethink' which Orwell depicts as the basic use of propaganda. Recalling his own wartime experience, Empson was later to argue, in *Milton's God*, that such work 'cannot narrow a man's understanding of other people's opinions', though it might conceivably 'narrow his own opinions' (p. 123). Milton was also a seasoned propagandist, with much experience of the kind of subtle and roundabout argumentation that Empson imputes to *Paradise Lost*. His mind was sufficiently devious, yet clear enough about its own mixed motives, to support the rationalising arguments of a critic like Empson. In *Complex Words*, Empson looks to his semantics for a counter-argument to Orwell: that 'the human mind . . . is not irredeemably lunatic and cannot be made so' (p. 83). The same applies to Milton, in whom 'unaided reason' and 'normal sentiment' are held up as adequate to balance the effects of his 'appalling' theology. This attitude seems less doggedly perverse when viewed in the light of Empson's previous semantic researches. In the spirit of *Seven Types*, he could express distaste for the feelings involved in a religious sonnet of Donne, yet admit (in a footnote) that his reaction 'has little to do with the ambiguity in question' (p. 146n). In the later books, this dissociation of moral and critical judgement would entirely beg the question. What his criticism now seeks is a workable basis for judging a poet's answerable motives, the bearing of which may not be straightforwardly evident in his 'official' language. When Empson speaks, in *Complex Words*, of the family of rationalist ideas which 'kept Christianity at bay', he is not referring only to church-and-state but to the whole tempting logic of Christian paradox which his favourite kinds of language confront and subvert.

This associates with Empson's obvious interest in the history of religious dissent, and his admiration for those who battled with Christian dogma on various grounds of individual conscience. Milton becomes the chief, because most deeply and publicly engaged, of a long tradition of reformers and dissidents, the line which Empson himself joins in *Milton's God*. The importance of 'intentions' is a topic of debate which itself forms a part of this moral history. W. K. Wimsatt brings the point home by taking up an opposite stand. Multiple meaning as a concept in criticism has its background, he suggests, in the schools of theology.[23] Unlike Empson, Wimsatt accepts this pedigree and the constraints and disciplines which go with it. But the interpretation of the scriptures down the ages has also produced—to Wimsatt's apparent discomfort—the heresy of 'intentionalism', or of claiming to know just what the prophet *meant* beyond the traditional figures of his speech. Wimsatt and Empson, as priest and heretic, are a pair nicely matched.

The chapter on Milton in *Some Versions* is itself an ironic variant of the rationalising approach which Empson holds in such high esteem. Bentley and Pearce, those wrangling literary scholars in the Age of Reason, are made to strike sparks off Milton's poetry by trying to suit it to their own tidy notions of thought and language. Empson does not seek to redeem Bentley's scholarly reputation; he defends the spirit of his criticisms but rarely the particular judgement. His purpose is to show that these critics were about as much attuned to Milton's poetry as Milton himself to the articles of faith which officially he was trying to defend. In each case the intellect revolted, refused to accept passively the subject it dealt with, and thus provided a strengthening source of heterodox opinion. Pearce and Bentley serve the role Milton's own conscience effectively fulfils in *Milton's God*. The poet's world is 'harsh and hypnotic', and Bentley's notes by comparison 'an irruption of firm sense' (*Some Versions*, p. 126). In the later book Empson comments, with a touch of probably unconscious hindsight, that hypnotism—on the evidence of modern psychology—cannot make us act contrary to our deepest moral convictions. The hypnotic power of Milton's religion, like that of his poetry, need not deter criticism from following out its rational assumptions.

MILTON, PASTORAL AND THE LEVELS OF CONSCIOUSNESS

Empson's approach to Milton's poetry raises two obvious questions. How far can Milton possibly have been aware of the kind of meaning that Empson attributes to him? And if such matters are beyond reasonable answer—which Empson would anyway deny—then what can be the basis for hoping to understand the articulate workings, or 'intentionality', of the poet's mind? Empson has had a good deal to say about the Freudian Unconscious, although his comments have mostly either denied its existence, or dismissed it as merely a 'product of definition'. But it is worth pursuing his various arguments, since the 'unconscious' in one guise or another is the ultimate resort of all those 'deep' confusions—paradox, symbolism, the cult of unreason—which Empson has so persistently questioned.

His reactions to Freud can be seen in some early reviews for *Granta*, where Empson often discussed books on psycho-therapy and kindred topics. The 'subconscious', he remarks in one such article, now has so many senses and uses that 'it is no pleasure to think of it as a simply existing noun'.[24] This comment is echoed in his article replying to John Sparrow, which appeared in *Oxford Outlook* at about the same time. Empson argues that 'to treat beauty as a simple noun', like Sparrow, inevitably 'stultifies the intelligence, abolishes criticism'.[25] These simplified notions restrict argument and prevent—it is a fair analogy—the creative play of meaning *within the word* which was Empson's idea of Ambiguity. Sparrow made 'thought', 'feeling' and 'value' separate entities; which 'patent simplicity of style', according to Empson, left him 'utterly at the mercy of his vocabulary'.

It was perhaps for this reason that Empson refused to naturalise his insights, to turn Ambiguity into a settled system of distinctions, or to posit any simple theory of literary meaning which would seem to compass the whole of an author's active intelligence. The same reservation is at work in *Complex Words*. In an anxious footnote on page 57, Empson is on guard against the charge of absorbing 'the living water of thought' to a mere system of 'fixities and definites'. He recalls the warning of Coleridge that 'too much definiteness of terms is a bad thing, wasting "the vital and idea-creating force", and preventing "originality"'. Intelligence operates beyond the reach of any system of ideas, or subconscious 'rules', which could be offered to explain it.

One cannot help feeling there is a double edge to Empson's tribute when he calls Ezra Pound 'such a clever man', with such 'natural good feelings', that he has not needed to do any 'original thinking' for many years.[26] This reflection comes from the essay 'Rhythm and Imagery in English Poetry', which presents among other things the case for a rationalist criticism against the Imagist aesthetic descending from Pound and Eliot. So far as an image preoccupies the poet's or critic's attention, it excludes all possibility of rational exchange. Like the total acquiescence in paradox, or the subconscious viewed as a 'simple noun', the literary image as Pound conceived it amounted to a denial of the reasoning process in poetry. Jean-Paul Sartre, in his book *Imagination*, states in philosophic form the problem recognised by Empson. If an image is assumed to consist only in its 'sensory content', it must logically be 'expelled from thought'. And again: 'if an image has a purely sensory content, perhaps one could think *on* it but never *with* it'.[27] Sartre therefore views the imaginary 'unconscious' as a kind of store-case invented to hold a limitless supply of inertly existent 'images'.

The only kind of image which Sartre finds compatible with genuine Imagination—also called 'imaginative intending'—is something more qualified and paradoxically self-conscious. Sartre speaks of the image's 'awareness of itself', its 'self-transparency', existing as it does 'only to the extent that it knows itself'.[28] These are somewhat clumsy locutions, betraying (at least in translation) the problematic nature of his subject. Empson handles the problem with less obvious strain by allowing it to figure implicitly in the critical encounter with poetry. In the essay 'Rhythm and Imagery', he returns to Marvell's 'The Garden' in order to show that a simply 'visual' reading—one which proceeded on Imagist assumptions—would reduce the poem to patent absurdity. He takes Marvell's 'image' of the ocean, which the poet compares to the mind and its contents, and points out that the effort to *picture* this relation is riddled with plain contradictions. These puzzles also emerge, rather less explicitly, from the chapter on Marvell in *Some Versions*. The ocean is at once surface reflection (conscious knowledge) and hidden depths (the 'unconscious'), with all their fantastic shapes and correspondences. Yet at some point there must occur 'a transition from the correspondences of thought with fact to those of thought with thought, to find which is to be creative' (p. 104).

The image gives a curiously literal meaning to Sartre's idea of 'transparency', while at the same time denying its own apparent status as a concrete object of perception. The tensions here are germane to the argument, the hint of paradox and play of contra-dictions, which—in Maxwell's suggestive stanza—permit the mind a measure of escape from its own inherent limitations. This passage of Empson has an intricate depth of imaginative mean-ing. It forms his response to the quality, found in Marvell and largely missed in Wordsworth, of a creative mind both richly self-aware and fully in posesssion of its critical faculties. The main debt of Pastoral to Ambiguity is evident in the movement, traced in Marvell's image, from relations of 'thought with fact' to those of 'thought with thought'. Ambiguity releases the language of poetry from the 'simple noun' idea of proper meaning, and delivers it up to the creative play of self-conscious irony and argument. It allows for those regions of witty but *rational* reserve within which poetic imagination and critical reason have their inseparable scope.

Empson's critique of Imagism takes a more obviously moral colouring in *Milton's God*. T. S. Eliot and his following are the chief offenders in Empson's view. 'So long as you gave Mr. Eliot pictures of someone being tortured his nerves were at peace, but if you gave him an image of two people making each other happy he screamed' (p. 30). This combines Empson's objections to the Christian ethic of sacrifice with his mistrust of the Imagist aesthetic which allowed Eliot to criticise the verbal inconsistencies of Milton's poetry while accepting without question its religious arguments. Again it is the Imagist refusal to *reason* about poetry, and the assumption of a like-minded refusal on the poet's part, which Empson finds so suspect and evasive.

This objection is very typical of Empson's way of thinking. Ambiguity was the first challenge to a philosophy of meaning and value which discounted the multiple and shifting resources of verbal intelligence. In *Complex Words*, as we have seen, this argument is taken further and comes to include a logical account of the scope and conditions of verbal implication. When the method meets a stumbling-block in Milton's use of 'all', the case simply proves the inherent contradiction between Empson's rationalising bias and the obscure economies of the Freudian unconscious. His critique of literary Imagism turns on the same clash of attitudes. The image or symbol, naïvely accepted as such, takes hold of the mind at a level of undifferentiated meaning which puts it out of reach of rational self-understanding. Where Ambiguity refused to naturalise or simplify the idea of literary meaning, *Milton's God* rejects the conformist attitude of a criticism which bases itself, with single-minded piety, on a religious myth of origins. The politics of Milton's imagination, as Empson conceives it, are those of creative intelligence in general.

These reflections on the nature and concept of imagery can be usefully pursued into the whole vexed question of the 'politics' of Empson's Pastoral. Christopher Caudwell, the English Marxist critic, objected to Empson's criticism on philosophic grounds. 'Since words are fewer than the objects they symbolise, . . . poetry itself is correspondingly cloudy and ambiguous. This ambiguity, which Empson takes to be the essence of poetry, is in fact a by-product.'[29] This implies a one-to-one relation between words, meanings and objects which amounts to the 'simple noun' idea of semantic economy. Caudwell equates it with a doctrine of socialist realism which he opposes, in orthodox fashion, to the elaborate mystifications of modernist and formalist influence. Elsewhere he expresses the conviction that modern poetry has 'moved away from concrete living' into 'the development of its own technique'.[30] Ambiguity in Empson's sense, the creative plurality of meaning, would loosen the word from its proper place in the materialist economy of reference.

Sartre is among those recent Marxist philosophers who have attempted to reconcile Marxism with a more flexible and qualified account of literary meaning. To their way of thinking, the tendency to *naturalise* meaning—to limit the play of significations—can only lend support to existing realities, and arrest the productive conflicts of historical awareness. This leads Sartre to criticise the forms of 'psychological' realism adopted by many modern authors and critics. He draws the relevant distinction by comparing the creative techniques of Faulkner and Dos Passos. Faulkner's characters have their psychology supplied, as it were, 'fixed and immutable, like an evil spell . . . they bear it within them . . . it is a *thing*'.[31] In Dos Passos, on the contrary, 'the story of a single life . . . crystallises into the social, and the problem of transition to the typical is thereby resolved . . . Each of his characters is unique. What does it matter since he *is* Society?'[32] Pastoral exemplifies the second set of options. Empson argues—in the first chapter of *Some Versions*—to the same effect as Sartre, that there is no need with this understanding to try to present a 'working-man type'. The limitations of what Empson calls 'proletarian literature', basing his definition on the current pronouncements of the Soviets, are replaced by the idea of the creative artist as a 'complex' individual, mediating the demands of art and social conscience through his own, detached but compassionate ironic vision.

In Chapter 2 I mentioned Raymond Williams' accusation that Pastoral had always tended to erect class-divisions into a 'natural order', propped up by its own 'metaphysical sanctions'. As Empson treats it, the *genre* has precisely the opposite character. The traditional 'metaphysics' are to some extent retained, as in the problems of 'the one and the many' and the cognate machinery of intellectual puzzles. But these conceits are always subject to a higher, more self-conscious dialogue of motives, more closely related to (although not completely determined by) the consciousness of class divisions. In one of his notebooks, probably kept about 1966, Empson writes that Donne's Neo-Platonism is not swallowed whole by the poet.[33] It is much more a matter of 'respecting the claims of the poor; regard for social justice, an attempt to make less of a brutal farce of the doctrine of the goodness of God'. In fact the metaphysics have the very unmetaphysical, democratic purpose of cutting away these supernatural sanctions and thus giving everyone a fair claim to independent knowledge. The remnant metaphysics of Pastoral need not totally engross the mind but should, as in 'The Garden' and Shakespeare's 'The Phoenix and the Turtle', provide the spur to its rational self-exercise.

Paradox, metaphysics and themes of the 'deep' subconscious are always something of a problem in Empson's criticism. The unconscious mind, with its obscure economies of guilt and repression, gives no hold for the kind of rational argumentation which Empson most values in poetry. In *Complex Words* he is eventually forced to find a sort of 'Freudian symbol' in Milton's use of 'all', since the word evokes such a deep and contradictory range of meanings. But in Pastoral these conflicts of motive are partly resolved in terms of the series of metaphors which project a more complex and rewarding 'psychology' for artist and critic alike. Empson's chapter on the Alice books is commonly called a classic Freudian reading; but really it is something different, and something more. He remarks (p. 206) that 'Wonderland is a dream, but The Looking-Glass is self-consciousness'. The essay raises some larger questions about Freudian psychology than those critics realise who quote the rather pat account, the gamut of Freudian symbolism, which Empson gives of Alice's descent into Wonderland. 'Self-consciousness' is at least as important as 'dream' in the Pastoral approach to Lewis Carroll.

The real debt to Freud in this chapter is Empson's allowance —not explicitly stated, but effectively organising his argument— for the 'decomposition' of imaginary characters in Alice's dreamworld. 'The qualities held in so subtle a suspension in Alice are shown at full blast in the two queens' (p. 227). And these turn out to be the regular complementarities of Pastoral, always within reach of the 'complex' individual prepared to analyse his own ambiguous motives. The White Queen becomes an 'inclusive' figure, somehow gathering in herself all the 'decomposed' characters of Carroll's imagination. She contains, like Marvell's poem, 'the mysteries of self-knowledge, the self-contradictions of the will, the antinomies of philosophy' (p. 232). Empson disagrees in an earlier chapter (p. 59) with the orthodox Freudian view—represented here by Ernest Jones—that 'decomposition' and its allied effects result always from a 'regular repression', or a conflict of 'deep' psychological origins. This approach can only deal with literary cases in terms of myth and symbol—that is, by restricting itself to a region of the author's psychology where his own reason and conscience are scarcely at home. For Empson, on the contrary, the basic myth and its adequate *interpretation* may have an inverse relation of complexity. The fluid psychology of Pastoral is an indication that authors may mean more than they know without the critic's having to appeal to a deep and unavowable source of motivation. Creativity entails the paradoxical power of the mind to reflect so intimately on its own equivocal workings that no firm line can be drawn any longer between 'conscious' and 'unconscious' levels of expression.

In *Some Versions*, Empson counters the idea of a 'collective unconscious' with the model of a communal intelligence which he describes (p. 59) as 'a small public opinion'. The ideal example is a good theatre audience, diverse in its tastes and opinions but unified by 'the mutual influence of its members' judgements'. This 'sensibility held in common' is the theme which emerges in *Complex Words* as the 'common sense' of secular reason. In Pastoral terms, an equation is drawn between the interchange of responses in a diverse but communicative audience, and the mixture of ideas and feelings in a single intelligent reader. This state of awareness is both required and, to some extent, *produced* by the divisions of class-interest which make up 'public opinion'. George Steiner has pointedly observed that where Empson notices 'the complex play of irony', the Marxist critic would probably record 'a dialectical conflict between a poet's thesis and his actual vision of things'. In both kinds of argument, the writer's intentions are given a manifold social interest which keeps them clear of the Aladdin's cave of 'deep' unconscious motive. Both explanations credit the artist with a truth-telling power of recognition. Empson, however, would allow more subtlety of implicit self-knowledge to the poet who is able to mirror in himself the social conditions of complex awareness.

In recent years, the problem of the Freudian 'unconscious' has been forced upon Empson's attention by the alliance he sees between Symbolist doctrines and the whole 'Neo-Christian' movement of opinion. He has tended to repeat, with a somewhat more polemical obviousness, the line of reasoning from *Some Versions* which replaced the notional Unconscious with an image of society at large. Thus he argues that the 'problem of incest', in Webster's play *The Duchess of Malfi*, arose only because 'Freud expected audiences to be unconscious' and the critics, in their turn, 'did not know what an Elizabethan audience would be unconscious of'.[34] He goes on to argue from the social make-up of such an audience, its class-divisions and interests in common, to a working notion of how it must have reacted and hence to a better idea of the dramatist's practical intentions. This is not merely to put the clock back, ignore the insights of Freud and adopt the scholar's 'period' approach. The case for Empson's reading—here as with 'sense' and its relatives in *Complex Words*—rests upon the larger validity of an interlocking set of attitudes found, most typically or explicitly, in a certain period of literature. The Elizabethan and the Augustan, Pastoral and Complex Words, represent in different ways the same rationalising attitude, itself a constant in human experience transcending local origins.

Empson has not denied the importance of either Freud or Marx as a part of the modern background of intellectual awareness.

He now tends to think of himself, half-seriously, as 'one of the old buffers who were always made fretful' by the overwhelming trilogy of Marx, Freud and Darwin.[35] It was these thinkers who first suggested that man the conscious agent was less in control of his own thought and destiny than he liked to imagine. But Empson's 'fretting' was never so desperate as to prevent his criticism from staking out a credible claim for human dignity and freedom. The predicament, as it struck Empson at the time of *Seven Types*, was hinted at in Freud's paper on 'Moral Responsibility for the Content of Dreams' (1925). Freud rules that the paradoxes of moral determinism, implicit in his theory of the Unconscious, are a part of the complexity which attaches to all moral judgement. 'If anyone is dissatisfied . . . and would like to be better than he was created, let him see whether he can attain more in life than hypocrisy or inhibition'.[36] In *Seven Types* Empson discovers, interprets and even admires certain tactics of human 'hypocrisy'; those which Hugh Kenner can easily dismiss as mere gestures of the humanist intellectual, his back to the wall, assailed by sceptical doubts. In *Some Versions*, especially the paraphrase of Shakespeare's sonnet 'They that have power', Empson states the most complex and ironic variant of this generous accommodation to social 'hypocrisy'. 'I must praise to you your very faults, especially your selfishness, because you can only now be safe by cultivating them further' (p. 85). Where Freud finds reason for a stern rebuke to human pretensions, Empson characteristically discovers a ground for renewed forms of sympathy and trust.

This is the force of Empson's comment, in *Seven Types*, that the 'unconscious' may well be 'a convenient fiction or product of definition' (p. 103). Moral values, like meaning itself, can only be rationally entertained by suspending belief in the pre-determined nature of human impulse, and opening oneself to the ambiguous promptings of sense and reason. In Empson's scattered comments on the poetry of Dylan Thomas, one senses a certain baffled reasonableness, a straining after the poet's commonsense attitudes, which seems to involve the same set of puzzles about the role of his 'unconscious' motives. In a 'London Letter', published in America in 1937, Empson spoke of a Welsh poet, presumably Thomas, whose poetry fed upon events which 'involved the universe but happened inside his skin'. He goes on to suggest that Thomas is 'wasting his opportunities as a Welshman and ought to make full use of a country in which he could nip across the classes'.[37] Empson implies that some kind of political interest, or at least a sense of the practical problems involved, would help Thomas to break out of the painfully closed circle of his symbolist communings. Marvell is the obvious example, in *Some Versions*, of a poet whose political feelings, although perhaps too complicated for his own recognition, enabled him to make more intelligible sense of his 'metaphysical' themes. The 'London Letter' makes the point more directly with regard to the left-wing English poets of the pre-war decade. The current high sales of Auden and Spender reflect, Empson says, not a sense of direct commitment on the part of the reading public, but 'an obscure safety and bafflement in moving from the poem to consider what the country could possibly do'.

Empson's own poems of the pre-war period have something of this 'baffled' quality; always articulate, sometimes seeming to chatter on regardless, but never giving way to the threatening mood of despair. In 'Courage Means Running' (*Collected Poems*, p. 56) there is even an echo of the 'London Letter': politics are seen as raising 'bafflement to a boast we all take as guard'. These poems are attempting to find, in the absence of straightforward loyalties and commitments, at least an answerable poise or attitude which might measure up to an impossibly demanding situation. The poem is itself an object of puzzlement. It does not engross or dictate to the reader's intelligence but, on the contrary, sets it to work more freely and self-critically. Empson recommends to Thomas what he had discovered in Marvell: an imagination inward but circumspect, given to public themes but conveying their complexity only by a measure of shrewdly self-occupied reserve. The poet of 'The Garden' has all these brave opposites in play: engagement and detachment, imagination and reason, subconscious depth and witty, reflective surface.

Ambiguity and *Pastoral* show Empson coming to terms with the difficult legacy of Freud and Marx. They retain what might be called a latent 'archaeology' of conflict and desire, a matter of occasional mood in *Seven Types* and a source of endless metaphorical themes in *Some Versions*. To some extent the resulting ideas are naturalised, or made the subject (as in Gray's 'Elegy') of artificial comparisons with nature, somehow belonging to the collective unconscious. The apparent 'universality and imperson- ality' of Gray's style claim by implication that 'we ought to accept the injustice of society as we do the inevitability of death' (p. 12). But Empson typically goes on to recognise that many readers, 'without being communists', have been 'irritated by the complacence in the massive calm of the poem'. There is, Empson concedes, a 'kind of cheat in the implied politics', although what is said is undeniably 'one of the permanent truths'. This kind of divided response is familiar from Empson's dealings with Wordsworth, and from those chapters of *Complex Words* which push the semanticist close to his limits. In Pastoral there is always an intriguing tension between the broadly Marxian politics of motive and the more 'metaphysical' —or largely sub-conscious—machinery of meaning.

But Pastoral also possesses a kind of teleology or mediating process whereby literature, with its increasing burden of self- knowledge, comes to include and actively *interpret* the sources of its own discontent. One of Empson's book-reviews in 1937 contained some relevant comments on the notion of 'directive purpose', a principle of psychology 'opposed to Mechanism, Determinism or blind chance'.[38] This seems to be the principle at work in Pastoral, where the crudely deterministic philosophies, both of Marxism and Freudianism, are replaced by the develop- ment of a *genre*, a metaphor and a potent set of ironies; until finally the White Queen of Carroll's elusive fiction sends mean- ing and value 'through the ceiling as if it were quite used to it' (p. 232). Throughout Pastoral the increasing complexities of social attitude—the imaginative politics of literature—take up the burden of expressing, relieving and even obscurely *justifying* the inherent compromise of the *genre*.

Empson describes the last, dissociated phase of Pastoral where 'there is jam only in the future and in our traditional past' (p. 232). The process of development has been wrenched apart by its own momentum, much like the civilisation described in Empson's poem 'Reflections from Rochester', which tunnels so far into dangerous self-knowledge that it collapses all the tradi- tional safeguards of reason. The chapter on *Alice* is a drama of consciousness poised between the opposite poles of neurotic isolation and giddying social change. It opens with an emphasis on Freud, on Carroll's repressed sexuality and the fact that this Version—'the child as swain'—is 'more open to neurosis than the older ones, . . . less hopeful and more a return into oneself' (p. 205). It closes with the spotlight on Carroll's creatures, Alice and the White Queen, who embody the opposite despair—ideas and values, creations of the intellect, running wild in the Empyrean of pure thought.

This seems the best way to read the rather loosely attached pieces of Freudian argument in Empson's dazzling chapter on the Alice books. The unconscious mind is not the 'simple noun', or handy storehouse of meanings and images, usually assumed by literary critics. It stands rather in a changeable, ambiguous and essentially *dramatic* relation to the whole history and project of interpretation in Pastoral. Anthony Storr, in a recent book on art and psychology, puts forward a theory which suggests that there might even be a basis in mental physiology for the cultural phenomenon which Pastoral, especially late Pastoral, seems to articulate. Storr observes that in humans, as in no other animal, childhood experience is largely contained in an 'old' brain, an early growth, which lacks connection with the 'interpretative cortex' of the adult. Consequently, the formative experiences of childhood 'can never be either retrieved as memories or altered by comparison with subsequent experience'.[39]

This genetic biology provides at least a suggestive parallel to the history of Pastoral. The sequence of Empson's book, culminating in the chapter on *Alice*, shows an increasing estrangement between the subterranean workings of human instinct and the compensating subtleties of intellectual power. Storr deduces from his biological evidence that discontent is intrinsic to the human condition. Empson is likewise continually led from details of local interpretation to some such generalised mood of resignation. 'The isolation even of a life rich in intimacy' is among the central feelings of the *genre*. The Freudian unconscious enters this history, in its later phase, as a regressive, primitive drive toward neurotic individualism, more cut off than ever from the pathetic strategies of intellect which try to contain it.

This offers an interesting background to Empson's more recent comments on the 'objective correlative', some of which I quoted in Chapter 1. The only real use of Eliot's theory is, Empson thinks, in dealing with problematic cases like that of 'The Ancient Mariner', which actually make a point of some strained, ambiguous relation between the subconscious mind (the Mariner's obscure guilt) and the rational, explanatory level of plot and theme. It would therefore be possible to say of *Alice*, as Empson says of 'The Ancient Mariner', that it does not effectively provide an 'objective correlative'. The judgement would no longer be rooted in Eliot's Bradleian idealism, but in a phenomenology of expression which seeks out the subjective logic of literary meaning, along with its conflicts of instinct and reason. The 'Mariner' is a good example because it asks us to imagine its dramatic purpose, in the narrative and the telling, as that of expiating a guilty conscience. Empson treats the poem as an heroic record of the poet's battling conscience, struggling with the half-accepted Christian theology of unearned guilt and punishment.

In Empson's approach to Coleridge one can see the connection between his secular moral outlook and his attitude to questions of Freudian psychology. Writing in *Granta* as an undergraduate, he was already finding something to deplore in the way that Adler superimposed an idea of 'the good'—or a theory of morality—on the standard notion of the Freudian unconscious. Adler, Empson thought, had merely 'picked up the most respectable ideas of the good' and then 'stolen fire from the scientific altar' to validate them.[40] Moral values, he seems to imply, can only be drawn from, or created at, some higher level of consciousness where their bearing on human relations, and their accountability to reason, are able to be judged.

The same issue is raised by Empson's 1958 essay on Fielding's *Tom Jones*.[41] Far from any evidence of moral confusion, Empson detects in Fielding a generous refusal to believe that a character's 'subconscious' motives are of much use in explaining his genuine reasons for action. The essay is partly polemical. It starts out by attacking 'the current orthodoxy of despair', and goes on to debunk the supposed 'incest-theme' in Fielding, along with other manifestations of the critical pietism which, in Empson's view, invariably goes with a taste for scandalised sexual revelations. It is aimed, in short, at the leading assumptions of Freudian psychology as put to the service of symbolist criticism. The essay is also, more than incidentally, a running reply to the Chicago Critics' approach, exemplified in R. S. Crane's article 'The Concept of Plot and the Plot of *Tom Jones*'.[42] This compartmentalised theory of literature, with its appeals to Aristotelian law, strikes Empson as a rigid and lifeless set of prescriptions. Crane's account he considers efficient in its way but finally 'trivial'. Later in his essay Empson distinguishes Fielding's 'plot', which at some points is 'rigged' and contrived, from 'the reaction of character to plot', which should (he thinks) be the critic's main concern.

This strikingly resembles the 'dramatic truth' proposed by Coleridge in 'The Ancient Mariner'; to display those feelings (Coleridge hoped) which would 'naturally accompany such situations, supposing them real'.[43] Empson's reading of *Tom Jones* breaks down the novel's monolithic 'plot' in much the same way that his account of Coleridge—and poetry in general —cuts across the preconceived boundaries of form and creating mind. It is interesting that another of the Chicago critics, in the same volume of essays, addressed himself to a wholesale attack on Empson's idea of poetic Ambiguity.[44] Empson offends the Aristotelian sense of priorities by assuming that the intensive play of meanings in literature defines its quality more exactly than any received ideas of formal classification. Thus Empson's examples of Pastoral, as well as Ambiguity, are drawn almost randomly from poetry, drama or fiction, so far as these serve to illustrate the developing theme. Their generic identity is less important than the overarching sequence which—more or less convincingly—sets them in order. For Olson, the Chicago spokesman, this is a monstrous confusion of realms. Empson's muddles are rooted, he argues, in the very idea of Ambiguity. Language is 'merely a medium, a material, never a form'. Mimetic poetry—the highest order—can only be ambiguous when 'the exigencies of representation demand that it be so'. Language is merely a 'device of disclosure', the accessory to a literary form already existent *in posse*.[45]

Olson's objections to Ambiguity show a strange resemblance

to those of Christopher Caudwell. Both critics state what amounts
to a case for the 'simple noun' or one-to-one economy of reference. Olson goes further in asserting that the poem, as a
linguistic object, has no more complexity of meaning than 'an
axe, a bed, a chair'. It is 'a certain kind of product', and it is up
to the Aristotelian critic, with his typology of forms, to determine the kind. This generic *a priori* is as much in conflict with
the working assumptions of Empson's criticism as the theory of
reference behind it. Olson's philosophy of poetic 'mimesis'
corresponds to the Imagist ideal of unmediated concrete perception. Empson would doubtless agree with P. N. Furbank, who
has sharply criticised the Imagist theory of poetry, that such a
line of argument finally amounts to 'a vote of no confidence in
the word'.[46] Furbank compares the Imagist doctrine—at least in
the extreme form propounded by Hulme—with the idea of the
philosophers in *Gulliver's Travels*, who elected to dispense with
verbal language and to carry about with them all the material
objects needed to signify their intentions. Olson surpasses the
sages of Lagado in asserting that poetry, let alone plain language,
is sufficiently employed in simply reproducing 'an axe, a bed, a
chair'.

When Empson objects to the 'concept of plot' in Crane's
terminology, he is once again questioning the rooted conventions
of formalist thinking. A *priori* notions of meaning and form,
like those of image and symbol, presume in the reader of literature a passive acceptance of subconscious values and patterns
which ultimately resist the active, reasoning mind. 'Plot', in this
strictly delimited sense of the word, is hardly distinguishable
from 'myth'. As Empson understands it, plot is a more inclusive
and many-levelled structure of awareness, allowing us to see
both the characters' reactions to unexpected turns of event and
the author's play of judgement in revealing those reactions.
Thus Fielding's intentions in *Tom Jones* are viewed in the light
of his 'double irony'—more a mood than a mere 'technique'—
which makes the novel in effect yet another version of Pastoral.
This approach has its parallel in the chapter on *King Lear* in
Complex Words, where characters' intentions get 'farcically
twisted' by the unforeseen consequences of their actions. We
have seen already how this stress on the practical logic of events,

in Empson's criticism, tends to modify and broaden the insights obtained by a purely 'verbal' analysis. Plot and situation are a part of that commonsense appeal to a larger context of human experience which Empson has always opposed to the narrowing techniques of formalist method. Above all, the interest of plot, in this extended sense, is the scope it gives to intelligent deduction of an author's conflicting motives and purposes.

POETRY AND NARRATIVE: THE 'PLOT' DIMENSION

In his piece on the Yeats 'Byzantium' poems, Empson suggests that the poetry makes better sense if one tries to disregard the 'symbolism' and to treat it instead as a kind of 'science fiction' narrative.[47] This remark is perhaps less baffling if one sees that Empson is attempting to restore the working confidence in rational explanations which he seeks of poetry in general. To understand the 'plot' of Yeats's poems is to treat them as a complicated and mysterious, but not ultimately *irrational*, document of imaginative history. This is the background to several of Empson's most recent and controversial arguments. In particular it helps to explain why his essays on Donne, with their bluntly polemical edge, seem so remote from the interests of Empson's earlier criticism. Their express purpose is to 'rescue' the poet, firstly (as in 'Donne the Space Man')[48] from the revised estimate of Eliot, and secondly (in the essays on textual history) from the post-Grierson editors whose readings, Empson thinks, largely serve to implement the critical views of Eliot.

Empson has to defend not only Donne's intellectual qualities, which Eliot, in his later remarks, tried to play down, but also the critical relevance of the poet's biography and the 'actual situations' out of which he was writing. This latter is the main point of his case against Helen Gardner, who inclines (with Leishman and others) to impute to day-dream and fantasy many of the poems which Grierson regarded as containing facts of biography. Empson identifies his arguments with Grierson's 'definitive' text, an attachment doubtless dating from his Cambridge days when, as he recalls elsewhere, he was imitating the poems in that edition 'with love and wonder'.[49] What Empson discovered from Donne in his own poetry, he now wants to restore to the currency of critical opinion. How Donne's influence had its part in such poems as 'Camping Out', we may guess from a comparison he used, much later, to describe the involvement of intellect in the Joycian 'epiphany'. The experience, he suggests, is like that of an ideal theatrical production: 'an absorption so absolute that all other experience seems to have dropped away from you, as in the act of sex'. Yet in this 'the reasoning mind is fully involved . . . Sherlocking, as well as in some way generalising'.[50] The sexual image here is something more than a playful comparison. Poems like 'Camping Out' have a sense of real-life occasion, and a zest of argument carried by sexual imagery, which invite the kind of attention that Empson —on principle—would give to Donne.

Empson sees a betrayal of Donne's poetry in the scholarly attempt to put it all down to wish-fulfilment and erotic fantasy. Such a theory 'makes Donne a feebler kind of man than he was' and thus encourages 'a thorough misreading of the poems'.[51] These feelings are of course not the whole of Empson's case, and he argues in considerable detail from the evidence of Donne's biography. Doubtless he would show the same contempt for any critic who suggested that his own poem 'Camping Out' was simply a conceited day-dream, unconnected with anything in Empson's actual experience. His poems, and the discovery of Donne which inspired them, had their background in a Cambridge of literary interests which did not consider such questions —as they are considered now—beyond the scope of competent enquiry. Richard Eberhart, in his retrospective article on Empson, recalls the popular scandal and speculations which surrounded the appearance of 'Camping Out', with its thinly-veiled personal background.[52]

When Empson argues that Donne's love-poems are 'true', in the sense of drawing upon the poet's actual experience, he is also claiming that they represent a balanced and commonsense attitude to life which critics can ignore only at the cost of distorting his character. This is the basis of Empson's quarrel with Eliot. It emerges in a roundabout way from the chapter on 'Sense and Sensibility' in *Complex Words*. One of the book's reviewers[53] thought that Empson was having an obscure joke at the reader's expense when he tried to show that Eliot, in his early formulations of metaphysical 'wit', was 'going through an independent process of thought' with the original machinery of 'sense' (p. 253). Eliot had spoken of the poet's intellect as being 'at the tips of his senses'. Empson agrees with this formula, but strikes a shrewd blow by removing its air of paradox and claiming it as a model of rational 'complex' semantics. 'Sense' and 'wit' are shown to interpret themselves, through the context of their usage, as vehicles of applied critical reason. When Empson came to write this chapter, Eliot had long since renounced his earlier views on Donne, and was now insisting that 'thought' as such played no important part in his poetry, and that Donne's 'scepticism' was merely an amusing intellectual game. Against this apostasy, so repugnant to Empson, the rationalist view of 'sense' has its own polemical point.

Empson's reply to this review of *Complex Words* was perhaps the most indignant and spirited of all his published correspondence. Strickland seemed to accuse him of 'cooking up a fatuously tiresome mass of spoof'. On the contrary: the book, its ideas and communicative interest were everything to Empson. 'When it was done I felt Nunc Dimittis; I was free, I was ready to die.'[54] This seems a distinctly creative sense of elation, the reasons for which I have already suggested in connection with the rationalising impetus of *Complex Words*. But a part of the energy in Empson's rejoinder is that of a resounding *tu quoque*. The achievement of the book goes essentially with its deep-grained character of a reproof to the dominant trend in criticism represented, on this occasion, by Strickland's 'fatuous' response. The orthodoxy betrayed by these 'indistinguishable young men' (old Empson was just back from China) is plainly that of Eliot's critical influence, the effects of which Empson was increasingly learning to dislike.

So, when Empson tries to restore the 'Twenties view of Donne's love-poetry, this involves a recognition of what the poet claimed for the 'senses' as well as the 'intellect'. Such is the amalgam of commonsense and reason which, as Empson expounds it from Pope, is to become 'adequate to the task of criticism'. The essays on Donne are still concerned, in a general way, with the associative family of meanings in 'sense'; a rationalism rooted in man's sensual nature and opposing itself—like the youthful, sceptical

Donne—to the instituted values of Christianity. Donne is assumed to be an independent thinker whose poetry at its best conveys a total reaction to the various predicaments—of mind and bodily nature—in which he found himself. The essays on Donne show the wider, less specialised bearing of the humanist philosophy of 'sense' laid out for inspection in *Complex Words*. In particular they show how Empson's militant 'intentionalism' —his appeal to the poet's experience, his character and likely outlook—connects with the interests of his more 'theoretical' writing.

Empson's reading of Coleridge sets out from the same assumptions about the poet's experience, and its relevance to his poetry, as the essays on Donne. He argues, partly on the basis of Allsop's testimony, that the poet was never able to throw off completely the religious doubts that made him turn to Unitarianism, during his early years, as a doctrine which helped to soften the idea of Christian 'redemption'.[55] Empson agrees that the myth can be somewhat civilised by assuming that Christ is decently independent of God, and thus not a party to his obscure 'satisfaction' in the sufferings imposed by divine providence on innocent humanity. If Christ, on the other hand, is mystically united with the Godhead, then God may be logically absolved from 'punishing' his son—since God and Christ are the same person—but Christ must be seen to condone by his sufferings the long-term plan for the punishment of all mankind. These Christian metaphysics are the source of all the paradoxical worryings which Empson discovered in Herbert, and which the rationalist ideas of *Complex Words* are intended to 'keep at bay'. Unitarianism and other 'heretical' ideas are important to Empson because they let us see how Coleridge—or indeed Milton—tried to come to terms with the 'appalling' theology of Christian tradition.

Empson considers Coleridge, like Donne, to have faced these problems most squarely in his early, sceptical years, and to have fallen later into a state of shuffling acceptance and guilt-ridden orthodoxy. He recounts some episodes from the Notebooks which show the chronic infirmity of a mind largely possessed by irrational fears and half-digested dogma. Such conflicts belong, presumably, to the 'deep unconscious' of Coleridge's mind. But these are less important, Empson argues, than the clashes of doctrine and feeling which provide the intelligible *themes* of Coleridge's most successful poems. This lends an additional interest to the 'plot' of 'The Ancient Mariner', in so far as the poem enacts, in its very telling, the desire to give a point and significance to the teller's private anxieties. In 'Donne the Space Man', Empson finds the problem of the Christian Atonement—the idea of man's redemption through Christ's exemplary suffering—covertly explored by imagining how it would apply to the inhabitants of other worlds. So with 'The Ancient Mariner': the narrative is a means of stretching the mind to see all round the human implications of religious doctrine. The plot of the poem is more relevant, or more accountable to civilised reason, than its content of undifferentiated 'symbols'.

One finds exactly the reverse set of priorities in W. H. Auden's Christian interpretation of 'The Ancient Mariner'.[56] Auden's whole approach acknowledges what he calls 'the necessity of dogma'. He justifies the deaths of the ship's crew on account of their 'irresponsible fickleness'. This done, he can admit the fact that 'they have to be got out of the way' if the allegory is to take its proper course. This means in effect that the plot of the poem is merely a series of more or less useful props upon which to hang the religious doctrine of unearned guilt and divine retribution.

'Plot' has the same inclusive function in Empson's treatment of *Paradise Lost*. Milton, like Coleridge, is given the benefit of the sceptical doubt, and found to be struggling for a sane and workable version of Christian mythology. Milton's politics, his dissenting views on religion and changes of conscientious tack, are all involved in the narrative dimension which Empson brings to the poem. So far as divine Providence is concerned, 'plot' takes on its secondary meaning of 'intrigue' or 'malicious scheming', with God as the on-stage director of a wholesale comedy of errors. Milton is assumed, like Donne, to be writing out of a total situation which involves every possible trick of argument, every shade of moral and political conscience, in the process of supposedly 'justifying' the ways of God to man. In an appendix to the second edition, Empson presents a detailed and, on the face of it, not very flattering account of Milton's activities as a propagandist on Cromwell's behalf. He even undertakes to prove that Milton was involved in forging the heretical prayer which, attributed to King Charles's authorship, helped to secure his indictment and execution. The point of all this is to underline the fact that Milton was a man of genuine political cunning, whose mind would not have been too simple or other-worldly for the kind of diplomatic intrigue which Empson discovers in *Paradise Lost*.

There is a great difference between Milton's devious brinksmanship, as Empson reconstructs it, and the disengaged politics of Marvell's 'The Garden'. Yet they are both examples of the broadening narrative context which Empson sees as an essential part of the poet's communicative temper. *Some Versions* is by no means the only place in Empson's criticism where political interests, treated for the most part as a matter of intelligent compromise, seem to define the very nature of imaginative reason. In Empson's essay on *Hamlet*, the hero is described as possessing a 'curious generosity of the intellect'; he puts on 'a tremendous display of top-class behaviour' and thus seems to claim 'a peculiar status as an aristocrat after the practical status has been lost'.[57] Hamlet is in effect another 'version' of Pastoral, a complex individual set about with simple but impossible issues of choice. The real *Hamlet*-problem, Empson argues, is 'a problem about his first audiences'. The hero's struggles of conscience have curious political overtones, like those which defined and qualified the elusive *genre* of Pastoral. Empson suggests, doubtless with reference to Eliot's comments on *Hamlet*, that there should perhaps be 'some mediation between the surface and the depths'.[58] But this, for Empson, is basically a puzzle about the mental reach and diversity of an Elizabethan audience, which seems to have been more supple and variously conscious than its modern counterpart. This social perspective allows Empson to discuss the problems of *Hamlet* as they might have struck a contemporary, without pursuing them into regions of conflict, such as Eliot divines, in Shakespeare's conjectural subconscious. Likewise, in his essay on *The Spanish Tragedy*, Empson reads the play as refracted through the interests of a lively theatre audience 'keeping half an eye on the ghost . . . while the ghost watches the actors and the actors watch the play-within-a-play'. The audience provides an image, or working notion, of dramatic 'involvement' as a unity of multiple but connected interests.

The internal mechanics of Kyd's drama provide a good example —almost a convenient parody—of Empson's extended notion of 'plot'. His approach also throws light on the implicit philosophy of mind which treats the creative faculties of poet and reader alike as being structured, in some sense, like an ideal theatre audience. This constant appeal to a wider background of human interests is perhaps the most notable feature of Empson's criticism in recent years. It represents a down-to-earth insistence on the practicalities of plot and situation, conceived almost as a hierarchy of complicating motives and meanings. Nothing in the poet's formative experience, his ideas or the history of his practical choices, can be deemed irrelevant to the intellectual challenge of his poetry.

THE RATIONAL BIAS: SOME LIMITING CASES IN EMPSON'S CRITICISM

Beyond this point it is perhaps not worthwhile or profitable to follow out the logic of Empson's assumptions. I have argued that Pastoral and Complex Words both provide, in their different ways, an imaginative focus or 'subjective correlative' for the organising interests of his criticism. Milton's God and the more recent essays have a good deal in common with these earlier patterns of thought. But it is one thing to point out these interesting connections, and quite another to assume—as perhaps I have suggested—that the later work is altogether as convincing. The problems are fairly obvious. Where putative 'symbols' are concerned, Empson apparently asks us to ignore them on principle, and make what we can of the poetry by his own usual standards of commonsense judgement. In apparent cases of 'deep' religious conflict, we are required to deplore the effects of Christian theology but to find it (as Empson can scarcely deny) a source of rich and fruitful ambiguities. To this extent there is some reason, at least in the later criticism, for the reiterated complaint of reviewers in Scrutiny—I quote R. G. Cox—that Mr Empson 'notoriously allows his intellect to get out of touch with his sensibility'.[59] The strategies of Pastoral and Complex

Words imply their own provisional balance of reason and imagination, like the complex adjustments which Empson discovers in 'sense' and its relatives. But Cox's judgement cannot be easily dismissed when it comes to assessing the latest turns of Empson's argumentative style.

There is a typical twist of imputed motives in the article which Empson based on the recently-published facsimile manuscript of Eliot's *The Waste Land*.[60] Eliot, he thinks, had gradually forced himself to accept the most orthodox and conscience-racking form of Christian belief. His father, on the other hand, was a Unitarian, and thus managed to avoid what Empson considers the appalling implications of God being 'satisfied' by his son's individual suffering. Eliot therefore, resenting his father's more accommodating faith, had a comprehensible reason for the conflicts of motive evident in his poetry (and also, incidentally, for his curious insistence on Hamlet's emotional problems). Empson begins his review with the grudging concession that *The Waste Land* is one Symbolist poem which does seem to justify the programme. But he then proceeds to cut away the Symbolist assumptions by providing other, more or less distracting explanatory props.

This line of argument raises the same problems of credibility as *Milton's God* and the essays on Donne and Coleridge. One is sometimes tempted to apply to Empson the criticism which he once made of a scholarly work on Marlowe: that such 'flip literary judgements' took only one side of the subject in view, whereas 'the whole point of dramatic poetry is to keep both sides in view at once'.[61] The divided response is often at work in *Seven Types*, although there it is mostly carried off by the quickness and pliancy of Empson's critical address. He describes the agile movement, in a poem of Crashaw, between 'the sacrificial idea' and 'incest, the infantile pleasures and cannibalism'—a monstrous and lurid 'short-circuiting of the human order' (p. 221). But in this case he moves on quickly to a passage from Dryden which hints at the same themes only to translate them into a mood of easy-going sensible acceptance. The 'machinery of analysis' would, Empson feels, be wholly misapplied in this case. Dryden's readers probably thought the performance 'curious' and even 'graceful'—an achievement of wit in the commonsense mode. The sheer pace of argument and flow of examples enable Empson to shelve for the while the awkward question of Crashaw's peculiar genius.

This problem is more insistent in the latest writings, where Empson is consciously at grips with a whole modern revival of Christian opinion. There is an unintended irony in Ransom's suggestion that Empson's critical methods might best be applied to modern poetry; the 'tortured and dead serious' kind of poem which 'intended to be a theology and not a work of art'.[62] If this seems an odd prescription, from a critic who (as we have seen) wants to keep theology and poetry carefully apart, it is worth noticing the exact terms of Ransom's loaded suggestion. He baulked at Empson's reading of Herbert because there his methods seemed likely to rationalise the sources of Christian paradox beyond the limits of acceptable faith. If the conflicts in modern poetry are 'tortured and dead serious', they are nevertheless, in Ransom's view, a matter of individual psychology, not to be confused with the dangerous subtleties of argumentation which a critic like Empson can tease out of Herbert's poetry. It was natural for Ransom to take alarm at the subversive 'seriousness' which Empson showed in talking about Herbert and the seventeenth-century poets in general. Yet apart from such scruples of religious conscience, it is clear that Empson was on much firmer ground in his dealings with Herbert than in the later essays where theological questions are raised into a full-scale drama of motive. Somehow, in *Seven Types*, the paradoxes of Herbert's poetry hardly enter the embattled regions of deep psychological guilt. Instead, they lead to the reflection that 'only the speed, compactness and isolation of Herbert's method could handle impulses of such reach and complexity' (p. 231). This comment could equally apply to Empson's own working method, which manages—by sheer 'compactness' and energy—to handle the complicated nexus of feelings in Herbert's sacrificial imagery.

There is a certain cat-and-mouse interest to this curious exchange of priorities between Empson and Ransom. It was doubtless correct, on Ransom's part, to feel that Empson's methods would draw him, by a kind of inexorable logic, to the poetry of neurotic guilt and conflict which has lately claimed his attention. Kenneth Burke, in *The Rhetoric of Religion*, shows how the inbred language of paradox tends to generate a prototype theology. The Christian ideas of sacrifice and atonement are, he suggests, 'intrinsic to Order verbally guided'. The religious prohibition 'is in itself a condition of temptation, since the negation contains the principle of its own annihilation'. There is always present in such verbal logic 'an inducement to round out the symmetry'.[63] Empson reaches some similar conclusions in the course of a passage in *Seven Types* (pp. 194–6), which examines the logic of antithetical words in a series of examples drawn from Freud. Such words, Empson says, are 'fruitful of irrationality', yet also appeal to the 'fundamental habits of the human mind'. They often bear witness to 'a rather sophisticated state of language and feeling' (p. 195). There is a similar 'logic of negation' in the process of reasoning by which Eve, in Empson's account of *Paradise Lost*, converts the meaning of Satan's temptation into a test of what she thinks may be God's more 'generous' plan. The very idea of forbidden knowledge induces a desire to 'round out' the complicated scheme of things by seeing beyond irrational taboos to a larger, more accommodating system of judgement. This rationalised psychology of choice is related to the puzzlings over 'primal opposition' in *Seven Types*. In both cases, Empson is finally less concerned with deep paradoxical sanctions than with the play of motives and practical reasons which makes them a subject of rational argument.

It is fair to say that Empson's imagination thrives on the ambiguous middle-ground of secularised religion. His criticism does, in a sense, lay itself open to the suggestive logic of religious paradox; and he does place a large and increasing stress on the role of religion in bringing out man's contradictory drives and aspirations. But these essential interests don't have the relation that Ransom conceives (or will allow) them to have. He directs Empson to his 'manifest destiny' in the study of modern poetry, where tortured psychology is a kind of substitute for the more dangerous questionings of heterodox faith. Empson refuses to hedge around divinity in this saving fashion. In discussing the psychology of religious belief, his moral and intellectual objections are too much a part of Empson's critical faith to be kept within tactful bounds. His criticism up to *Complex Words* has a way of containing and managing its quarrels with Christianity, so that Empson's rooted convictions are less obviously in conflict with the poetry he admires. Ambiguity moves over easily enough from 'the anthropological idea of opposites' to 'psychological idea of context', and in so doing clears the way for what Empson calls some 'moderate and sensible' examples of the verbal machinery in question. But *Milton's God* and the later essays are so explicit in their anti-Christian arguments that it becomes much harder to equate Empson's attitude with that of an express but unprejudiced rational enquiry.

Seven Types could be said, in retrospect, to avoid the real questions posed to Empson's method by the deeper complications of modern poetry. The analysis of Eliot's ambiguous syntax in 'A Game of Chess', falling within the second type, is specifically a matter of 'local texture', and is less concerned with questions of idea and attitude than any other passage of comparable length in the book. Ten years later, in the course of a review, Empson mentions *The Waste Land* only to remark, rather lamely, that 'a frightful tension' in the poet's mind may require 'a frightful concentration of style', and that anyway this is perhaps 'an odd thing to try to do'.[64] Altogether Empson seems to have fought shy of any real involvement with Eliot's poetry, just as—until recently—he had said very little to the point about Eliot's criticism. Now he feels obliged to take on the 'Neo-Christian' influence, with all its associated background of ideas, in a way which provides no escape into the larger, more stimulating air of his previous writing.

For one reason or another, Empson finds it difficult to deal on satisfactory terms with Eliot's modernist poetic and the critical presumptions which have grown up around it. P. N. Furbank, in his book on the subject, declares that the words 'image' and 'imagery' are 'charged with all the paradoxes about works of art but none of their nature'.[65] Empson would seem to have reached the same conclusion, regarding not only 'imagery' as such but the tenets of Symbolism and the whole mental economy —the divided 'conscious' and 'unconscious'—which they entail. But to take Empson's recent line of argument, and to 'explain' Eliot's critical theories by reference to his psychological conflicts, is to fall into the same closed circle of privileged explanations. In his critical 'credo' of 1950, Empson remarked on the 'fallacy' (not deducible, he hoped, from his own criticism) that poetic value is directly related to the extremity of a poet's psychological conflicts. He quoted Wordsworth's warning dictum: 'The gods approve/The depth and not the tumult of the soul'.[66] But it is not so easy to avoid such assumptions, especially with Eliot's example in view, and even more for the critic, like Empson, who is bent on making sense of private or neurotic conflicts in a way which turns them effectively into a measure of the poet's moral heroism.

In the same article, Empson is prepared to talk for convenience about the poet's 'pre-conscious' as the region of his mind where conflicts of motive might be supposed to reside. This, however, is mainly in order to recall 'the distinction from the deep Freudian subconscious'. This distinction is supported in *Seven Types* by the idea that the 'subconscious' may be in effect a 'structure of past judgements', the *intentionality* of which—to expand on Empson's argument—gives it a more actively intelligent role than the alternative formula. In this sense Ambiguity avoids the paradoxical conclusions of Eliot's creative philosophy. In *Complex Words* the semantics of 'sense' contain a more effective, because more self-supporting, critique of Eliot's assumptions. But since *Milton's God*, Empson has been conducting a more open campaign of counter-argument which leaves him, one might almost say, at the mercy of that 'simple noun' notion of the unconscious which he first detected in the arguments of Sparrow.

Empson describes the characters of Pastoral as possessing an ironic awareness which 'brings to mind the whole body of their difficulty' so that 'it may give them strength to escape from it' (p. 56). The same applies to the literary critic, whose 'strength' derives from his sense of the compromised nature of human understanding. He has to assume at some point, as Empson says of *The Beggar's Opera*, that distinctions between 'conscious' and 'unconscious' motives are somehow no longer relevant: the poet's mind is less 'impeded' than we are, and the over-awareness of Freud may simply get in the way of an adequate response. This mediation between surface and depth is perhaps the main function of Pastoral irony. The more difficult business of applying this standard to modern poetry is evident in a comment of Empson's on the purpose of Eliot's notes for *The Waste Land*.[67] It is not a valid objection, he argues, that the notes offer purely private associations. Only by being given such details can the reader be prevented from seeking out, or needing the reassurance of, 'symbols' and obscure depths of meaning. J. L. Austin, the linguistic philosopher, argues to somewhat similar effect that the failure of belief in 'other minds' can only encourage the sceptic to push his questioning to 'profounder depths' of fruitless speculation.[68] If the mind is conceived as a bundle of 'subconscious desires', lacking all intelligible meaning and connection, then there is nothing to prevent the more extreme forms of irrational scepticism. Austin's, however, is a curative argument, aimed at philosophers who might be beguiled by the tempting logic of the solipsistic doubt. Empson is in the much more difficult position of trying to explain away the mysteries of a poem which offers itself, on the plainest terms, as a product of the 'deep' subconscious. I have shown how the notes to Empson's own poems are a genuine part of their intellectual challenge, containing as they do a variety of themes and attitudes which often contribute to the main line of thought. The same applies to the rational prose virtues, or background of practical experience, which Empson discovers in the poetry of Milton or Donne. But it is not so clear what it means to tell the reader that Eliot's symbols are a kind of obstructive mystification, best got over by making what he can of the poet's rather *ad hoc* commentary.

The problem is aggravated by the fact that Eliot's notes seem hardly more than an elaborate joke at the reader's expense. It is little help toward the rational assurance that Empson wants to be told by Eliot that his images derive from this or that source of casual reading. *The Waste Land* is a total and self-confirming exercise in Symbolist poetics. As such, it throws a curious paradox into Empson's manner of approach. It is hard to know whether Empson is rejecting the Symbolist programme in general, and criticising Eliot for his failure to communicate properly, or whether he is trying *as far as possible* to put off accepting its irrationalist background of ideas. However one looks at it, there is a hint of indecision at the heart of Empson's arguments. He is no longer working with that adaptable but convincing sense of an author's intentions, whether 'conscious' or not, which characterised his earlier criticism. *Milton's God* gives rise to the same uncertainties. Many readers will conclude that the book takes its bearings, not from any credible portion of Milton's own mind, but from the quite distinct Empsonian standards of rational humanism. In *Some Versions*, these were neatly attached to the mediating figure of Bentley, whom Empson could afford partly to defend, partly to ridicule. In *Milton's God* the strategies of Pastoral, of a complex and reciprocal tradition, are simply beside the point. Empson now imputes the entire drama of conflicting motives to Milton's own mind, a reading which concentrates all the problems of 'intention' onto the poet's subconscious and its relation to his official creed.

These contradictions are increasingly evident in Empson's criticism, sometimes even in his occasional turns of phrase. Such is the disarming use he often makes of wholehearted but mutually exclusive terms of judgement. Wordsworth's poetry, where its paradoxes test Empson's logic to the limit, seems to be making an 'obscure but splendid claim'. *Paradise Lost* reveals a tortured psychology at once 'splendid and appalling'. Empson is, I think, well aware of the strained though productive division between his sense of poetic value and his idea of moral good. More recently, however, the effect of this awareness has been to underline the central paradox of Pastoral—the ambiguous virtues of 'complex' interpretation—at the cost of its imaginative breadth and subtlety.

Having spent the greater part of this book in arguing for the logic and consistency of Empson's criticism, it may seem odd to have devoted the last few pages to emphasising its inherent limitations. But these are not intended merely as negative remarks. They accept what has always been the characteristic strength of Empson's work—its rationalising motive—and show that the continuity survives where the method, by its very nature, runs onto difficult ground. By recognising this, one can arrive at a better understanding of the complicated interests, and the implicit morality, of Empson's critical thinking.

6

Literary 'Values' and Modern Humanism: Empson's Work in Perspective

In a letter published in 1957, Empson took up the defence of Restoration comedy against the indignant John Wain and others of 'our fiercely moral young men'. Whatever their depravities, the plays were at least on one level 'looking for a more reasonable and contented relation between the sexes'.[1] This tone of un-illusioned moral hopefulness is that which interprets eighteenth-century usage, in *Complex Words*, as something more than a cynical currency of mutual abuse. Wain's 'fierce' and rooted morality seems less hopeful, in the long run, than an attitude which accepts and builds upon the inherent variety of human satisfactions. This is to apply the imaginative truth discovered in Pastoral: that for 'real goodness' to survive in an imperfect world, 'its acts must be imperfect' (*Some Versions*, p. 194).

Empson's humanism is a mood of chastened but generous and tolerant allowance. It emerges most clearly from the three short chapters on 'Theories of Value' which make up an appendix to *Complex Words*. 'Human pretensions need to be exposed because a great deal of cruelty is due to self-righteousness; a noble mind will not assert that its good actions are truly generous, but will recognise the variety of its satisfactions.' This leads on to the liberal understanding that 'we under-rate our neighbours if we do not see the painful complexity of their situation' (p. 433). Such is the philosophy which Empson has persistently opposed to 'Neo-Christian' virtues of self-abnegation and religious con-straint. The 'typical products of our time', Empson thinks, are 'avid for self-sacrifice' (p. 428); and it seems therefore that an ethic of enlightened self-interest is in need of rational defence.

This outlook is often identified, in Empson's writing, with the idea of Bentham that morality consists in consulting 'the greatest happiness of the greatest number'. In *Milton's God* Empson argues that the Benthamite theory 'feels healthier than any holy one', and goes on to observe that the only 'metaphysical evil', since it throws a paradox into Bentham's whole argument, is the happiness caused in some people by inflicting pain on others. Sadistic pleasure comes to seem the one great exception to the 'variety of human satisfactions' which Empson can both accept and admire. *Complex Words*, as we have seen, makes something of a test-case of Swinburne's poetry, with its latent sadistic tonings, and likewise of Housman's masochistic strain of irrational despair. But the problem is posed more squarely in *Milton's God*, where Empson can hardly escape the conclusion that Milton's mind, or a part of it, was in some way 'satisfied', like God the Father, by the sacrificial cravings of religion.

Empson speaks up for the Benthamite 'calculus of interests', though he is fully aware of its ultimate problems. It is the same attitude, in *Seven Types*, which encourages the reader of poetry to follow out the logic of his own deep responses without worrying too much about disturbing them at the source. In *Milton's God* he is even more determined to reassert the claims of a rational ethic, at the possible cost of throwing its problems into more dramatic relief. He recalls that it was Richards, in his *Principles of Literary Criticism*, who applied the main ideas of Bentham to the moral *and* the aesthetic dimensions of poetry. Empson may not have fully accepted Richards's philosophy, especially the 'emotive' doctrine of meaning which he derived from the Benthamite notion of satisfied 'impulse'. But Empson has always been ready to acknowledge the soundness of such appeals to human satisfaction, the more so when he is faced, as of late, with the widespread acceptance of irrational theories of value.

If Empson was alarmed by the fierce moralism of John Wain, he has come to be even more suspicious of Dr Leavis and his attitude to moral and literary 'values'. Empson makes the point in *Milton's God* by way of answering Leavis's attack on Bentham. 'I feel now, even more than I did at the time, that Dr. Leavis brought moral confusion upon his many followers by the denunciations in *Scrutiny* of Professor I. A. Richards's treatment of Benthamism as fundamental' (p. 260). Leavis is found among Empson's opponents at this point because he, like the Christian apologists, sets up as a defender of ultimate values which exclude all appeal to unaided human reason. It is no coincidence that 'Benthamite' has become one of Leavis's most frequent terms of abuse, directed at everything which he feels to be responsible for the present-day decline in cultural values.

When Empson was asked, for a critical symposium, to give some account of 'value' in poetry, he appeared to avoid the issue. Estimates of value, he said, ought to emerge 'from the analysis as a whole', being part and parcel of the critic's considered response.[2] This argument, once again, comes down on the side of the 'analytic' reader, prepared to investigate his reasons for reacting as he does, and not allowing the problem of literary 'values' to get in the way of his primary response. In *Seven Types*, the whole issue is neatly fenced off by the non-stop activity of Empson's mind as it tries to make sense of a mass of demanding examples. He seems to be working things out so rapidly and continuously, with so little time for satisfied reflection, that the question of final judgement is conveniently postponed.

The reference to Bentham in *Milton's God* is a part of that intellectual drama of rational dissent which Empson finds everywhere at work in Milton's poetry. In *Some Versions* he called it the 'terrific fancy' of Milton's theme, his heroic determination 'to hold everything before the searchlight of the conscious will' (p. 147). If the critic falls back, like Leavis, on a sense of established values, and declines—on principle—to argue their validity, then the poetry loses its power of actively engaging and resisting his faculties of reason. It may be, as John Casey has argued,[3] that criticism finds its judgements bounded by a sense of irreducible values; that the critic is no more able than the philosopher to explain or logically justify the grounds of his ultimate convictions. Scepticism, says Wittgenstein, is 'not irrefutable but *obvious nonsense* if it tries to doubt where no question can be raised'. Leavis takes the same stand in refusing to enter argument about the central values of his criticism. But this is not a principle which must, or should, set limits to the exercise of the critic's rational mind. It is a philosopher's argument, having more to do with the concept of criticism, suitably generalised, than with the critic's practical business. When Empson puts it that values should emerge 'from the analysis as a whole', he is precisely insisting on the critic's independence, as a giver of explanations, from any such limiting and mystified realm of value.

Empson's faith in analysis, as a fit state of mind in which to appreciate poetry, goes with his Benthamite belief in the rational accountability of literary 'values'. In *Seven Types* there is no attempt to judge various poets according to individual merit. The concept of Ambiguity, as Empson more than once remarks, has no machinery of its own for 'putting in' a judgement of value. What we gather of Empson's opinions and preferences comes entirely from the sense of involvement which he brings to his various examples, and then from the fruitfulness of the encounter. Likewise with *Milton's God*, where the sheer resistance of the poet's 'terrific fancy' calls out the utmost in his critic's powers of argument. Bentham's crudely quantitative measure of human satisfactions is transformed by Empson into a habit of rational allowance which gives full scope to the complicated background of all moral judgement.

When Leavis refuses to 'philosophise' about judgements in criticism, he rests his case on the 'immediate sense of values' which makes up the critic's claim to authority.[4] Eliot likewise deplored the intrusion of philosophic arguments into criticism. His 'perfect critic' is one who shows 'intelligence itself swiftly operating the analysis of sensation to the point of principle and definition'.[5] In each case the critic's refinement of sensibility is thought of in terms of in terms of a gradual process, bounded on the one side by his 'immediate' response, and on the other by his principled ideas of value. His education is a long-term progress of adjustment, not to be suddenly or radically advanced by a single testing encounter. Eliot and Leavis both offer a body of criticism firm in principle, secure in its historical viewpoint and largely self-validating in questions of literary value. There is not much room in this philosophy for the kind of two-way questioning exchange which Empson expects of poetry. Eliot's position is stated clearly enough in his famous sentence from 'Tradition and the Individual Talent': that 'the conscious present is an awareness of the past in a way and to an extent which the past's awareness of itself cannot show'.[6] At first sight this resembles the Pastoral gambit of 'putting the complex into the simple'.

But it differs in one essential point: that Empson never ceases to credit his subjects with all the imaginative shifts of attitude which they evoke in himself, the Pastoral critic. His intelligence is constantly being tried to the limit, and provides no footing for the kind of assured and authoritative judgement which Eliot and Leavis demand.

For Leavis, the more immediate the critic's response, the more sure and convincing his sense of values. In his reply to Wellek, Shelley becomes a test-case for the critic impelled to move on from sensuous impression, not into theory or justifying argument but straight to a combined aesthetic and moral judgement. Inevitably, in reading Shelley, 'the literary critic finds himself becoming a moralist'. Leavis concentrates his criticisms on the ode 'To a Skylark'. He finds Shelley's poetry confused and insincere, since its imagery contains such a mass of conflicting impressions that the mind is unable to hold it in a single, accommodating picture.[7] It is interesting to find Empson, in *Seven Types*, defending Shelley against T. S. Eliot's rather similar line of attack. He agrees that the imagery is often rather hazy, but suggests that this may communicate a mood of excitement and urgency which could not be expressed by any simpler means. The problem is essentially 'one of focus', as always in difficult poetry where 'the range of ideas' and 'the difficulty of holding the right ones in the mind' are so great (p. 160). Where Leavis moves directly from baffled response to limiting judgement, Empson typically keeps an open mind and looks to the *reasons* for Shelley's disordered imagery. The poem advances in theme from 'natural beauty' (with all its heightening sensory confusions) to 'an intellectual apprehension of it' (p. 159). And the critic to some extent matches this process in his own understanding when he recognises that 'the grammatical disorder of the verses is a very proper expression of the doctrine they convey'.

Eliot's visual preoccupations are just as evident in his essays on Milton, where he charges the poet with failures of tact and consistency in his images of Hell and the Garden of Eden. Empson, as we have seen, treats these arguments as a mere distraction from the crucial problems of Milton's theology. What he finds so offensive in Eliot's approach is the fact that Eliot mounts his whole argument on the least *accountable* aspect of Milton's imagination. Eliot's objections can be traced back to Hulme and his Imagist philosophy of poetic truth. Every man, says Hulme, 'sees a little differently'; and to express this difference, he must have 'a terrific struggle with language, whether it be with words or with the techniques of the other arts'.[8] Poetry is 'sincere', which in Hulme's terminology means 'visually accurate', only when 'the whole of the analogy is necessary to get out the exact sense of the feeling or thing you want to express'.[9] This adds an almost heroic dimension to the requirements of Eliot and Leavis, where 'sincerity' is likewise equated with 'concrete' presentation, and has little to do with the poet's intellectual basis of belief. Empson, on the contrary, thinks Milton at his best when most occupied with the conflicts of theme and idea which his religion forces upon him. For the same reason, he finds much to admire in the intellectual shifts and devices by which a poet like Shelley tried to come to terms with his own state of feeling and his sense of isolation from a sympathetic audience. The ideas in his poetry were 'obvious' to Shelley—they were indeed 'the main cause of the excitement he was translating into lyrical terms'—but they also needed to be 'explained and kept in his conscious mind' (*Seven Types*, p. 160). Thus the poem's comparative obscurity, its real but *understandable* confusion, reflects the poet's 'peculiar relation to ordinary people'.

This reflection points forward to Pastoral, where the artist as 'complex' individual has to adapt ironically to the simpler satisfactions of his public at large. It may also remind us of Empson's curious admission in *Complex Words*, that the 'emotive' part of a poet's meaning is often a 'pretence of humility', not to be taken at face value. It relates to the normal habits of language much as the Romantic poet, in Shelley's conception, related to the rest of humanity. If the critic is to respond with full generosity to Shelley's poetic ideals, he has to make allowance for the queer shifts of attitude which make up the background of his social philosophy. Empson looks to Pope, in the *Essay on Criticism*, as a poet who writes with a steady sense of moral conviction, and a knowledge that his readers will more or less share his assumptions. With Shelley, the process is more obscure, since it is more tied up with all the paradoxes of Romantic individualism. But this is no reason, Empson thinks, to write off the obscurities of Shelley's style as mere confusions of thought or language.

The importance of Bentham's critique of satisfactions is that it offers an imaginative focus—a 'subjective correlative'—for poetry which seems, like Shelley's, to be forced into a posture of ironic self-defence and isolation. It is a way of acknowledging the rich variety of human motive, even where its reasons are self-contradictory and tend to obstruct communication. There is evidence of this line of thought in the marginal notes which Empson made in his copy of Richards's *Principles*, at about the time he started to publish his essays toward *Complex Words*. At one point Richards denies, from his own psychological viewpoint, the 'vulgar' notion of an absolute choice in human affairs between the short but happy and the long but mediocre life. To the question 'whether they prefer a long life or a joyous one', most people (Richards believes) would sensibly reply 'that they find very satisfactory a life which is both'. Empson, however, comments uneasily that this seems to 'evade the theoretical issue'. Later he remarks more flatly: 'it is for the short good life and the long medium life (and the martyr) that you need the positive definition of the number of impulses satisfied'. Richards describes people who are 'paralysed' by their rich but confused mentality; while the poet, on the other hand, is freed into plenary self-expression by the lucid balance of his psychology. Empson briefly notes his objection: that 'artists commonly live in muddles'. The poet may indeed worry himself into privacy or plain neurosis. But Empson seems equally convinced that some kind of mental drama, or internalised conflict of motives, is the basis of all communication in the arts.

These weightings of the Benthamite equation have an obvious bearing on Pastoral. They connect with the elemental drama of the scapegoat or primitive hero, sacrificed to the good of the nondescript multitude. In later, more civilised versions, this role is taken over by the 'complex' individual who repeats in himself the sacrificial image of doomed and noble isolation. Empson finds the same curious interest in the poems of Rochester—a type of the suicidal rake—and, more recently, in the figure of Kastril from Jonson's *The Alchemist*. Kastril, Empson feels, 'deserves to escape . . . from the suicide into which he is driving imself with frank cries of pain and fear'.[10] It is difficult to imagine Jonson's roughcast yokel sustaining this powerful impression in the theatre. Empson has ennobled his character mainly, I think, to counteract the prevailing trend of cynical interpretation, the effect of which (he believes) is to reduce characters to mere stage 'types' in the service of an orthodox morality. But it also casts an interesting light on the problems which Empson discovered in applying Bentham's rationalised psychology of impulse. Kastril is assimilated, like the characters in *The Beggar's Opera*, to a philosophy of human motive which squarely accepts the variety of possible aims and desires, while admitting that their conflicts may become almost 'suicidal'.

Empson is applying the same generous principle when he finds Shelley's 'muddles' to be mainly a product of his 'peculiar relation to ordinary people'. The poet is, for better or worse, a more sensitive and suffering creature than the rest of mankind. Whether this is a genuine difference of temperaments, or whether it is largely a product of Romantic mythology, is not the real point at issue. What counts is the critic's appreciative sense of all the complexities of feeling and attitude which go to the making of a poet's creative identity. The same principle is at stake when Empson gives full rein to the rationalising side of Milton's imagination, or to Donne's covert arguments for freedom of religious conscience. The morality of Empson's criticism lies in the sense of priorities which he announced clearly enough in *Seven Types*: one which attaches more importance to the idea of working things out, in a rational and sympathetic way, than to any orthodox scheme of judgement and values. For all its paradoxical implications, Bentham's philosophy is the nearest to a full-scale statement of Empson's critical morality. It is present in a more demonstrative way in the recent essays, where Empson approaches his various authors—Donne, Coleridge or Joyce—with the express determination to find 'decent feelings' at work.

We have seen already how Empson's humanism tends to give a certain twist to the conventional idea of tragic values in drama. His chapter on *King Lear*, in *Complex Words*, concludes that the play derives its sense of tragic completeness from the fact that 'the general human desire for experience has been so glutted' (p. 157). This appeals unmistakably to something like the Benthamite register of satisfactions. In his earliest reviews for *Granta*, Empson is already suggesting that a commonsense philosophy of values tends away from tragedy towards, at the extreme, a sense of the inherent *comedy* of human aspirations. Of Strindberg's *The Spook Sonata* he remarked that human experience might indeed often be dreadful, but that when treated 'with an adequate view of life', or with 'sufficient energy to excite respect', the artistic result would seem quite different. Instead of an 'apologetic and meaningless apocalypse', it might turn out a 'rousing, though bitter and uncomfortable to the tender-hearted, farce'.[11] This ironic concession to the 'tender-hearted' has its parallel in *Seven Types*, where Empson's methods are addressed to those unafraid of submitting their delicate responses to the searchlight of conscious investigation. Tragic 'values', or the spiritualised ethos which supports them, must be to some degree transformed by a rationalised critique of human interests.

George Steiner has described this shift of attitudes, which he sees as fundamental to modern humanism, as a movement beyond the realm of tragedy to a state of 'dialectical awareness' which would find 'high comedy' its natural mode of expression.[12] He also suggests that the working out of this 'dialectic' tends to concentrate on the *language* of drama—its semantic implications —and not so much on its universal, or metaphysical, sanctions. Steiner's argument is of course highly speculative, and he doesn't go as far as Empson in applying it to the detailed process of critical judgement. But it does strikingly support the impression one has, in reading *Complex Words*, that Empson is expressing a humanistic outlook which largely revalues the tragic morality of self-surrender and renunciation.

By contrast, Leavis's philosophy of values finds its clearest expression in his essay 'Tragedy and the Medium'.[13] According to Leavis, it is a mistake even to raise such questions outside the discussion of tragedy itself, or the greatest examples of its kind. Tragedy enacts the confrontation between man's assertive ego and the sense of impersonal destiny which drives him on to heroic self-sacrifice. By the same token, there is no room in this philosophy for the critic who would seek to rationalise the basis of tragedy, or to work out its practical implications for the life of normal desires and involvements. It is for this very down-to-earth sense of priorities that Bentham provides at least a working basis of assurance.

Pastoral likewise stops short of tragedy. It looks for a wider, more generous background of sympathies than the tragic identification with 'the one' as against 'the many'. Bentham's calculus of interests may not totalise in the straightforward manner which he imagined, but it serves for a good basic index of the human predicament involved. Empson can understand the motives of the Russian communists who, he reports (p. 13) now 'disapprove' of tragedy. There was apparently a Russian performance of *Hamlet* which the audience 'spontaneously' decided to treat as a farce. Empson is not concerned to defend their reaction, or even to present it (like Steiner) as something in the nature of a modified world-view. What fascinates Empson is the whole range of adaptive manoeuvres by which poets have fitted their imaginative vision to the social requirements of their art. Communist morality is a wholesale prescription, along Benthamite lines, for 'the greatest good of the greatest number'. It faces the artist with an ultimate choice between the introverted pleasures of his solitary craft and the comfort—which is also a 'waste of his powers'—in bowing to the socialist creed. This paradox is at the heart of Empson's chapter on 'Proletarian Literature' in *Some Versions*. It connects on the one hand with what he had written about Shelley in the earlier book, and on the other with those cryptic remarks about Bentham in his copy of Richards's *Principles*. One might perhaps call this a 'tragic' philosophy, in so far as it views the most gifted individuals as unable, through sheer strength of mind, to achieve the conditions of a full and unimpeded emotional life. But this is to ignore the allowances of humour and mutual toleration which make up the Pastoral complex of feelings. In the end it is the ironic latitudes of Pastoral, and not its paradoxical themes, which define the character of the *genre*. The problem is not solved, from Empson's point of view, by appealing to an altruistic code of values, rooted in the idea of tragic fulfilment, vicariously witnessed and approved. Bentham's hypothetical calculus, despite its crudity, takes Empson closer to the truths of experience obliquely expressed through the phases of Pastoral.

In the course of *Seven Types* there is a passage on 'form' and 'value' in poetry which puts Empson's case in rather puzzling terms. The notion of 'organism' is connected, for Empson, with the principle that '$n+1$ is more valuable than n for any but the most evasively mystical theory of value' (p. 132). In this case one would expect to find 'more important cases of ambiguity where several ambiguities are put together'. This quantitative theory of value is partly a defence against the larger, 'metaphysical' versions of Ambiguity which critics were to hold up in condemnation of Empson's 'finicking' examples. I have already explained how such arguments lend themselves to formalist doctrine, by providing a realm of ontological values where the inbred workings of 'paradox' or 'irony' assume canonical status. Empson's formula of '$n+1$' is a vague but useful reminder that the critic must never be so much impressed by his own machinery of judgement that he closes his mind to the sheer variety of literary values. Again, there is a hint of the Benthamite calculus of interests, the idea that criticism is best employed in working out the fullest range of implications for a given context of experience. Empson is reluctant to theorise about literary 'values' because they tend to preempt the moral question and narrow the critic's powers of rational sympathy. One is reminded of that curious passage in which Empson refuses to accept the suggestion of Shelley, that 'form' is in some way 'its own justification'; 'it sustains itself, like God, by the fact that it exists' (*Seven Types*, p. 161). The critic is evading the difficulties of his subject if he allows the poem to maintain such a perfect indifference to the complications of human life.

Edmund Blunden took Empson to task for what he thought the tactless and patronising tone of the comments on Shelley in *Seven Types*. Empson replied with some diffidence: 'I was wondering whether the tone of the passage was all right (that is a curiously large part of the business of a critic . . .)'.[14] In a book review, published at about the same time, Empson makes this problem of attitude the basis of a generalised distinction between critical methods. 'Analytical is more cheerful than appreciative criticism (both, of course, must be present) precisely because there is less need to agonise over questions of tone . . .'[15] It may be better or more generous, from the 'analytic' stand-point, to give the poet full credit for the range and variety of his possible meanings. But genuinely to 'appreciate' his complex satisfactions, the critic has need of a certain forebearance—a quality of analytic tact—which points up the limits of his critical 'method'. Pastoral and Complex Words are each a kind of solu-tion, on its own pragmatic terms, to the paradoxes inherent in this contrast between 'analytic' and 'appreciative' criticism. The Pastoral critic is one who makes a virtue of necessity by applying the vigorous breadth of his judgement to what must seem, on the face of it, a deceptively 'simple' subject. In the same way, the idea of 'appreciative pregnancy', in *Complex Words*, allows the critic to make full use of his analytic powers while assuming the poet to have had in mind the most generous sense of a word's capabilities. With *Milton's God* and the recent essays, this 'appreciative' habit of response is more frankly a matter of looking for 'decent feelings' where an author's moral beliefs are involved. There is, nonetheless, a real connection between these later issues of interpretative conscience and the problems raised over 'tone' and method in the wake of *Seven Types*. If Shelley was a test-case for Empson's dealings with Ambiguity, he is likewise present as a moral example in *Milton's God*. Empson joins his critique of Christianity to what he calls the 'sturdy eighteenth-century rationalism' of Shelley's moral philosophy. The Romantic poets were the first to recognise that Milton's God was cruel and perverse, and that the poem needed interpreting in the healthier light of commonsense moral decency. Shelley is the spokesman for an enlightened tradition of dissent which, Empson says, 'deserves that name quite as much as the opposing tradition' (p. 14).

It therefore seems true to say that Empson's methods in criticism, while they resist any single or absolute measure of value, do represent an active and continuing moral debate. In *Seven Types* the issue is deliberately postponed, giving rise to a mood of chastened perplexity which sometimes finds its way into Empson's style of paraphrase. Thus in Eliot's 'Whispers of Immortality': 'Value and *a priori* knowledge are not known through sense; and yet there is no other mode of knowledge. No human contact is possible to our isolation, and yet human contacts are known to be of absolute value' (p. 79). This commentary evokes the 'sense of isolation' which becomes such an important part of the Pastoral set of feelings. Its pathos connects with the idea that values, for all their vital importance, cannot be derived from any straightforward process of argument. At its simplest this merely states the philosophic truism that there is no logical relation between an 'is' and an 'ought'. But with Empson the problem is a source of imaginative puzzles which both engross and frustrate the human intelligence. Thus Pastoral discovers that 'value is outside any scheme for the measurement of value because that too must be valued' (p. 23). Once again, this throws a paradox into Bentham's system of moral reckoning. Yet it also supports the crucial idea which Empson develops in his chapters on Pastoral drama: that real communication is always a matter of 'satisfying impulses', and that an audience is 'more completely interested' if *all* possible responses are somehow called into play (p. 49). Provided one resist the impulse to erect it into a premature moral absolute, Bentham's theory is a true and reliable index of human satisfactions.

This principle is stated more bluntly, as a matter of plain common sense, in the Appendix to *Complex Words*:

> No doubt the falsity of the pretence that all men are equal entails a certain risk, and the same for impulses, but there is less risk in it than in any attempt to prejudge their different values, because this is certain to be an 'interested' one (p. 422).

This is not a cynical attitude, but one which allows in a realistic way for all the varieties of human gratification. Empson goes on to argue that people are in general 'fairly well-supplied with other-regarding impulses, if they are not actually taught to suppress them' (p. 422). And if this sounds a piece of vague liberal hopefulness, the examples are there—in words like 'sense' and 'fool'—to support the generalities of Empson's argument. The idea that self-fulfilment may not be merely selfish, since it helps one to understand other people's interests, is present in much of Empson's writing. Reviewing some poems by George Barker in 1935, Empson drew the comforting moral that 'all thoughtful egotists come to disbelieve in the individual'.[16]

This connects in turn with the sympathetic 'energy of judge-ment' which, as Empson describes it, converts the feelings of tragedy into something more akin to stoical humour. In *Othello*, the power of Emilia's death-scene comes from our sense that 'she ties up a variety of sacrificial virtues into a bundle labelled "mere coarse frankness"' (*Complex Words*, p. 228). In this, one can see how the 'sacrificial virtues', which played such an ambigu-ous role in Pastoral, are lifted into the liberating air of Empson's 'appreciative' semantics. His essay on Pope has the telling re-mark that 'great powers are seen most clearly in a suicidal freedom; they create their own destruction' (p. 92). Again, this looks back to Pastoral, and echoes what Empson has said else-where about the lyrics of Rochester and—more improbably—the character of Ben Jonson's Kastril. But Pope's self-occupied dia-lectics of 'wit' are typically redeemed, in Empson's view, by the stabilising influence of 'sense'. In *Seven Types* he had already complained that much recent criticism of Pope had 'contented itself with saying how clever it was of the little fellow to be so rude' (p. 125). The approach in *Complex Words* does justice to both the painful complexity and the saving generosity of Pope's singular style. The *Essay on Criticism* is caught in the same paradoxical situation as the 'analytic' critic; obliged to mediate between the claims of unassisted reason and the 'tone' of an adequately sympathising mind.

If one fails to recognise the conflicts inherent in Empson's method, one is likely to conclude—with Kenner and the others —that mere 'ingenuity' has taken the place of responsible judgement. It is only by following out the results of his method, as tested through all kinds of practical encounter, that one gains a sense of Empson's moral engagement. More than any other critic of his time, he has taken up the challenge of modern rationalism, with all its philosophic problems, and explored its implications for the practice of literary criticism. If I have seemed to labour the 'analytic'/'appreciative' dualism, it is because this problem is at the heart of Empson's writing, and because he has made it the practical focus of a good deal of in-explicit moral debate. At the simplest level, there is no under-standing without a measure of self-involvement: 'unless you are enjoying the poetry you cannot create it, as poetry, in your mind'. The 'act of knowing' is itself 'an act of sympathising'; and criticism, like the sciences, has to accept that the object is altered by our observation of it. The same applies to moral judgements. Empson's attitude is perhaps best illustrated by a comment on Shakespeare in *Seven Types*. 'It is not "tout comprendre", in his view, it is merely to feel how a man comes to be a working system, which necessarily creates a degree of sympathy' (p. 138). The limits of analysis, the mistake of expecting to understand everything, apply as much to the moral imagination as to critical method in general.

This lesson is drawn more explicitly in several of Empson's recent articles. Usually it is addressed to critics whose moral convictions have blinded them, in Empson's opinion, to the real generosity of an author's feelings. Such is Empson's reply to the 'cynical' interpreters of Jonson's *The Alchemist*:

> The term 'values', it seems well to point out, has the serious function of helping us to recognise the variety of the world. The chief use of reading imaginative literature is to make you grasp that different people act on different beliefs, whereas the chief use of critical jargon is to obscure the basic facts, making you feel at home where you are not.[17]

The 'jargon' in question is mainly the device of imputing a 'subtle irony' which degrades Jonson's characters into mere satirical types. This particular fashion of *tout comprendre*—to recall *Seven Types*—is just the opposite of trying to understand 'how a man comes to be a working system'. It might be considered a more devious and insinuating version of the sanctified rhetorics of irony and paradox invented by formalist critics.

Against these habits of conformist principle, Empson stresses the importance of recognising other 'systems of value' and not trying to delude oneself into feeling 'at home' with an author's viewpoint. This idea is raised into a point of principle in *Milton's God*. When Empson calls the poetry 'splendid and appalling', or compares it with a piece of Benin sculpture, his intention is to jolt the reader's mind into recognising the immense, unhomely *strangeness* of Milton's imagination. 'Understanding that other people are different is one of the bases of civilisation, and this use for a story is as much a culture-conquest as the idea of God' (p. 94). This admission of the dark side of Milton's religion—its origins in sacrificial craving—is as much a part of Empson's response as the moral revulsion it inspires. The several allusions to Aztec art have the same effect of acknowledging the possible varieties of human satisfaction, while attempting to preserve at least a civilised awareness of the horrors they occasionally present.

Reviewing Arthur Waley's *Secret History of the Mongols*, Empson felt that 'a large capacity to accept the assumptions of any world-view, without assuming any merit for our own' was the basic virtue of Waley's mind.[18] The same could be said of *Milton's God*, despite the value which Empson places on the rationalising temper of Western religious dissent. *Paradise Lost*, as he remarked in a later correspondence, is magnificent poetry because it confronts the human mind with 'a massive specimen of one of the ways it can go'.[19] Like the sacrificial imagery of *Pastoral*, or the cynical twists of *Complex Words*, this view of Milton prevents the interpreter from too easily imposing his own tidy notions of order. One finds the same openness to unsettling habits of thought in Empson's earliest writings for the Cambridge magazines. An article in *Granta* explains how Wyndham Lewis 'exhilarates by describing people with strong, well-marked systems of habit, absurdly unlike one's own. It gives a sort of courage, and makes you feel more competent, even to have imagined them'.[20] There is a similar cluster of feelings, half-admiring, half-resentful, about the figure of Shakespeare's unmovable patron as described in *Some Versions*. The puzzle of his exact relationship with the poet is deepened by the sense of baffled affection which the sonnets alternately celebrate and lament. In the end his remoteness and self-absorption are balanced against the splendour of his solitary strength. Human nature, it seems to be implied, 'may only be able to do good by concentrating on itself as an end' (p. 82). And if this must be called 'an evasion of the central issue about egotism', the evasion is at least a potent source of imaginative truths.

'This queer sort of realism', Empson concludes, 'is one of the main things he [Shakespeare] had to say.' The 'realism' is often within reach of the Benthamite equation, so that Empson can paraphrase at one point: 'all men do most good to others by fulfilling their own nature' (p. 83). It is 'queer', like the work-ings of Milton's imagination, because it brings out the perverse range of pleasures which are possible even on terms of rational self-interest. The counterpart of Shakespeare's tortured pleasure is the sadism which Empson describes in *Milton's God* as 'a remarkable object, carrying the only inherent or metaphysical evil in the world' (p. 260). Its claim to uniqueness seems to be the fact that a Benthamite ethic of gratified impulse would cover all cases except that of an active pleasure in cruelty. Empson's readiness to test such cases, from Shakespeare's vaguely maso-chistic ironies to Milton's 'appalling' theology, is a way of admitting the unfathomable queerness of human moralities. They may then become, like the Aztec parallels in *Milton's God*, a source of renewed strength and balance. Such experiences are valuable, Empson thinks, 'chiefly because we need to feel that, whatever we do with our own small lives, the rest of the world is still going on and exercising the variety of its forces' (p. 276).

ALTERNATIVE WISDOMS: EMPSON BETWEEN TWO CULTURES

I have tried to suggest, from a number of angles, the generous complexity of Empson's moral imagination. Convinced as he always has been of the basic right-mindedness of human reason, and the importance of rationalising questions of value, he has nevertheless insisted on the wide and often baffling varieties of experience. If the human mind is fundamentally sane and generous, as *Complex Words* for the most part suggests, then Bentham's critique of satisfactions is a matter of common sense and plain decent feeling. But in practice the equations have to be stretched around a great deal of difficult and contradictory evidence. In his early rejoinder to John Sparrow, who had criticised Richards for his Benthamite philosophy of values, Empson could afford to be flatly insistent on the virtues of a rationalised ethic. 'Certainly appreciation, that is, pleasure, is the object in view, but appreciation is not therefore immoral, as Mr. Sparrow seems to think: it is the purpose and index of morality: it is the difference between civilisation and barbarism.'[21]

His answer is effectively to collapse the distinction between 'analytic' and 'appreciative' orders of judgement, and to argue that they both give rise to the pleasures that come of an adequate understanding.

This, however, was an abstract and somewhat simplified statement of the case. *Milton's God* is the plainest example of Empson's recognition that, however 'civilised' its conscious morality, the mind still discovers an obscure fascination in the 'barbarous' pleasures of humanity. Empson approaches *Paradise Lost* with the same allowances for human nature—its tight-rope balance of instinct and reason—as he made habitually in *Seven Types*. Chief among these are the paradoxes associated with 'egotism' and its various implications. It is typical of Empson that, while pursuing these problems to their logical conclusion, he has often tried to take a wider view by recalling the various 'systems of value' on which the human mind can support itself. Empson's own experiences in China and Japan seem to have impressed him with the need for a world-view large enough to accommodate the alternative wisdoms of East and West.

The need to hold both cultures in view is frequently a main line of argument in *Milton's God*. Among the critics singled out for detailed reply, it is Yvor Richards whom Empson considers to have thoroughly missed the point of *Paradise Lost* by ignoring its wider moral bearings. Winters had expressed a frank impatience with the silliness of Milton's theology, the brutality of his moral feelings and the inflated quality of his language. One might have expected Empson to agree, at least with the argument that Milton's religion had a harmful effect on his moral judgement. In fact the reply is on a quite different tack, and brings out the mixture of feelings—mistrust and fascination, moral dissent and intellectual excitement—which characterises *Milton's God*. Empson points out that Christian theology is capable of various interpretations, some of which incline to a mystic or 'immanent' idea of God which presents fewer problems to the moral imagination.

If you deny that God is a person, as many people do, then you will not agree with Yvor Winters that the western intellectual activity has been profounder than the eastern; but you have to agree that the western theologians were trying to handle a real difficulty. (p. 94)

Empson is in mind of the 'eastern' tradition of ideas when he argues, later in the book, that Milton's God may be planning to 'abdicate', or merge his powers into the mystic's 'ground of all being'. If the idea seems rather far-fetched, it serves at least to indicate the heroic scale and variety of Milton's conscientious drama. It also provides, in speculative form, that 'use for a story' —a narrative trial of judgement—which Empson considers a 'culture-conquest' in its own right. Empson accepts both the inherent attractiveness of Eastern religious ideas, and the sheer fascination of Milton's attempt to make sense of their Christian counterpart. As for Milton's 'style', which Winters (like Leavis) holds up to scorn, Empson is convinced that its main peculiarities need to be judged in the light of a moral debate. He makes the point most firmly in a later correspondence with Leavis. If the poem is regarded as 'inherently nerve-racking in this peculiar way', then one should not have to feel that 'any separate justification is needed for its extraordinary style . . . the style is necessary for the effect'.

Paradise Lost is the crowning example, for Empson, of the Western mind at the height of its moral and intellectual temper. The God of Milton's poem is the utmost perversion of that spirit of moral self-dependence—the 'enlightened' individualism— which underlies *Complex Words*. Milton's powers of reason are chronically divided between the appalling rigours of the faith he is defending and the appeal, as Empson interprets it, of a better, but in some sense *evasive* doctrine of goodness. Empson's allusions to alternative systems of belief, though important for his case against Christian morality in general, have also to admit the magnificent energies of mind which are called out in Milton by his grapplings with God the Father. Empson cannot bring himself, like Winters, to merely dismiss the embattled tradition of Western Protestant dissent. Winters' reaction is too cosily sure of its own normality to do much justice to Milton's agonised style. In a book review which scolded another critic for his feebly conventional views, Empson described *King Lear* as 'magnificent and loony and true to life'.[22] He applies the same standards to

Paradise Lost, and is often impelled to give imaginative credit for what his moral feelings, plainly enough, find simply repulsive.

There is often this curious ambiguity about Empson's appeal to alternative systems of belief. He warns Christian critics that 'they should not expect an informed Asian or indeed African to feel much reverence for their interesting God' (p. 242). If not to be 'revered', the belief is at least 'interesting'; for the reason, among others, that it managed to inspire such a singular achievement as Milton's poem. Empson seems all the more conscious of Milton's predicament for his own experience of Eastern religions and their quietist moral philosophies. During his years in China and Japan, Empson wrote a number of articles on aspects of Asiatic culture which typically move from aesthetic appearances to moral implications. In a piece on 'The Faces of Buddha', Empson reflects on the idea that 'you have to be somehow satisfied as well as mortified before entering repose', a feeling which he thinks 'goes deep into the system and perhaps into human life'.[23] This apparently combines the ethic of fulfilment with the ironies learned from Pastoral; the sense that life is inherently wasteful of human powers, and that it needs a broad and forgiving humour to see why this should be so. The Buddha's face 'is at once blind and all-seeing . . . sufficient to itself and of universal charity'. Its passive omniscience seems to comprehend the sufferings of the world in the same way that God's 'abdication', as judge and tormentor, redeems his role in *Paradise Lost.* What the Buddha represents in the end is 'the humorous goodwill of complete understanding'.

Empson has more than once expressed his sympathy for the Buddhist philosophy of life, with its promise of reconciling will and reality, self-interest and the claims of detached intelligence. This feeling emerges from a passage in *Complex Words* where Empson describes the sources of emotional power in a ballad's simple refrain. 'Life went on, and in a way this seems a cruel indifference to her human suffering, but it lets us put the tragedy in its place, as we do when we sing about it for pleasure' (p. 347). The irony here is one which takes the measure of human pain without detaching itself so completely that it loses contact with the sense of a shared condition. Such, as we have seen already, is the mood of words like 'fool' and 'honest' when used with generous intent. Empson is always ready, in *Complex Words*, to check the tenor of his judgements against what he has found to be the tolerant wisdom of the East. 'Fool' in particular seems to encode the same kind of feeling that Empson discovered in Buddhist art. A Chinese student, Empson tells us, 'wrote that he had not supposed the good-humoured paradox to be European at all; it was more likely to be a translation from some oriental philosopher' (p. 110). I have argued the importance for Empson's semantics of the claim that their 'machinery' would hold good for any language, given that its speakers possessed the requisite range of elementary feelings and sympathies. It is clear nonetheless that some kind of cultural mediation is going on when Empson comes to assess their ethical background. In the section on Theories of Value, he remarks half-seriously that his arguments are meant as a 'go-between' for Richards's individualist philosophy and the beliefs of Pali Buddhism. As a matter of commonsense wisdom this means that 'some impulses not merely selfish are necessary for mental health and general content' (p. 425).

It is the ironic magnanimity of the Buddha, and not the creed of ascetic self-denial, which Empson finds so valuable. By imagining a good beyond the cravings of individualism, it enables the mind to weigh its experience with a genuine breadth of disinterest. In *Milton's God*, Empson is not content to leave such redeeming philosophies to the rival religion of the East. He argues that Christianity has also produced its share of 'civilised' spokesmen, some of whom—like the Cambridge Platonists—arrived at an almost Buddhist conception of the deity. What the Platonists meant by God is very nearly 'what Fielding meant by the good impulses of Tom Jones' (p. 180). The comparison is an odd one, but it makes Empson's point that religions are open to a wide range of uses, some of them humane and sensible, others narrow and vindictive. In *Complex Words* he takes it for a 'commonplace' that Christianity and Buddhism alike have always been interpreted in various ways, producing in turn 'a kind of shrubbery of smaller ideas . . . which also may be a half-conscious protest against the formulae, a means of keeping them at bay' (p. 158). Neither religion, in its orthodox form, seems to Empson a sufficient basis for the efforts of civilising reason.

Empson has occasionally complained about critics who regard him as having picked up some colourful notions in China and Japan, and applied them as a straightforward curative to Christian religion. The poet Alan Brownjohn portrayed him, 'the man with the Chinese beard', looking on impassively at an Aldermaston rally.[24] This popular image contains some truth but not—as I have tried to show—the most important and general truth about Empson's attitudes. He himself rebutted the critics' presumptions in a correspondence of 1956, entitled 'Mr Empson and the Fire Sermon'. Explaining his use of the Buddhist text as a preface to the *Collected Poems*, Empson denied that he had meant it as a straightforward statement of belief.

> You might say that it is present as one extreme of the range of human thought, because the poetry often tries to take the position 'what I'm saying is admitted to be true, though people look at it in different ways'; but even so, it is pretty remote, and not appealed to.[25]

This implies once again that the essential exercise of a rational mind is to see all round, or as far round as possible, the various beliefs by which men have lived. Buddhism may be better than Christianity in so far as it managed to escape 'the Neolithic craving for human sacrifice'. All the same, Empson feels, 'it should be applied cautiously, like the new wonder drugs'.

The assumption here, as in much of Empson's thinking, is that rival ideas have their own claims to truth, which taken altogether may help to subdue the inveterate pride of isolated beliefs. In *Milton's God* Empson remarks that it often happens, with another man's critical opinion, that 'one needs to consider why it seemed so true, after apparently rebutting it' (p. 128). This mixture of sturdy dissent with a feeling of irresistible admiration is perhaps the most striking quality in Empson's later criticism. It assumes on principle that a poet like Milton was as much aware of the problems of belief, and the range of his intellectual choices, as the critic who has to make sense of imaginative fictions. The critic can only respond in kind by entertaining the whole variety of creeds which may have presented themselves, from whatever source, to the poet's questing imagination. Sometimes this involves a covert appeal to the poet's 'subconscious' which fails to achieve (as I suggested in Chapter 5) a sufficient or credible psychology of motives. But with Empson at his best, such doubts are dispelled by the enlarging sympathy which he brings to bear on the conflicts of faith and reason. There is much in *Milton's God*, especially the bits of homely paraphrase, which makes the book seem an elaborate joke against Milton's 'appalling' beliefs. Critics have mostly been inclined to take it as a kind of clownishly intellectual parody, with Empson as well as Milton emerging the victim of his own sceptical wiles. Yet parody can also be the source of an ironic strength which, as Empson showed in *Some Versions*, helps one to accept the baffling varieties of human belief. Hence the most curious of all Empson's mediating tactics: the approach to Milton through Bentley and Pearce, where risking one's intellectual dignity is almost the precondition of moral good faith.

These ideas are implicit in *Seven Types*, where Empson refers more than once to the state of indecision in modern awareness which makes it impossible for the critic to assume any single or ultimate basis of judgement. Cultured individuals, Empson suggests, nowadays tend to hold 'all the beliefs, however contradictory, that turn up in poetry' (p. 242). If it is not to produce a widespread failure of moral nerve, this relativism needs to be treated with all the respect of an informed and diverse philosophy of values. It is to this end, I think, that Empson has continually balanced his judgement between moral extremes, like those in *Milton's God* which attach on the one hand to Christian tradition at its most exclusive, and on the other to Buddhism at its most appealingly remote. Empson's way is to admire an author for his courageous handling of notions which, if he accepted them simply at face value, would cramp and pervert his moral imagination. He speaks of Joyce in a recent essay as presenting himself like 'an avatar of the needed culture-hero, as it might be of Vishnu or the Buddha'.[26] This is not to imply that Joyce's highest good was a passive escape into 'eastern' mysticism, or indeed that Empson would much admire him on that account. He goes on to say that the same ideas were current among 'radical reformers' of the sixteenth century, who refused to believe (like orthodox Christians) that 'there is no basis for goodness except as derived from one Atonement'. Even when it surfaced in what

Empson calls 'the Victorian "wisdom of the East" ', this philosophy provided at least as much basis for independent thought as for vague escapes into woolly-minded mysticism.

One could say that Empson's use of these far-fetched parallels, like his treatment of Milton's theology, reduces the subject to a kind of solemn parody. Yet the intention, and often the achieved effect, is to set them up in a generous light as interesting cases of the human mind doing all it can to make sense of the world. In an article of 1937 on 'Ballet of the Far East', Empson admitted that 'there seems a touch of caricature about this account, but you have to parody things to describe them'.[27] The ballet struck him as containing in some sense 'the other half of the truth about the world'. But describing this truth for Western readers is a process which involves an almost Pastoral sense of ironic distance. And indeed, it is in Pastoral that Empson steers the most fruitful and difficult path between the ideas associated with the great religions. The chapters on Marvell and Shakespeare are particularly rich in figures of thought which Empson derives, more or less explicitly, from the paradoxes of Christian and Buddhist tradition. His reading of 'The Garden' is at one point a virtual exercise in the mystic's philosophy of self-transcendence by inward contemplation of external nature. Empson records (p. 99) that he was sent to the poem in the first place by I. A. Richards's treatment of this theme in his book on Mencian philosophy.[28] But again, Empson seems to hold off from the engrossing logic of paradox which the poem's arguments invite. In Chapter 2 I described this habit of reserve as a way of rescuing the poem from the inbred 'metaphysical' sanctions which lent themselves (as James Smith had demonstrated) to a formalistic concept of meaning. For the present purpose, it is equally clear that the 'Buddhist' notions which Empson discovers are one side only of the poem's complex activity, and that what he calls 'the tricks of the style' (p. 119) are not to be regarded as ultimate truths of being.

Empson maintains, as always, a commonsense check on the tendencies of language to run wild in puzzles of its own inventing. Richards's arguments from Mencius were a main support for the context-theory of meaning which he developed in later books, and which Empson found reason to criticise in *Complex*

Words. According to Richards's commentary, the 'emotive dress' of Mencius' language is more important than any definite meaning his words might seem to possess. The Mencian concept of 'nature' is a cover-term for both human nature and the natural world it inhabits. A way is thus opened for the kind of wholesale idealism which Empson briefly entertains in his chapter on 'The Garden'. For Richards, it offered a fully-digested philosophy of mind (developed in his later work on Coleridge) and a theory of meaning to support it. The Mencian concepts of 'nature' and 'being', with their expansive semantics, are the basis for a generalised rhetoric which (as Richards remarked in an essay on 'The Chinese Renaissance') treats ideas as 'tools to be judged by the work they do'.[29] This pragmatism is much akin to the vaguely suggestive idealism which Empson found so disturbing in Wordsworth's poetry, and which he tried to rationalise in *Complex Words.*

It seems, then, that Richards was readier than Empson to take his Chinese experience as a source of alternative wisdom, and apply it wholeheartedly to the problems of philosophy at large. Empson remained very much aware of Richards's theories, and used them, even in *Complex Words,* as a means of occasionally checking his own line of argument. At one point he quotes Richards's warning (from *Mencius on the Mind*) that 'we may give a word a far more elaborate sense than it really has' by ignoring its emotive or purely rhetorical overtones. But he still goes on to argue that such an approach, if pressed too far, disables the critic's judgement by cutting away the props of rational understanding. Despite their inherent suggestiveness, the ideas of Mencius are no more binding or ultimately valid than the mystical equations of Wordsworth or the Buddhist paradoxes of 'The Garden'. The deep-grained rationalism of Empson's thought makes it impossible for him simply to accept such potent analogies as a means of escaping the logical commitments of the Western philosophic temper.

This is all the more striking if one remembers that most of the essays toward *Complex Words* were written during Empson's periods of teaching in China and Japan. The experience seems to have pointed his interests in a quite different direction from those of Richards. What seems to have impressed itself on

Empson's mind was the practical problem of finding a basic, explanatory language to communicate the meaning of English poetry to students unfamiliar with its background of ideas. Basic English provided one possible solution, and Empson appears to have tested its claims in a highly practical manner. With Japanese students, he later recalled, 'where their writing went out of sight in the undergrowth the only thing to do was to put down in Basic two or three of the possible senses'.[30] Of course it was Richards, together with C. K. Ogden, who developed the idea of Basic English and first encouraged Empson to put it to work. But Richards allowed his two great interests to develop more or less separately. Perhaps it was hard to reconcile the idea of Basic as an English esperanto with the claims for Chinese philosophy as a source of alternative wisdom. At any rate, it was Empson who, in a number of essays and reviews, tried out Basic as a workable tool of applied critical method.

One striking example is a piece on Wordsworth which attempts to pin down the difference in quality between the first text of *The Prelude* and the poet's later revisions.[31] The first version is demonstrably better, Empson thinks, because Wordsworth is using language with a proper respect for its limits of intelligibility. The argument is more often carried by verbal implications which seem to be 'taking his ideas to bits'; a process which lends itself 'not quite by chance' to the analyst's attempt to 'put it into Basic'. In the later version he imposes a mystical world-view which makes its points more rhetorically and, for this reason, 'takes it much further away from Basic'. The effect is like 'turning the guns round from firing at the Germans and pointing them against the French' (the article was published in 1940).

It is evident from this that the idea of 'putting it into Basic', or something very like it, was a part of Empson's programme for *Complex Words*. It is present for that matter in *Seven Types*, where Empson observes that 'the only way to say a complicated thing more simply is to separate it into its parts and say each of them in turn' (p. 249). My real point here is that Empson's experience of Far-Eastern cultures made the business of rational explanation seem all the more urgent and general a problem. As so often with Empson, there is a need both to recognise the irreducible strangeness of alternative systems of belief, and to see how they work on the available basis of a commonsense pushed to its simplest definitions. From the ethno-linguistic point of view, *Complex Words* is very much a product of European language-philosophy. Its stress on subject-predicate logic, or semantic 'grammars' which replicate the structures of syntax, stands in absolute contrast to the thinking of cultural relativists like the linguist B. L. Whorf.[32] Whorf and his disciples argue that the logic of European grammars, far from reflecting any 'universal' laws of thought, restrict the speaker to a limited and 'mechanistic' view of reality. From this standpoint, the conventions of European syntax—subject, verb, object—are just one means, and perhaps not the best, of ordering our perceptions. The Hopi Indians, according to Whorf, have a far more flexible grammar of concepts which allows them, for instance, to dissolve the age-old European puzzles about 'form' and 'content' in philosophic argument.

Whorf's demonstrations have much in common with the lessons which Richards draws from Mencius. They encourage the mind to step outside its native culture, and to treat the main problems of Western thought as a kind of local aberration. Although Empson has often found use for such suggestive ideas, he has remained on the whole very much attached to the philosophic assumptions of Western rationalism. One of the uses for Basic, he suggested, was as 'a way of separating statement from form and feeling (it may then be used at school for "paraphrases"). . .' This makes a point of maintaining—even sharpening—the categorical distinctions which Whorf would seek to transcend. Moreover, it holds out for the virtues of 'paraphrase' in virtual isolation from 'form' and 'feeling'; an idea which places the maximum distance between Empson's rationalising outlook and the purist philosophies of modern criticism. Indeed, the New Critics were somewhat in tune with Richards's Mencian doctrines when they based their rhetorics of meaning on an inclusive form-concept which barred the way to paraphrase and prose explication.

Richards later recalled that he had allowed Coleridge (and presumably Mencius) to lead him 'out of literary criticism' into more expansive regions of enquiry.[33] Empson chose a different path, and one which constantly directed his attention to the characteristic problems and themes of Western intellectual history. The Buddhist paradoxes of *Pastoral*, like the far-flung analogies in *Milton's God*, are treated always as one possible extreme of human thought, not to be taken as a straightforward means of irrational escape. They are held in the steady critical light of a mind which accepts, as its own formative background, the intellectual compass of Western civilisation. Of the third Type of Ambiguity, Empson remarked that 'its most definite examples are likely to be found . . . among the seventeenth-century mystics who stress the conscious will, the eighteenth-century stylists who stress rationality . . . and the harmless nineteenth-century punsters . . .' (p. 103). The third Type, as we have seen, was the one which raised most problems about Empson's method, and which led on directly to the researches of *Complex Words*. In this passage of confident predictions, Empson in effect sketches out the working ground of most of his later criticism, including *Milton's God*. Those Western mystics who 'stressed the conscious will' are for Empson a meeting-point of cultures, an example of the mind at full imaginative stretch between the various choices of existence.

I have tried to convey, in this final chapter, both the range and the central preoccupations of Empson's criticism. He has never allowed himself to be sidetracked into the kind of specialised theoretical activity which so much occupied the American New Critics, and is nowadays the hallmark of modern French structuralism. He is very much the 'practical' critic, even in *Complex Words*, where the theorising tends to fall away when successfully put to work. Empson once remarked, in reviewing a work of philosophy, that 'the human mind must labour against unknown forces which make the obvious invisible to it, and does this best by an arduous churning of facts and theories'.[34] This states as clearly as possible the relation which exists in his own work between the 'facts' of a diverse literary knowledge and the theory which attempts to relate them. The connection may not be tidy or always comprehensible: nor indeed *can* it be if the critic is faced (like Empson on Wordsworth) with poetry which eludes his rational assumptions. Richards's *Philosophy of Rhetoric* set Empson wondering 'how far he could change men's opinions who made them more conscious about language'.[35] But at least, if the mind has to labour against 'unknown forces' of delusion, it is helped by being made more conscious of its inherent liabilities. Empson goes on to notice 'the obscure sense of power, the hint of magic normal in poetry, which continually reverberates in Dr. Richards's work . . .' Richards, he implies, may well have the imaginative root of the matter; but there is still some need for a mode of understanding which takes full measure of the intellectual problems involved.

It is typical of Empson's way with ideas that Coleridge, as well as Bentham, offers some fruitful suggestions of method for *Complex Words*. Bentham and Coleridge have usually been seen (by Mill to begin with, and lately by Leavis) as representatives of the two great opposing traditions of nineteenth-century thought. Richards himself followed Mill's change of heart by converting, in mid-career, from Bentham's to Coleridge's guiding example. For Empson, these thinkers are not so much opposite numbers as useful extremes by which to measure the achievements of human reason. Bentham goes to the heart of the matter by posing the question of rational self-interest in a simplified but strong and reliable fashion. Coleridge provides the counter-example of a philosophy which exalts the idealised aspects of imaginative reason, yet still needs to be taken on its practical merits as a means of interpreting the world. Reviewing Richards's *Coleridge on Imagination*, Empson pointed out that 'however Coleridge brought off his poetical achievement, it is only in so far as the theory admits this heartily that it can claim to interpret his intention'.[36] The critic is in much the same position as Coleridge himself, unable to know the value of his theories except by their fruits in a finer, more generous understanding.

This all goes to demonstrate the central idea of Empson's criticism, that one ought to accept any likely 'theory', however remote or problematic, which throws some light on an author's practical intentions. Such was the attitude in *Seven Types*, and so it has remained through all Empson's later criticism. Where he has hit upon seemingly far-fetched ideas—like the Buddhist analogues of Pastoral, or the Aztec comparisons of *Milton's God* —his purpose is always to give full credit to the sheer resourcefulness of human imagination. Theory is worthless if it fails to make room for the different ideas which other, perhaps less conscious minds have brought to their own experience. Empson has himself given voice, often indirectly, to the central topics in modern philosophic debate. His criticism is a real (and so far unacknowledged) contribution to the discussions of language, truth and logic which have so much preoccupied current philosophy. Where I have suggested parallels with Husserl or Wittgenstein, the point has been not to claim any direct influence, but to show how Empson has pursued his own insights into similar regions of enquiry. He has steadily refused to go along with literary movements of fashion which evade the problem of rational belief in an age of dominant scepticism. For this, and much besides, he will surely go down as one of the finest and most resourceful critics of his time.

Appendix

Complex Words and Recent Semantic Theory

In my account of *Complex Words*, I have not attempted to deal with Empson's semantic theories from a strictly logical point of view, since his 'bits of machinery' are used in a fairly ad hoc manner, and are anyway a tool of practical criticism, not formal philosophy. However, my reading of a recent book on semantic theory by Jerrold J. Katz[1] has convinced me that Empson's logico-linguistic arguments, laid out rather casually in his first two chapters, are in fact capable of being re-stated in the formal mode which Katz suggests. Empson's example might yet inspire, as I have argued in various connections, a more answerable theory of literary language than those which currently dominate the field.

Katz proposes to treat the main problems of semantics (synonymy, translation, the laws of inference and lexical definition) as matters of right reason and analytic knowledge. He mounts a convincing defence of this argument against the sceptical outlook of W.V.O. Quine,[2] whose principle of the 'indeterminacy' of radical translation—the non-existence of semantic constants—would deny the validity of all Katz's theories. There is an interesting parallel here with the issue of intention (what Cleanth Brooks calls 'the heresy of paraphrase') in literary criticism. Empson's equations, the minimal units of logical statement, support a rationalistic philosophy of language similar to that which Katz advances. Quine would have it that all such generalised theories of semantics, at least when applied to natural languages, involve a choice of analytic terms which must, in the last resort, be purely arbitrary. The forms of predicative logic are not, he argues, a direct and universal bridge between natural language and analytic reason. They are elements, but not the absolute foundations, of intelligible discourse. Their place in the linguist's reckoning has to be supplemented, Quine suggests, by some idea of 'how to construe them in terms of domestic and foreign dispositions to verbal behaviour'. This closely resembles the various forms of emotivist and behaviorist approach—that of I. A. Richards in particular—against which Empson has defined his critical thinking. Katz's rejoinder to Quine, which invokes 'canonical all-purpose elements of paraphrase',[3] arrives by logical argument at the same position which Empson takes in *Complex Words*.

Of course, Katz's premises are those of a highly conceptualised philosophic programme and not, like Empson's, developed through coping with the inherent diversity of 'natural' usage. If Empson is, as I have tried to show, 'doing philosophy' in a genuine sense of the word, it is clearly not the kind of philosophy which Katz and Quine are officially concerned with. It is clear, however, from what Katz has to say about the rationale of meaning and definition, that philosophy of language cannot be held separate from practical issues of semantic interpretation. This accounts in part for the curiously reflexive quality of *Complex Words*, by which its seemingly arbitrary method—the machinery of logical equations—finds itself confirmed and anticipated by the complex intentionality of literary language. For Empson, who is primarily a literary critic, these complexities of interest are naturally imputed to the language he examines. Katz's approach is necessarily rather different, since he works at the one extreme with distinctions based on the simplest of object-sentences, and at the other with logical concepts at a high degree of abstraction.

There are, however, several points of philosophic contact where Katz's arguments might fill out the background to Empson's more commonsense approach. He, like Empson, employs an extended notion of logical 'entailment' to provide a criterion of definitional equivalence (or paraphrase) which goes beyond the confines of strict (redundant) analyticity. This recalls the speculative portions of Empson's chapters on metaphor and 'pregnancy', where he attempts (as we have seen) to reconcile the apparent prescriptivism of his logical semantics with a more flexible and 'creative' sense of linguistic possibility. Katz draws a relevant distinction between *logical* truth, in the narrow sense acceptable to a philosopher like Quine, and the *analytic* properties

of language that offer a wider and more workable basis for
reasoned interpretation. The status of logical truths depends on
'the structure of truth conditions alone', which in turn amounts
to 'a vacuous requirement which cannot help but be met'. With
'analytic' propositions, in Katz's sense, their status derives from
'the relation between the truth-condition and the presupposition'
—the context, that is, or intelligible background of meaning.[4]
Of course this calls for any number of further definitions, but
the approach it suggests—the appeal to an open but answerable
range of expectations—is also that which reconciles the logic of
Empson's equations to all the variety of literary meaning. There
may be some danger, as Empson more than once remarks, of
the logical 'machinery' taking over the work of imaginative,
sympathetic reading. The chapter on Pope finds a unique
justification in the poet's own style for pushing such analysis
almost to the point of a self-supporting system of equations. But
Empson remains very much alive to the temptations of his
method, and in practice achieves something like the distinction
which Katz maintains between formalised logic and semantic
open-endedness.

I have not attempted to assess the proposals in *Complex
Words* for a system of applied lexicography based on the logic of
Empson's equations. The chapter on dictionaries is somewhat
remote from the book's main literary interests, although Empson's
use of the O.E.D. as a critical instrument has, I have suggested,
a distinctive and methodological character. His ideal lexico-
grapher would have to be also an accomplished critic and
philosopher of language: performing the sensitive task of recreating whole families of associated meaning, defining their
distinctions and at the same time working to clarify his own
investigative logic. Katz intends a similar procedure when he
rejects 'lexical definition' (by synonyms) in favour of 'theoretical
definition'. He and Empson concur in their wish to provide (in
Katz's words) 'a dictionary entry which represents each one of
its senses in the form of a theoretical construction, a *reading*,
that is composed . . . of symbols expressing language-independent
constructs . . . drawn from the theoretical vocabulary of
empirical linguistics'.[5]

The theoretical portions of *Complex Words* are too sketchy

and marginal, as they stand, to sustain more than this suggestive outline of their philosophic import. The book does, however, hold out the real possibility—strengthened by Empson's practical insights—of a new and beneficial liaison between criticism and the methods of linguistic philosophy.

Postscript by William Empson

Most of this book was shown to me as it was written, and I offered minor corrections of fact or intention. I became liable to wonder whether my work deserved such devoted scrutiny, or at least to wish I had not written so confusedly that it was needed. And then, when the whole book was shown me in page proof, all this patience turned out to have sharp limits: anything I had printed for the last quarter of a century was irrelevant nonsense, to be dismissed briefly with a sigh. There had been an earlier book, giving a chapter to Empson among other literary critics, which had expressed the same point of view though without such tactful coolness, so Mr Norris did not come as a shock. And of course I would be absurd if I told my critic to alter his opinion, especially after he has praised me so warmly. But I am glad of an opportunity to assure the reader that I do not look at it in that way myself. Also that I have not been entertaining myself with frippery in my old age; I have not even felt a change in my line of interest. I have continued to try to handle the most important work that came to hand.

In 1953, having returned from China, I started teaching in England, so that I had to attend to the climate of opinion in Eng. Lit. Crit., if only because of its effects upon the students. This was the peak of the neo-Christian movement, which has now largely subsided; perhaps it was already subsiding by the time I was prepared to attack it, but even so I was not making a fuss about nothing. The change left the bleakness of aestheticism all the more apparent, especially from its assurance that no one has feelings or judgements different from those of a literary don —there isn't anyone else, or there shouldn't be. Max Beerbohm spoke of the sound of contented munching from a field of academic critics, and the perpetual swish-swish of their white-wash brushes. The expert scholar, who by a skilled technique has disproved a libel or scandal against a long dead author, is allowed almost complete immunity; scrutiny of his technique is felt to be presumptuous and ill-natured (why do you *want* to do it? my friends ask me). But I think that the views of Helen Gardner on the love poems of Donne are themselves a libel on him, and the supposed technical proof of them wins credit only because it is obscure. Marvell in his last phase as a populist was brave and consistent to marry his landlady, and the proof by Tupper that he didn't, which has been accepted for forty years, falls to bits as soon as you pick it up—though I grant you that you need to go to the Records Office to realise just how bad it is. But I can hardly grumble at such opinions not being accepted, because I am so behindhand in publishing tidy arguments for them. I adopted a policy, while in employment, finding so many odd jobs on my hands, of leaving the complete versions to be written after retirement; and now I hope I may be spared for a long enough time.

But these details about experts, though useful as supporting evidence, are only a consequence of the main fact; the experts would not arrive at such forced conclusions if the general prejudice of the Lit. Crit. Establishment did not demand them. A good small example, I thought, crops up when Mr Norris remarks that I must be wrong about Kastril in *The Alchemist*, because he is obviously a yokel. I had said that the play has a happy ending because Kastril is saved; the landowner admires the unscrupulous businessman so much that he abandons his class-duty of duelling. A 'yokel' would never have felt tormented by this obligation, even if he had by accident inherited £3000 a year. The play is very severe against ladies and gentlemen and their customs, and a modern audience readily enjoys that; but Jonson is also like Dickens in expecting you to love his eccentrics—it is enough entertainment to see them troop on and each do his gimmick over again. Thus the view of T. S. Eliot, that you are meant to regard them all with icy contempt, is completely upside down; and it has become a rigid dogma of the pundits of Eng. Lit., without ever once having been accepted by an audience. Surely, when things have got as loony as that, it becomes a duty to speak up; even though it feels less momentous than propounding a theory of Ambiguity.

January 1978

Bibliographical Note

Since I have referred, in the course of this book, to a large number of Empson's publications—some of them in passing and once only—it seemed best to provide a sufficient note for each reference and to omit the usual list of 'primary sources'. Where the same article is referred to more than once in a short space of text, the subsequent notes are duly abbreviated, I hope without causing confusion. My task has been much simplified by the fact that there exist already two valuable bibliographies of Empson's writing, to both of which readers can easily refer. The first, by Peter Lowbridge, appeared in the special Empson number of *The Review* (Nos. 6 & 7, June, 1963), and covers most of the necessary ground up to 1962. The second, and more detailed, is by Moira Megaw in the book *William Empson: the Man and his Work* (ed. Roma Gill: Routledge and Kegan Paul, 1974). This carries the record up to 1973, with a good deal of additional information on the reviews and articles which Empson published as an undergraduate in Cambridge magazines. I am glad to acknowledge help from both these sources in checking my own references.

Notes

INTRODUCTION

1 Muriel Bradbrook in *Shakespeare Survey* (1953), p. 55.

1: EMPSON AND PRESENT-DAY CRITICISM

1 Cleanth Brooks, 'Empson's Criticism', *Accent* (Summer 1944), pp. 208–16.
2 Empson, 'Answers to Comments', *Essays in Criticism* (January 1953), pp. 114–20.
3 Empson, 'The Shores of Light', *Sewanee Review* (Summer 1955), pp. 471–9.
4 John Crowe Ransom, 'Mr. Empson's Muddles', *Southern Review*, vol. IV (1938/9), pp. 322–39.
5 Cleanth Brooks, *The Well Wrought Urn* (New York, 1947), p. 138.
6 T. E. Hulme, *Speculations* (London, 1924), p. 124.
7 Empson, preface to J. R. Harrison, *The Reactionaries* (London, 1966), p. 11.
8 Empson, 'Rhythm and Imagery in English Poetry', *British Journal of Aesthetics* (1962), pp. 36–54.
9 Ludwig Wittgenstein, *The Blue and Brown Books* (Oxford, 1964), p. 70.
10 Brooks, op. cit. p. 237.
11 Empson, 'The Structure of Complex Words', *Sewanee Review* (April 1948), pp. 230–50.
12 Wittgenstein, op. cit. p. 78.
13 Stanley Cavell, *Must We Mean What We Say?* (New York, 1969), p. 94.
14 J. L. Austin, 'The Meaning of a Word'. In *Philosophical Papers* (Oxford, 1961), p. 43.
15 F. R. Leavis, Epilogue to *New Bearings in English Poetry* (2nd edition, London, 1950).
16 Cavell, op. cit. p. 85.
17 Empson, review of *The Way of Deliverance* by S. Hanayama, *New Statesman* (17 Sept. 1955), pp. 337–8.
18 Empson, 'Feelings in Words', *The Criterion*, vol. XV (1936), p. 199.
19 Cavell, op. cit. p. 43.
20 Georg Lukacs, *Writer and Critic* (London, 1970), p. 11.
21 Winifred Nowottny, *The Language Poets Use* (London, 1962), p. 156.
22 Philip Wheelwright, 'On the Semantics of Poetry', *Kenyon Review*, vol. II (1940), pp. 264–83.
23 Geoffrey Hartman, *Wordsworth's Poetry 1787–1814* (New Haven, 1964).
24 Empson, review of *Collected Poems* and *Under Milk Wood* by Dylan Thomas, *New Statesman* (15 May 1954), pp. 635–6.
25 Empson, 'O Miselle Passer', *Oxford Outlook*, vol. X (1929), pp. 470–8.
26 Hugh Kenner, 'Alice in Empsonland', *Gnomon* (New York, 1975), pp. 249–262.

27 Recounted in I. A. Richards, 'William Empson', *Furioso*, vol. I (1940), special supplement.

28 Empson, 'Reflections on Shakespeare', an offprint shown me by the author, but the source of which—possibly an Eastern university journal—I am unable to trace.

29 Ernst Kris, *Psychoanalytic Explorations in Art* (London, 1953), pp. 245–250.

30 Empson, 'Tom Jones', *Kenyon Review*, vol. XX (1958), pp. 217–49.

31 See for instance Elder Olson, 'William Empson, Contemporary Criticism and Poetic Diction' in *Critics and Criticism*, ed. R. S. Crane (Chicago, 1952).

32 Walter Stein, 'Christianity and the Common Pursuit' in *The Northern Miscellany of Literary Criticism* (1953), pp. 47–63.

33 Empson, 'Donne in the New Edition', *Critical Quarterly*, vol. VIII (1966), pp. 255–80.

34 Stanley Fish, *Self-Consuming Artifacts* (California, 1972), p. 417.

35 Empson, 'Empson, Adams and Milton', *Partisan Review* (November/December 1954), pp. 699–700.

36 Empson, reply to Roger Sale, *Hudson Review*, vol. XV (1967), p. 538.

37 Michael Polanyi, *The Tacit Dimension* (London, 1967), p. 25.

38 Austin, op. cit. p. 64.

39 Empson, review of *Why Mr. Bertrand Russell is not a Christian* by H. G. Wood: *Granta* (June 1928), p. 481.

40 See for instance Empson, 'These Japanese', *The Listener* (5 March 1942), pp. 293–4.

41 Empson, review of *The Secret History of the Mongols* by Arthur Waley, *New Statesman* (13 March 1964), p. 410.

42 R. P. Blackmur, *A Primer of Ignorance* (New York, 1967), p. 79.

43 Empson, review of *Dublin's Joyce* by Hugh Kenner, *New Statesman* (11 August 1956), pp. 163–4.

44 Empson, 'The Theme of *Ulysses*', *Kenyon Review*, vol. XVIII (Winter, 1956), pp. 26–52.

45 Empson, 'Ballet of the Far East', *The Listener* (7 July 1937), pp. 16–18.

46 Susanne Langer, *Mind: an Essay on Human Feeling* (London, 1967), p. 147.

47 Robert Graves, *Poetic Unreason* (London, 1925), p. 82.

48 Ortega Y Gasset, *The Modern Theme* (London, 1931), p. 93.

49 Empson, 'The Variants for the Byzantium Poems' in *Essays Presented to Amy G. Stock* (University of Rajasthan Press, 1965), p. 136.

50 E. H. Gombrich, *Meditations on a Hobby-Horse* (London, 1965), p. 43.

51 Empson, 'The Ancient Mariner', *Critical Quarterly*, vol. VI (1964), pp. 298–319.

2: BEYOND FORMALISM: PASTORAL AND THE 'SUBJECTIVE CORRELATIVE'

1 Allen Tate, *The Forlorn Demon* (Chicago, 1953), p. vii.

2 John Casey, *The Language of Criticism* (London, 1966), p. 170.

3 Frank Kermode, review of *Further Speculations* by T. E. Hulme, *Essays in Criticism*, vol. VI (1956), pp. 460–6.

4 Frank Kermode, 'Survival of the Classic' in *Shakespeare, Spenser, Donne* (London, 1973), p. 175.

5 Geoffrey Hartman, *Beyond Formalism* (Oxford, 1970), p. 365.
6 William Van O'Connor, 'Tension and the Structure of Poetry', *Sewanee Review*, vol. LI (1943), pp. 555–75.
7 Herbert J. Muller and Cleanth Brooks, 'The Relative and the Absolute: an exchange of views', *Sewanee Review*, vol. LVII (1949), pp. 357–77.
8 Cleanth Brooks, *A Shaping Joy* (London, 1971), p. 142.
9 Empson, review of *The Dyer's Hand* by W. H. Auden, *New Statesman* (23 August 1963), pp. 592–3.
10 James Smith, 'The Metaphysical Conceit', *Scrutiny*, vol. II (December, 1933), pp. 222–39.
11 Walter J. Ong, *The Barbarian Within* (New York, 1961), p. 24.
12 Tate, op. cit. p. 77.
13 Michael Roberts, *T. E. Hulme* (London, 1938), p. 158.
14 L. T. Lemon, *The Partial Critics* (Oxford, 1965), p. 4.
15 Cleanth Brooks, 'Hits and Misses' (review of *Complex Words*), *Kenyon Review*, vol. XIII (1952), p. 669.
16 William Archer, 'Poetry and Beliefs', *Experiment*, no. 5 (Cambridge, 1928), p. 35.
17 Empson, review of *Modern Poetry and the Tradition* by Cleanth Brooks: *Poetry* (Chicago), vol. LV (1939), p. 154.
18 Stuart Hampshire in *The Morality of Scholarship*, ed. Northrop Frye (New York, 1967), p. 54.
19 Empson, 'Hamlet When New', Part One, *Sewanee Review*, vol. LXI (1953), pp. 15–42.
20 Allen Tate, 'The Fallacy of Humanism', *The Criterion*, vol. VII (1928), p. 668.
21 Monroe K. Spears, *Dionysus and the City* (Oxford, 1970), p. 24.
22 F. R. Leavis, review of *Seven Types*, *The Cambridge Review* (January 1931), reprinted in *The Cambridge Mind* (London, 1970).
23 Graham Hough, *An Essay on Criticism* (London, 1966), p. 41.
24 Empson, review of *Triforium* by Sherard Vines, *Cambridge Review*, vol. L (23 November 1928), p. 161.
25 R. P. Blackmur, *A Primer of Ignorance* (New York, 1967), p. 18.
26 Frank Kermode, *The Sense of an Ending* (London, 1968), p. 174.
27 Laurence Lerner, 'An Essay on Pastoral', *Essays in Criticism*, vol. XX (1970), p. 293.
28 Hartman, op. cit. p. 78.
29 Ibid. p. 57.
30 Kermode, 'Survival of the Classic', p. 175.
31 Murray Krieger, *The Play and Place of Criticism* (Baltimore, 1966), p. 55.
32 Blackmur, op. cit. p. 162.
33 Arthur Mizener, review of *Some Versions*, *Partisan Review*, vol. V (June 1938), p. 58.
34 Tate, op. cit. p. 111.
35 Raymond Williams, 'Pastoral and Counter-Pastoral', *Critical Quarterly*, vol. X (1968), pp. 277–90.
36 C. K. Ogden, *Opposition* (Bloomington, 1932), pp. 78–9.
37 John Wain, 'Ambiguous Gifts', *Penguin New Writing* (1950), pp. 116–28.
38 John Bayley, 'Against a New Formalism', *Critical Quarterly*, vol. X (1968), pp. 60–71.
39 Empson, review of *Poems* by George Barker, *New Statesman* (18 May 1935), pp. 720–2.

40 Empson in conversation with Christopher Ricks, *The Review*, nos. 6/7 (1963), pp. 26–35.
41 W. Muecke, *The Compass of Irony* (London, 1969), p. 129.
42 Ibid. p. 158.
43 Empson, review of *The Pre-War Mind in Britain* by C. E. Playne, *Granta* (April 1928), pp. 375–6.
44 J. Hillis Miller, 'The Still Heart: Poetic Form in Wordsworth', *New Literary History*, vol. II (1971), pp. 297–310.
45 Hartman, op. cit. p. 115.

3: COMPLEX WORDS AND THE GRAMMAR OF MOTIVES

1 E. D. Hirsch, Jnr, *Validity in Interpretation* (New Haven, 1967).
2 R. E. Palmer, *Hermeneutics* (Evanston, 1969).
3 See F. R. Leavis, *Revaluation: Tradition and Development in English Poetry* (London, 1936).
4 Georg Lukacs, *History and Class-Consciousness* (London, 1970), p. 155.
5 Frederic Jameson, *The Prison-House of Language* (Princeton, 1972), p. 82.
6 Empson, review of *As You Like It*, *Granta* (November 1928), p. 120.
7 Empson, *Granta* (February 1928), p. 43.
8 Empson, 'Virginia Woolf' in *Scrutinies*, II (ed. Edgell Rickword), pp. 204–216.
9 Empson, review-article in *Granta* (October 1928), p. 63.
10 Empson, reply to W. W. Robson, *Oxford Review*, vol. I (1966), pp. 77–9.
11 Ludwig Wittgenstein, *Notebooks 1914–1916* (Oxford, 1961), p. 25e.
12 E. D. Hirsch, Jnr, 'Three Dimensions of Hermeneutics', *New Literary History*, vol. II (Winter 1971), pp. 245–60.
13 Roman Jakobson, *Selected Writings* (The Hague, 1971), p. 213.
14 F. de Saussure, *Course in General Linguistics* (trans. W. Baskin, London, 1960), p. 131.
15 Hugh Kenner, 'Alice in Empsonland', *Gnomon* (New York, 1951), pp. 249–262.
16 Hirsch, 'Three Dimensions of Hermeneutics', p. 246.
17 Empson, review of Rochester's *Poems* (ed. V. de S. Pinto), *New Statesman* (28 November 1953), pp. 691–2.
18 Empson, review in *Granta* (March 1928), pp. 339–40.
19 Empson, 'The Shores of Light', *Sewanee Review*, vol. LXIII (1955), pp. 471–479.
20 F. R. Leavis, 'The Rhetoric of *Othello*' in *The Common Pursuit* (London, 1952).
21 Helen Gardner, *Religion and Literature* (London, 1971).
22 Colin Clarke, *River of Dissolution* (London, 1969), p. 10.
23 Empson, 'Lady Chatterley Again' (contribution to 'The Critical Forum'), *Essays in Criticism*, vol. XIII (1963), pp. 101–4.
24 Conor Cruise O'Brien, *Maria Cross* (London, 1953), p. 219.
25 Kenner, 'Alice in Empsonland', p. 252.
26 Empson, 'Feelings in Words', *The Criterion*, vol. XV (1936), pp. 183–99.
27 Empson, review of A. E. Housman's *More Poems*, *Poetry* (Chicago), vol. XLIX (1937), p. 228.

28 Empson, correspondence: 'Swinburne and D. H. Lawrence', *Times Literary Supplement* (20 February 1969), p. 185.
29 Empson, review of Christopher Ricks's *Milton's Grand Style*, *New Statesman* (23 August 1963), p. 230.

4: SEMANTICS AND HISTORICAL METHOD: THE PHENOMENOLOGY OF MEANING

1 William Hotopf, *Language, Thought and Comprehension* (London, 1965).
2 Ogden and Richards, *The Meaning of Meaning* (London, 1927), pp. 269–72.
3 Edmund Husserl, *Formal and Transcendental Logic* (trans. Dorian Cairns, The Hague, 1969), pp. 241–2.
4 Ibid. p. 210.
5 Donald Davie, *The Language of Science and the Language of Literature* (London, 1963), p. 93.
6 See Donald Davie, *Articulate Energy* (London, 1955).
7 Empson, review of *Purity of Diction in English Verse* by Donald Davie, *New Statesman* (13 December 1952), p. 274.
8 Cleanth Brooks, 'The Heresy of Paraphrase': in *The Well Wrought Urn* (New York, 1947), pp. 176–96.
9 Stanley Cavell, *Must We Mean What We Say?* (New York, 1969), p. 40.
10 Ibid. p. 43.
11 Empson, 'The Variants for the Byzantium Poems' in *Essays Presented to Amy G. Stock* (University of Rajasthan Press, 1965), p. 136.
12 Empson, *Granta* (November 1927), pp. 104–5.
13 Cavell, op. cit. p. 30.
14 Wittgenstein, *The Blue and Brown Books* (Oxford, 1964), p. 70.
15 Wittgenstein, *Notebooks 1914–1916* (Oxford, 1961).
16 Cavell, op. cit. p. 122n.
17 Scott Buchanan, *Symbolic Distance* (London, 1932).
18 Empson, in *Granta* (June 1928), p. 481.
19 T. E. Hulme, *Further Speculations* (ed. Hynes, Minnesota, 1955), p. 67.
20 Enid Welsford, *The Fool* (London, 1935), p. 169.
21 Empson, 'Literary Criticism and the Christian Revival', in *The Rationalist Annual* (1966), pp. 25–30.
22 C. S. Lewis, *Studies in Words* (Cambridge, 1967), p. 213.
23 Leo Spitzer, *Essays in Historical Semantics* (New York, 1948).
24 Leo Spitzer, *Linguistics and Literary History* (Princeton, 1948), p. 47.
25 Empson, 'Donne and the Rhetorical Tradition', in *Elizabethan Poetry: Modern Essays in Criticism* (ed. Paul J. Alpers, 1967), pp. 63–77.
26 Empson, 'Falstaff and Mr. Dover Wilson', *Kenyon Review*, vol. xv (1953), pp. 213–62.
27 Ibid. p. 246.
28 See W. W. Robson, 'Mr. Empson on Paradise Lost' in Robson, *Critical Essays* (London, 1966), pp. 87–98.
29 Philip Hobsbaum, *A Theory of Communication* (London, 1970), p. 119.
30 Empson, review of *King Lear in Our Time* by Maynard Mack, *Essays in Criticism*, vol. xvii (1967), p. 95.
31 John Crowe Ransom in *Critical Responses to Kenneth Burke* (ed. Rueckert, Minnesota, 1969), p. 156.

32 Cleanth Brooks, 'My Credo' (contribution to 'The Formalist Critics, a Symposium'), *Kenyon Review*, vol. XVIII (1951), pp. 72–81.
33 Empson, review of *George Herbert* by T. S. Eliot, *New Statesman* (4 January 1963), p. 18.

5: 'OTHER MINDS': THE MORALITY OF KNOWLEDGE

1 John Wisdom, 'Gods' in *Essays on Logic and Language* (ed. A. Flew, Oxford, 1951), pp. 185–98.
2 Thomas F. Merrill, ' "The Sacrifice" and the Structure of Religious Language', *Language and Style* (Autumn 1969), pp. 275–87.
3 See Ian Ramsey, *Religion and Science* (London, 1964), p. 79.
4 I. A. Richards, contribution to 'Religion and the Intellectuals: a Symposium', *Partisan Review*, vol. XVII (1950), pp. 138–42.
5 A. J. Ayer, *Language, Truth and Logic* (London, 1936), p. 171.
6 Empson, 'O Miselle Passer', *The Oxford Outlook*, vol. X (May 1930), pp. 470–8.
7 T. S. Eliot, *Knowledge and Experience in the Philosophy of F. H. Bradley* (London, 1964).
8 Ibid. p. 163.
9 Ibid. p. 36.
10 Edmund Husserl, *Formal and Transcendental Logic* (trans. Cairns, The Hague, 1969), p. 210.
11 Robert Graves, *Poetic Unreason* (London, 1925), p. 93.
12 Maurice Merleau-Ponty, *Phenomenology of Perception* (trans. Smith, London, 1962), p. 233.
13 Ibid. p. 267.
14 Empson, review of *The Selected Poems of Thomas Hardy*, *New Statesman* (14 September 1940), pp. 263–4.
15 Merleau-Ponty, op. cit. p. 440.
16 Paul DeMan, *Blindness and Insight: Essays in the Rhetoric of Contemporary Criticism* (London, 1971), p. 28.
17 Hugh Kenner, *Paradox in Chesterton* (London, 1948), p. 95.
18 Ogden and Richards, *The Meaning of Meaning* (London, 1927), p. 39.
19 W. M. Urban, *Language and Reality* (2nd edn. London, 1961), p. 678.
20 Cleanth Brooks, *The Well Wrought Urn* (New York, 1947). See especially his appendix, 'The Problem of Belief and the Problem of Cognition', pp. 226–38.
21 See T. S. Eliot, 'The Metaphysical Poets' and 'John Dryden' in *Selected Essays* (London, 1964).
22 Richard Sleight, 'Mr. Empson's Complex Words', *Essays in Criticism*, vol. II (Autumn 1952), pp. 325–37.
23 W. K. Wimsatt, Jnr, *The Verbal Icon* (Lexington, 1954), p. 268.
24 Empson, review of *An ABC of Adler's Psychology*, *Granta* (June 1928), pp. 519–22.
25 Empson, 'O Miselle Passer', loc. cit. p. 475.
26 Empson, 'Rhythm and Imagery in English Poetry', *British Journal of Aesthetics*, vol. II (January 1962), pp. 36–54.
27 Jean-Paul Sartre, *Imagination* (London, 1902), p. 116.

28 Ibid. p. 115.

29 Christopher Caudwell, *Illusion and Reality* (2nd edn. London, 1946), p. 204.

30 Ibid. p. 293.

31 Quoted in Benjamin Suhl, *Jean-Paul Sartre: the Philosopher as Literary Critic* (New York, 1970), p. 5.

32 Ibid. p. 26.

33 I am much indebted to Professor Empson for access to these notes.

34 Empson, review of *The Duchess of Malfi* (critical essays, ed. Clifford Leech), *Essays in Criticism*, vol. XIV (1964), pp. 80–6.

35 Empson, 'Rhythm and Imagery in English Poetry', loc. cit. p. 36.

36 Sigmund Freud, 'Moral Responsibility for the Content of Dreams': *Collected Papers*, vol. V (London, 1950), p. 157.

37 Empson, 'London Letter', *Poetry* (Chicago), vol. XLIX (1937), pp. 218–22.

38 Empson, review of *In The Realm of Mind* by C. S. Myers, *Spectator* (20 August 1937), pp. 324–5.

39 Anthony Storr, *The Dynamics of Creation* (London, 1972), p. 159.

40 Empson, review of Adler, loc. cit. p. 522.

41 Empson, 'Tom Jones', *Kenyon Review*, vol. XX (1958), pp. 217–49.

42 In R. S. Crane, ed., *Critics and Criticism* (Chicago, 1952).

43 Coleridge, *Biographia Litteraria* (ed. Shawcross, London, 1965), vol. II, ch. 14, p. 5.

44 Elder Olson, 'William Empson, Contemporary Criticism and Poetic Diction' in *Critics and Criticism*, ed. R. S. Crane (Chicago, 1952)

45 Ibid. pp. 69–71.

46 P. N. Furbank, *Reflections on the word 'Image'* (London, 1970), p. 93.

47 Empson, 'The Variants for the Byzantium Poems' in *Essays Presented to Amy G. Stock* (University of Rajasthan Press, 1965).

48 Empson, 'Donne the Space Man', *Kenyon Review*, vol. XIX (1975), pp. 337–399.

49 Empson, 'Donne in the New Edition', *Critical Quarterly*, vol. VIII (1966), pp. 255–80. See p. 256ff for Empson's comments on the later Eliot and his attitude to Donne.

50 Empson, 'Insets and Epiphanies', *New Statesman* (18 June 1965), pp. 967–9.

51 Empson, 'Donne in the New Edition', loc. cit. p. 269.

52 Richard Eberhart, 'Empson's Poetry', *Accent*, vol. IV (Summer 1944), pp. 195–207.

53 Geoffrey Strickland, 'The Criticism of William Empson', *Mandrake*, vol. II (Winter 1954/5), pp. 320–31.

54 Empson, reply to Strickland, *Mandrake*, vol. II (Winter 1955/6), pp. 447–8.

55 Empson, 'The Ancient Mariner', *Critical Quarterly*, vol. VI (1964), pp. 298–319.

56 See W. H. Auden, *The Enchafed Flood* (London, 1951), p. 28ff.

57 Empson, 'Hamlet When New', Part 1, *Sewanee Review*, vol. LXI (1953), p. 41.

58 Ibid. p. 203.

59 R. G. Cox, review of *Seven Types* (2nd edn): *Scrutiny*, vol. IV (1947/8), pp. 148–52.

60 Empson, review of Valerie Eliot, ed., *The Waste Land: a Facsimile of the Original Drafts*, *Essays in Criticism*, vol. XXII (1972), pp. 417–29.

61 Empson, review of *Christopher Marlowe* by F. S. Boas, *Life and Letters*, vol. XXVI (1940), pp. 173–5.

62 John Crowe Ransom, 'Mr. Empson's Muddles', *Southern Review*, vol. IV (1938/9), p. 334.

63 Kenneth Burke, *The Rhetoric of Religion* (Boston, 1961), p. 218.

64 Empson, review of *Modern Poetry and the Tradition* by Cleanth Brooks, *Poetry* (Chicago), vol. IV (1939), pp. 154–7.

65 Furbank, op. cit. p. 140.

66 Empson, 'My Credo: the Verbal Analysis', *Kenyon Review*, vol. XII (1950), pp. 594–601.

67 Empson, 'Answers to Comments', *Essays in Criticism*, vol. III (1953), p. 118.

68 J. L. Austin, 'The Meaning of a Word' in *Philosophical Papers* (Oxford, 1961), p. 83.

6: LITERARY 'VALUES' AND MODERN HUMANISM: EMPSON'S WORK IN PERSPECTIVE

1 Empson, 'Restoration Comedy Again', *Essays in Criticism*, vol. VII (July 1957), p. 318.

2 Empson, 'My Credo: the Verbal Analysis', *Kenyon Review*, vol. XII (1950), pp. 594–601.

3 John Casey, *The Language of Criticism* (London, 1966).

4 F. R. Leavis, 'Literary Criticism and Philosophy: a reply', *Scrutiny*, vol. VI (1937), pp. 59–70.

5 T. S. Eliot, 'The Perfect Critic', in *The Sacred Wood* (London, 1928), pp. 1–16.

6 T. S. Eliot, 'Tradition and the Individual Talent', in *Selected Essays* (London, 1964), p. 16.

7 Leavis, reply to Wellek (loc. cit.).

8 T. E. Hulme, *Speculations* (ed. Herbert Read, London, 1924), p. 119.

9 Ibid. p. 138.

10 Empson, 'The Alchemist', Hudson Review, vol. XXII (1970), pp. 595–608.

11 Empson, *Granta* (November 1928), p. 154.

12 George Steiner, 'Literature and Post-History' in *Language and Silence* (London, 1969), p. 344.

13 F. R. Leavis, 'Tragedy and the Medium' in *The Common Pursuit* (London, 1952).

14 Empson, 'Shelley' (reply to Edmund Blunden's review of *Seven Types*), *Nation and Athenaeum* (29 November 1930), p. 291.

15 Empson, review of *Studies in Elizabethan Imagery* by Elizabeth Holmes, *Criterion*, vol. IX (July 1930), pp. 767–74.

16 Empson, review of *Poems* by George Barker, *New Statesman* (18 May 1935), pp. 720–2.

17 Empson, 'The Alchemist' (loc. cit.).

18 Empson, review of *The Secret History of the Mongols* by Arthur Waley, *New Statesman* (13 March 1964), p. 410.

19 Empson, reply to W. W. Robson's review of *Milton's God*, *Oxford Review*, no. 3 (1966), pp. 77–9.

20 Empson, review of *Time and Western Man* by Wyndham Lewis, *Granta* (October 1927), pp. 285–6.

21 Empson, 'O Miselle Passer', *Oxford Outlook*, vol. X (May 1930), pp. 470–478.

22 Empson, review of *This Great Stage* by Robert B. Heilman, *Kenyon Review*, vol. XI (1949), pp. 342–54.
23 Empson, 'The Faces of Buddha', *Listener* (5 February 1936), pp. 238–40.
24 Alan Brownjohn, 'William Empson at Aldermaston', *Penguin Modern Poets*, no. 14 (1969), p. 20.
25 Empson, 'Mr. Empson and the Fire Sermon', *Essays in Criticism*, vol. VI (October 1956), pp. 481–2.
26 Empson, 'Joyce's Intentions', *Twentieth Century Studies* (November 1970), pp. 26–36.
27 Empson, 'Ballet of the Far East', *Listener* (7 July 1937), pp. 16–18.
28 I. A. Richards, *Mencius on the Mind* (London, 1932).
29 I. A. Richards, 'The Chinese Renaissance', *Scrutiny*, vol. I (1932/3), pp. 102–13.
30 Empson, review of *Basic Rules of Reason* by I. A. Richards, *Spectator* (14 June 1935), pp. 1024–6.
31 Empson, 'Basic English and Wordsworth' (broadcast talk), *Kenyon Review*, vol. II (1940), pp. 449–57.
32 See B. L. Whorf, *Language, Thought and Reality* (New York, 1956), p. 238ff.
33 I. A. Richards, *So Much Nearer* (New York, 1970), p. 6.
34 Empson, review of *The Foundations of Empirical Knowledge* by A. J. Ayer, *Horizon*, vol. III (March 1941), pp. 222–3.
35 Empson, review of *The Philosophy of Rhetoric* by I. A. Richards, *Criterion*, vol. XVIII (October 1937), pp. 125–9.
36 Empson, review of *Coleridge on Imagination* by I. A. Richards, *Criterion*, vol. XIV (April 1935), pp. 482–5.

APPENDIX: COMPLEX WORDS AND RECENT SEMANTIC THEORY

1 Jerrold J. Katz, *Semantic Theory* (London, 1972).
2 See W. V. O. Quine, *Word and Object* (Massachusetts, 1960).
3 Katz, op. cit. p. 285.
4 Ibid. p. 184.
5 Ibid. p. 244.

Index

The entries under 'Empson' are limited to (a) the more extended discussions of his books, and (b) the most important of his articles and reviews. Since everything here is treated in relation to Empson's critical interests, only a single entry—under their own name—is provided for each of the numerous authors alluded to.